War Eagles

Books by
Philip J Riley

CLASSIC HORROR FILMS
Frankenstein, the original 1931 shooting script
Bride of Frankenstein, the original 1935 shooting script
Son of Frankenstein, the original 1939 shooting script
Ghost of Frankenstein, the original 1942 shooting script
Frankenstein Meets the Wolfman, the original 1943 shooting script
House of Frankenstein, the original 1944 shooting script
The Mummy, the original 1932 shooting script
The Mummy's Curse the original 1944 shooting script (as Editor in Chief)
The Wolfman, the original 1941 shooting script
Dracula, the original 1931 shooting script
House of Dracula, the original 1945 shooting script

CLASSIC COMEDY FILMS
Abbott & Costello Meet Frankenstein, the original 1948 shooting script

CLASSIC SCIENCE FICTION
This Island Earth, the original 1955 shooting script
The Creature from the Black Lagoon, the original 1953 shooting script (editor-in-chief)

THE ACKERMAN ARCHIVES SERIES - LOST FILMS
The Reconstruction of London After Midnight, the original 1927 shooting script
The Reconstruction of A Blind Bargain, the original 1922 shooting script
The Reconstruction of The Hunchback of Notre Dame, the original 1923 shooting script

CLASSIC SILENT FILMS
The Reconstruction of The Phantom of the Opera, the original 1925 shooting script

FILMONSTER SERIES - LOST SCRIPTS
James Whale's Dracula's Daughter, 1934
Cagliostro, The King of the Dead, 1932
Wolfman vs Dracula 1944
Lon Chaney's Dracula - 1930
Bela Lugosi's Frankenstein 1931
Frankenstein, a play 1931
War Eagles (as editor) 1939

AS EDITOR
Countess Dracula by Carroll Borland
My Hollywood, when both of us were young by Patsy Ruth Miller
Mr. Technicolor - Herbert Kalmus
Famous Monster of Filmland #2 by Forrest J Ackerman

FILM DOCUMENTARIES
A Thousand Faces - as contributor (Photoplay Productions)
Universal Horrors - as contributor (Photoplay Productions)
Mr. Riley has also contributed to 12 film related books by various authors
as well as numerous magazine articles and received the Count Dracula Society Award
and was inducted into Universal's Horror Hall of Fame

An anonymous live actor shares the frame with one of Marcel Delgado's and George Lofgren's exquisite stop-motion eagle models, via the magic of Willis O'Brien's stop-motion animation, in this still printed from the legendary lost test reel for War Eagles. Image courtesy of Bob Burns.

WAR EAGLES

The Unmaking of an Epic

An Alternate History for Classic Film Monsters

Edited by

Philip J. Riley

Hollywood Publishing Archives

Production Background
By

David Conover

BearManor Media

Published by:
    BearManor Media
    P O Box 1129
    Duncan, OK 73534-1129
    Phone: 580-252-3547 (Sandy Grabman)
    Fax: 814-690-1559
    benohmart@gmail.com

Screenplay by Cyril Hume from a story by Merian C. Cooper

The Editor would like to thank the following individuals who contributed and helped make this series possible. Carl Laemmle Jr., R.C.Sherriff, Stanley Bergerman, Gloria Holden, Jane Wyatt, Otto Kruger, Marcel Delgado, Robert Florey, Paul Ivano (Cinematographer), Paul Malvern (producer), Elsa Lanchester, Merian C Cooper, Patric Leroux, Bette Davis, Bela G. Lugosi, Sara Karloff, Technicolor Corporation, John Balderston II, Douglas Norwine, Loeb and Loeb Attorneys, David Stanley Horsley, Bernard Schubert, John Teehan, Ray Harryhausen, Ivan Butler, Ernest B Goodman (Universal Legal Department) Herbert Nusbaum (MGM legal Department

Author's Note: I interviewed the producers, directors, stars, cast and crew in the early to late 1970s. They were recalling events that happened 35-45 years previous and sometimes memory fades or events are recalled from their perspective point of view.

The purpose of this series is the preservation of the art of writing for the screen. Rare books have long been a source of enjoyment and an investment for the serious collector, and even in limited editions there are thousands printed. Scripts, however, numbered only 50 at the most. In the history of American Literature, the screenwriter was being lost in time. It is my hope that my efforts bring about a renewed history and preservation of a great American Literary form, The Screenplay, by preserving them for study by future generations.

Acknowledgments

This work would not exist were it not for the boundless enthusiasm, infinite curiosity and bold imaginations of many who came before me in search of Merian C. Cooper's lost cinematic dream. The small communities of film historians, studio archivists and stop-motion animators and enthusiasts who welcomed and encouraged my own efforts deserve the lion's share of credit, and I assure the reader that any contributions I have made along the way are due solely to the fact that I had the luxury of being an obsessed hobbyist while the real professionals were busy trying to earn a living. In the most literal sense, this book was written "on the shoulders of giants" and I thank the following for their continuing support, contributions, friendship and inspiration:

Forrest J Ackerman, James Aupperle, John M. Ballentine, Rudy Behlmer, Buddy Barnett, John Berg, Mark F. Berry, Ronald V. Borst, Ray Bradbury, Bob and Kathy Burns, W. Stewart Campbell, William Cappa, Ned Comstock and the staff of the Doheny Memorial Library at the University of Southern California, Michael Copner, John Creelman, Jim Danforth, James D'Arc, Curator of the Merian C. Cooper Collection at Brigham Young University, Jack Daves, Joe DeVito, Matt Dravitzki, Chris Endicott, Ernest D. Farino, Randy Fox, Lillian Gleason Garrison and Eleanor Grossman & The Duncan Gleason Archives, Ray and Diana Harryhausen, Barbara Hall and the staff of the Academy of Motion Picture Arts and Sciences Library, Bill Hedge, David Hume, Nelson Hume, Peter Jackson and the folks at Wingnut Films, Howard Jones, Tim Keegan, Gregory Kulon, Arnold Kunert, Dan Levitt and the staff of Larry Edmunds Bookshop, Carl Macek, George T. McWhorter, Curator of the Burroughs Memorial Collection at the University of Louisville, Joe Moe, John Moran and the staff of John Moran Auctioneers, Inc., Stephan Pickering, Jack Polito, David Raines, Harry Redmond Jr., Don Shay, Russell Shears, Douglas Turner, Mark Cotta Vaz, Tom Weaver, Robert Welch and Carl Wohlschlegel.

And last, but certainly not least, Philip J. Riley, whose dedication to the preservation of the art of screenwriting has produced such a great body of genre film history over the past 25 years. It was my greatest wish that the final draft of War Eagles be an integral part of this work, and Phil was the only editor who had the requisite passion, energy and experience to make it happen.

I also thank the following companies for their fine reproduction and restoration of the visual elements of the project:

The Kinetic Corporation and the staff of the Digital Imaging Division
Louisville, Kentucky

Isgo Lepejian Custom Photo Lab
Burbank, California

The Authors dedicate this book to
Forrest J Ackerman and Bob Burns

&

Willis O'Brien and Merian C. Cooper

INTRODUCTION

"He was thinking of doing something terrific. We went one day to the airfield to say goodbye to a mutual friend. Cooper was leaning on a fence with me and he said 'You know, I have an idea that is so much bigger than KONG. You thought KONG was big? Well, it is nothing compared to the idea I have now.'... He never did that film that he was dreaming of."

— Fay Wray, in an interview
with producer Rick McKay

What follows is a detective story.

A forensic investigation, if you will.

There's really no other way to define this tale. I've been described as a "film historian" by some, and, while that appellation is flattering, I can't honestly label this effort a work of film history because what Fay Wray reported above still holds true to this day. *War Eagles* was never made. Despite the efforts of a small army of brilliant artists and technicians, three of the most imaginative writers and scenarists of the era, one of the most powerful and instinctively brilliant producers in Hollywood and the financial backing of the richest studio in motion picture history, *War Eagles* became a casualty of its time. An epic and technologically groundbreaking fantasy film that fell victim to history and the very human folly of war.

And all of the witnesses, save for one extraordinary artist, are now dead.

Like them, *War Eagles* does not exist in what one might call corporeal form, but bits and pieces have survived: piles of yellowing paper, photographs curling with age and unstable bits of celluloid strewn quite literally around the world in dusty university basements and crumbling, condemned studio backlot buildings. Imagery culled from its screenplay has flickered, ghost-like, across theater and late-night television screens over the span of seven decades, while the milled steel skeletons of its titular heroes were disentombed from property warehouses and sold to the highest bidders on the auction block. An unrealized cinematic dream that many have called "one of the greatest movies *never* made," Merian C. Cooper's *War Eagles* has maintained a unique and compelling hold on the lives and imaginations of many in its 70-year struggle to simply *be*. Some of them are Academy Award-winning producers and directors, while others are special effects wizards working on the cutting edge visuals of today's fantasy blockbusters. Some are archivists and collectors who have protected and preserved the fragile evidence of lost cinematic worlds— and some are just life-long monster movie fans like me.

I first stumbled across one of production artist Duncan Gleason's beautiful *War Eagles* drawings in the pages of issue number 136 of Forrest J Ackerman's legendary *Famous Monsters of Filmland* magazine in June of 1977. I was only 13, but had been a devotee of fantasy and horror films for nearly a decade already. That summer I was deeply in the thrall of *Star* Wars, which was not only changing the lives of millions of filmgoers by transporting them to new levels of cinematic fantasy, but also altering the way that films were made and marketed as it shattered box-office records and propelled Hollywood into the special-effects-driven blockbuster cycle that dominates the business of filmmaking to the present day. *Famous Monsters* (or simply FM to the initiated) had been The Bible for monster-movie-crazed kids— including the precocious young director of *Star Wars*— for nearly 20 years by then, not only giving us our monthly ration of current and classic films from the likes of Vincent Price and the Unholy Trinity of Chaney, Karloff and Lugosi, but also spotlighting the behind-the-scenes work of genius craftsmen like Universal's makeup maestro Jack Pierce, *King Kong* co-creators Willis O'Brien and Marcel Delgado and the modern master of stop-motion animation himself, Ray Harryhausen.

Ray had a new film in release that summer as well, Columbia Pictures' latest installment in the much beloved Sinbad series, *Sinbad and the Eye of the Tiger.* Its dazzling poster art was featured on the cover of that issue, and I grabbed it off the drugstore rack with relish, as I did with all things Harryhausen-related. He was, and remains, one of my biggest heroes and I would not learn of the very important place *War Eagles* held in his life and career for many years to come.

But the first thing my eyes fell upon as I flipped through the magazine was this:

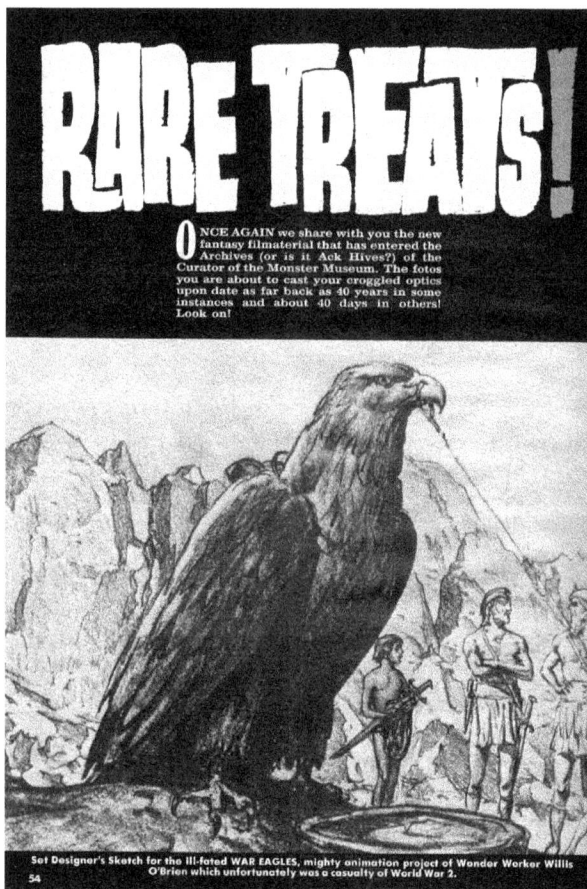

RARE TREATS!

ONCE AGAIN we share with you the new fantasy filmaterial that has entered the Archives (or is it Ack Hives?) of the Curator of the Monster Museum. The fotos you are about to cast your croggled optics upon date as far back as 40 years in some instances and about 40 days in others! Look on!

Set Designer's Sketch for the ill-fated WAR EAGLES, mighty animation project of Wonder Worker Willis O'Brien which unfortunately was a casualty of World War 2.

54

Image courtesy of Forrest J Ackerman & Warren Publications

It was my first glimpse of the fabled "What Might Have Been." An authentic movie - mystery that appealed to everything escapist in my youthful imagination. I immediately *needed* to know more about this compelling image that the editor had so romantically captioned "...the ill-fated WAR EAGLES, mighty animation project of Wonder Worker Willis O'Brien which unfortunately was a casualty of World War 2." It became an almost instant obsession with me. A sort of alternate reality counterpart to what was arguably my favorite movie of all time, the original *King Kong*. So I did—what was to a shy, pimply teen from the wilds of Kentucky—the unthinkable. I made a long-distance call to Mr. Ackerman.

What I learned when he picked up the phone, and have continued to uncover in the thirty- plus years since, is the basis of this report. To reveal more now, in what is simply the introduction, is to rob the saga of *War Eagles* of its powerful attraction, so I will step aside and allow the principals in this investigation to tell much of the tale in their own words. Most of what they said, wrote and crafted is collected here together for the first time, and a great many of these words and images have not been glimpsed by human eyes in a generation. As with any historical mystery, a fair amount of hypothesizing is involved. I have taken pains to clearly label what is established fact, what is educated guesswork and what is myth. My own somewhat Chandleresque narrative will intrude at intervals throughout to reveal a few instances of the wondrous adventure, mind-boggling serendipity and blind stupid luck that have played the lead roles in this search for a flickering lost world of light and shadow. It's a good story, replete with romance, wartime intrigue and all-too-real tragedy. The black-hearted villains seem to have come straight from Central Casting, and there are even a couple of mysterious informants who wish to remain anonymous.

As I said earlier, it's a detective story.

And the best part is that the case is still open...

David Conover, November, 2010

A Note on Screenplay Resources

Of the roughly 8 distinct script drafts and estimated 22 (and still counting) sets of revisions and changes for *War Eagles*, I have singled out three distinct drafts for primary story reference. They are:

"WAR EAGLES" From: Merian C. Cooper, dated Februry 11, 1939. No writer's credits are listed, but this early draft was penned by Harold Lamb and James Ashmore Creelman and is a facsimile of Willis O'Brien's personal copy of the script. From the collection of Gregory Kulon

"WAR EAGLES" by Cyril Hume, dated October 13, 1939. This is a unique copy of the original typescript with hand notations by Hume throughout. It is very likely the last draft he personally typed. From the author's collection.

"WAR EAGLES" by Cyril Hume. A draft cover-dated October 10, 1939 but incorporating changes made through February 20, 1940. It is the final draft and the closest to what a finished production of the film would appear to be. From the collection of Ray Harryhausen.

The final draft printed for inclusion in this book is derived from the last two Hume drafts listed above.

10

MODERN MECHANIX AND INVENTIONS

JULY

NOW 15¢
IN CANADA 20¢

SEE PAGE 32

DO WILD RADIO WAVES CAUSE AIR DISASTERS?
WORLD WAR CODE SECRETS — NEW SUMMER SPORTS

An image from the popular culture of the day that may have inspired scenarists for War Eagles? *The July 1933 issue of* Modern Mechanix *features an airship with some very odd accoutrements...*
From the author's collection.

Willis H. O'Brien, captured at a darker moment on the stage of 1933's Son of Kong.

Willis H. O'Brien

Where Eagles Dare: September, 1938...

Raymond Frederick Harryhausen had just recently turned eighteen and was one fortuitous meeting and a single phone call away from literally meeting his maker.

Settling into his senior year at Los Angeles' Manual Arts High School, he was a quiet, imaginative young man still in the thrall of a movie he'd seen at its premiere at Grauman's Chinese five years earlier, on March 24, 1933. The unmatched cinematic experience that was Merian C. Cooper's *King Kong* had all the impact of a religious epiphany on the youth's reeling mind that evening, and he had witnessed his own dreams of living dinosaurs, high adventure and soaring fantasy realized on the screen like nothing he'd ever seen before. Scouring every available (and frequently fictitious) account of the film's production, Harryhausen had finally learned the rudiments of a mysterious, painstaking technique labeled "stop-motion animation" and was deep into his own experimentation with the process in the garage of his parents' suburban home.

By century's end he would be the recipient of an honorary Academy Award and his name would come to personify movie magic like none before or since. But at present he was busy altering the contours of his mother's old fur coat to fit a model woolly mammoth, and spending his weekends in the company of a pair of similarly hyperimaginative misfits named Forrest J Ackerman and Ray Bradbury. They hung out at a downtown cafeteria called Clifton's, and one of the most frequent topics of discussion was the wizardry of one Willis H. O'Brien, the "Chief Technician" credited with bringing Kong and the other prehistoric denizens of Skull Island to life. Within a few short weeks, Ray Harryhausen would meet his hero in the flesh for the first time and it would alter their lives, and the future of fantastic cinema, forever.

Willis O'Brien—"Obie" to practically everyone he knew—was beginning to see daylight again. Moving into a small suite of offices on the MGM lot in Culver City, he was feeling the return of the old optimism and blooming energy that steady work brought to his life in its increasingly more infrequent bright periods. The new production that lay before him was to both provide him with the financial and artistic backing to conceive startling images previously unseen and unimagined, and to challenge his formidable technical abilities as nothing had ever done before. It was a fight that the fifty-two-year-old former boxer felt up to.

What should have been a meteoric career rise after the triumphs of both *The Lost World* and *King Kong* had instead been a five-year-long checkerboard affair of high times, spotty employment and deep tragedy. While in the midst of animation duties on RKO's quickly produced 1933 *Son of Kong* cash-in, he had suffered the worst that life had to offer. Both of his sons, fourteen-year-old Wiiliam and his younger brother, Willis Jr., had been murdered by his estranged wife, who then turned the gun on herself. It was a loss he would carry with him for the rest of his days, but it had also buoyed him with the grim knowledge that whatever else came his way, he could survive it. And more did.

Squeezed out of a better salary at RKO after his groundbreaking work on *Kong*, Obie began to distrust studio management and even briefly chaffed under the employ of his regular patron, Merian C. Cooper. He petitioned to have his name removed from *Son of Kong*'s credits, but Cooper insisted he get his due and it remained. Meanwhile, the rest of Hollywood, in one of its most curious character lapses, failed to do what it does best: Imitate success. The deluge of opportunities to create impossible beasts and sprawling

A very early pre-production War Eagles *watercolor by Duncan Gleason depicting the harvest sequence in the Valley of the Ancients.*
Image courtesy of the Duncan Gleason Archives

visuals on the scale of *King Kong* failed to materialize on O'Brien's doorstep. No one even *attempted* to make anything on the scale of *Kong*, and, twenty years later, with the arrival of the 1950's science-fiction big-bug-boom, producers would be unwilling to spend the kind of time and money required by O'Brien's levels of technical perfection. Cooper was the only one trying to recapture the "lightning in a bottle" that was his brainchild, and his RKO productions of *She* (which Obie had unfortunately sat out on) and *The Last Days of Pompeii* were entertaining spectacle, but little more. The beating of a giant-sized heart was missing from them.

Now happily remarried to his actual soul-mate Darleyne Prenett, Obie had drifted through close to two years of meager employment since Cooper had left RKO over similar financial disputes. He had even applied for the position of department head of Photographic Special Effects at Universal in 1937, with no success. Unfortunately, his letter of semi-application had revealed his limitations as a self-promoter, something that would dog him for the rest of his career. He wasn't far off the mark when he claimed he had been the sole developer of "animation with stop-action photography" but it wasn't strictly the truth either. Desperate times sometimes required desperate measures. When "Coop" had come calling again a few weeks back, Obie hadn't hesitated to once again hitch his fate to the star of his dynamic creative partner/producer/savior, and the outlook was rapidly improving. The promised lifting of what both men considered "The Curse of Kong" was looming in what passed for autumn air in Southern California, and they found themselves on the lot of the most powerful studio in Hollywood, and, for the first time, dreaming of a lost world in glorious Technicolor...

Mr. Martin Murphy,
Production Manager,
New Universal Studios,
Universal City, Calif.

Dear Sir:

Rather than take your time for an interview later in the week as you suggested, I am leaving this memorandum for your perusal - then you can let me hear from you at your convenience.

I have been told that Mr. Fulton is leaving your studio and because I have devoted twenty-three years to special photographic effects and have been connected with many of the biggest pictures requiring special effects, I am asking that you consider my application for that position.

My references are: Mr. William LeBaron of the above studio, Mr. John Hay Whitney, Mr. Jesse Lasky, Mr. Watterson Rothacker, Mr. Emerion Cooper, Mr. David Selznick.

I invented and developed many of the processes in common use today and my patents cover details of back projection for which I have been paid royalties by some studios including RKO and Selznick-International, although I have never sought to capitalize on these inventions as they were of great importance to the industry as a whole. The development of animation with stop action photography has been solely mine.

Among some of the pictures which you will recall are: "The Last Days of Pompeii", "King Kong", "The Lost World". Within the last thirty days I have finished five years with Selznick.

Will you give me an interview when the pressure has let up a bit?

Sincerely yours,
Willis H. O'Brien

723 N. Orlando,
Tel. Wy. 1484

14

Merian Coldwell Cooper

Merian Coldwell Cooper had, at forty-five, lived longer than he'd ever expected. A daring aviator—shot down and imprisoned by enemy forces *twice* during the era of The Great War—and an incurable adventurer, he had sublimated his desire for dangerous engagements into successful twin careers in business and film production. Cooper and his compatriot Ernest B. Schoedsack had turned Hollywood on its ear back in '33 when they unleashed their enormous simian on unsuspecting moviegoers, and the money and advancement that came afterwards had been almost effortless. Somewhere along the line he'd also found time to author three volumes recounting his adventures as well. He had trouble standing still.

A diminutive man who never hesitated to admit overachiever status, "Coop" had already made his name and his fortune, but the ever-expanding showman that ruled his

Cooper's Kong was almost banned in Germany for " aggression to the nerves and a provocation of the racial instincts of the German people..." What would the Reich's censors have made of War Eagles?

mind and heart (*Kong*'s Carl Denham wasn't even a *thin* disguise for his creator) was suffering. An early investor and zealous prophet for the Technicolor Corporation, he had worked hard to champion the coming age of full color in the motion picture industry, but was almost constantly thwarted by the small minds and timid imaginations of those above him on the studio ladder. He and Walt Disney were the only true believers in the future of the new three-strip Technicolor process, and Walt had won the race to bring it to its full potential with the release of his first feature-length animated film *Snow White*. Cooper had also been determined to top *King Kong* for the last 5 years, but nothing he had been allowed to produce had come close. The frustrations and budgetary restrictions of working within the system were wearing on him and had begun to take a physical toll. With the arrival of the truly "independent producer " still decades away, Coop had found himself sailing from one studio to another under a flag called "innovation" that, oddly, no one seemed to recognize anymore. What he had been celebrated for just a few years earlier, he now felt isolated by. After having a falling-out with old friend David O. Selznick over the future of a little western property called *Stagecoach*—Cooper and director John Ford were committed to both color and a relatively unknown actor named John Wayne, and Selznick didn't see either as a possibility— he'd resigned from Selznick International as quickly as he'd previously done at RKO.

In 1937, he jumped his own managerial ship and found a berth in Hollywood's most respected dreadnought, Metro Goldwyn Mayer. To work with Metro meant that you'd reached the top of your game, and the fluctuating film markets of the depression had left them almost entirely unscathed. Financially, they were completely solvent, but the unexpected death of their *wunderkind* head of production Irving Thalberg the previous year had shaken the stockholders, and an immediate hiring binge brought a flow of new blood into the old girl. They wanted producers who could produce, and Coop found himself happy to be back on the actual flight line again instead of playing budgetary politics somewhere upstairs. The only property he'd been shepherding so far was a pre- *Gone With The Wind* plantation potboiler starring Luise Rainer entitled *The Toy Wife*, but he had something very special percolating inside his prematurely bald head. Something Big.

Even bigger than *Kong*.

It held the promise of breaking the giant ape's grip on his stalled career and ushering in the age of Technicolor for a fantasy epic the likes of which no one had ever seen. It was a concept that drew elements from his own life into play with creations that only Willis O'Brien and his monkish crew of esoteric artisans could achieve. And, dangerously, it was a virtual call to battle for a world teetering on the brink of another war. Ever the Man of Action, Merian C. Cooper was on alert, and he didn't like what was happening in Europe...

On September 20th, 1938, he delivered a proposal to the heads of MGM.

WHITE EAGLE

or

WAR EAGLES

- - -

This story gives an entirely new and modern imaginative picture. I think it has greater box-office appeal than KING KONG, and will make more money.

In attacking a picture of this sort, the most important thing is the showmanship conception. For this showmanship the picture must have:

   a - A handling of the story which gives it the same
       quality of thrills and direct forward movement
       in action as a super-Western.

   b - One great showmanship spectacle scene which
       will be unforgetable - one which can be circus
       advertised - plastered on billboards - a
       substitute for a star name. In KING KONG this
       was King Kong himself as he stood on the top
       of the Empire State Building and was attacked
       and shot to death by airplanes.

   c - A central character which must be novel and
       fresh - such as Tarzan or King Kong.

In WHITE EAGLE these conceptions are more perfectly fulfilled than in any story on which I have ever worked:

   a - It will be handled as a super-Western of the
       air in which, instead of riders of the plains
       on horseback, we will have wild riders of the

air on giant prehistoric eagles. Just as Tom
Mix rode Tony, so our hero rides his great White
Eagle, - the fastest, fiercest, bravest bird
which the mind of man has ever conceived. In
other words, we have a Western of the air, with
a tribe of eagle riders, - with all the fighting
fierceness, thrills and excitement of Indians and
cowboys. We have a leader - our hero, riding a
huge, beautiful, brave bird of War - White Eagle.
This great White Eagle will stand out visually at
all times against the brown and black color of
the other eagles.

b - Our great showmanship scene will be a terrific
battle in the air over New York, between hundreds
of our eagle riders and squadrons of enemy airplanes
which are attempting to bomb the city. After the
destruction of the enemy airplane fleet, our hero,
on his great White Eagle, will land on the Statue
of Liberty for his last triumphant farewell to
the country of his birth. This fight is logically
and believable worked out.

c - Our central character will be like the Tom Mix-Tony
combination. It will combine our hero, an American
ex-aviator, and his steed - the great, beautiful,
fighting White Eagle.

****

Our hero is a young, athletic, daring army flyer. He is considered wild as a March hare, though a great aviator. One day he goes

too far on some daring foolish stunt. He is court-martialed and thrown
out of the army. He puts a bold face on the matter, but under this
careless exterior he really is deeply hurt. Army aviation has been his
life. He considers himseslf disgraced - - a man without a country.

As a reckless gesture towards Fate, de decides to fly around
the world single handed, flying from north to south, crossing both the
North and South Poles. All goes well until, in a hidden unknown region
over the gigantic mountain ranges in the great south polar ice fields,
engine trouble forces him down into a tremendous warm volcanic valley
twenty thousand feet deep. The plance crashes in the weird terrain of
a prehistoric land, and he is knocked unconscious.

From out of the sky, high above the fallen airplane, appears
a giant eagle. It circles about, then comes lower. It circles again
then glides down until it is only a hundred feet above the airplane.
Now we see that the great eagle is being ridden, like a horse of the air,
by a beautiful, exotic girl. The girl rides and manoeuvers her eagle
with all the grace of a splendid horsewoman on a spirited charger.
With typical feminine curiosity she brings her eagle down closer to the
plane, and then darts up as if frightened by the strange sight. Again
she comes closer. Finally she lands her great bird by the plane, and
dismounts. With graceful stride, she approaches the airplane and peers
through its shattered window at th eunconscious figure within. With
astonishment she sees it is a man. Finally she reaches in and, with
curiously light, graceful bestures, takes off his goggles and flying
helmet. She is fascinated by his blonde hair.

Now a great prehistoric beast comes through the forest to in-
vestigate th enoise of the crash. He is sniffing the blood odor form
the aviator's wounded arm. The beast has not yet seen aviator or girl,
who are hidden from him by the foliage, but he is following the blood
scent. Suddenly the eagle hears him. He utters a piercing cry. The
girl jumps from the plane to the ground, pulls from her belt a reed-like
instrument and blows into it, sounding a wild shrill note of alarm which
seems to pierce the very heavens.

The monster sees the crashed airplane, and charges. He begings
to tear at the plane as if it were human, not at first seeing the boy
within. The girl, at the first sign of his rush, runs to the eagle,
unslings her bow from the saddle, and plucks an arrow from her quiver.
She shoots the monster in th eneck. He turns towards her. It looks
as if both she and the boy will be killed. But at this moment a
circling swarm of gigantic eagles comes swooping down, answering her
call of alarm. We see that these great birds are ridden by men who
look like Indians. The men are astride saddles which are fastened to
the eagles' backs and cinched around their necks and under their wings.
They are armed with lances, bows and arrows, and long fighting swords.

And now, before th emonster can reach the girl, the eagles
of the air are diving by his head, their riders stabbing with spears,
and shooting arrows into him. The monster clutches an eagle in his
fierce claw and crashes him to the ground. But the attack continues
fiercely until finally the monster staggers and falls. Like a flash,
two eagles land, and their riders dismount and run in, hacking at the
monster with their great swords. He is killed.

Under the skilful direction of their riders, most of the other
giant eagles soar down to land near the boy and girl. Three or four
of them remain in the air, acting as scouts to watch for the approach
of other monster enemies.

The bird riders have landed. The leader is a stern old
warrior. He turns to the girl and with a gesture of anger orders her
to her eagle. She mounts and flies into the air. The other riders
are examining with curiosity the crushed plane and the unconscious
aviator, when suddenly there is a shrill whooping signal from one of
the flying scouts. Two other monsters are seen charging through the
forest towards the group of eagles and their dismounted riders, As they

approach, the leader of the bird riders lifts up the body of the
aviator, throws him across the pummel of his saddle, and the whole
group take to the air, circling upward. They fly some ten thousand
feet up, and then soar in to land on a natural cliff plateau which
projects cut from one side of the tremendouw inner wall of the crater.
This is their home.

It is now my purpose to show the life of these bird riders.
It will resemble that of a race of fighting, gallent trabe of horsemen,
except that instead of war horses, they ride war eagles. We will show
how these eagles are raised and trained. Instead of bronco busting,
we will show young eagles broken in to the saddle and conquered, etc.
It will be a Western with eagles instead of horses. We will also show
that this race of eagle riders are wonderfully likeable people - cheerful, handsome, daring, loyal - cast in a heroic mold, and yet with a
simple, roistering quality to their pleasures, after the type of
Vikings or other great clannish fighting peoples since the beginning
of time. Their women are beautiful, cheerful, gallant - fit mates for
a warrior race. They also fly the smaller and more docile eagles.

The little plateau is a paradise, except for one thing. It
has no food. It is necessary for the eagle people to gather the furits
and kill whatever meat they need in the prehistoric valley far below.
Whenever it is necessary to gather notural fruits, herbs and vegetables
from the valley, the women fly down to do this, but only after the men
have scouted out the safety of the landing place. They are protected
by warrior guards who have landed, and by warrior scouts from the air.
At the first sign of approaching danger from the monsters, they all take
to the air.

But there is another danger below - far more fearsome than the
monsters. There is a race of savage apelike men, drafty and cunning,

who build traps and snares, not only to capture the monsters, which they use in their arena battles to satisfy their degenerate blood lust, but also to capture the women of the bird people. Twice a year, in the full of the moon, these apelike men use these captured women as human scarifices to the prehistoric monsters, in a great, cavelike arena. These ape people are ruled by a gigantic, monstrous, semi-human figure who presides over the human sacrifices of the women.

Our aviator takes to the life of the bird flyers wonderfully. This is really flying! No riding behind the fumes of a gas motor. No enclosed box with its mechanical instruments. But the free, easy swoop and tremendous speed of the eagle himself. He becomes as expert as any of the tribe. He falls in love with the daughter of the war lord, or war chief.

The girl is captured by the ape people on one of the flights below, and is taken into one of the hidden caverns which the flying men have never been able to enter. The aviator, in a series of outstanding adventures, rescues her. This rescue takes place just as she is being swung like a pendulum over an Allosaurs, the apelike people laughing with high glee as the beast leaps and jumps after her body, just out of his reach in the middle of a huge natural cavern arena. The aviator kills the chief of the ape people in single combat, and escapes with the girl, bringing her back to the plateau above.

The old chief is dying, and the stranger, now one of themselves due to his heroic feat, is accepted by the eagle riders as their chief. He is betrothed to the daughter of the old war lord.

Now during his life among these people, and his adventures, I want to build our aviator as a sort of serious Connecticut Yankee, with th emechanical power of American to invent and construct things. Before the girl was captured, he has seen, in part of the volcanic crater, material out of which hand bambs could be made, and it is by making a natural hand bomb and using it that he has been able to break into the cavern of sacrifice and rescue the girl. He now constructs a tremendous quantity of bombs, and in a great battle he leads the bird people to the attack which finally wipes out the apemen below. They return triumphant to their homes on the cliffs.

There is a bgeautiful and strange wedding ceremony between the aviator and the girl. He, mouned on White Eagle, and she on her lovely smaller brown eagle, fly across the valley and higher up, to a little cove-like paradise which she has made her own particular place.

It is their wedding night, and the boy has told her of the beauty of some music. With parts of his former radio and his own inventive ability, he has at last succeeded in rigging up a receiving set on which he intends to surprise her with some radio concert music. However, when he turns on the radio for the first time to test it out, instead of hearing music he hears a radio broadcast by the President of the United States. He hears that America is at war, that the enemy has made an invention which destroys the power of every American engine and no American airplane can leave the ground. The enemy has threatened to destoy New York by air unless America surrenders and becomes a vassal state. The Prsident of the United States has been given forty-eight hours, and it is evident that he will refuse. America appears to choose death rather than to lose its freedom.

As he listens to the stirring words of the President, the boy's mind is already made up. He gathers the hundreds of warriors together, and in a stirring speech tells them that his own people in the far distant out world are threatened with a disaster.

There has been a religious taboo, disclosed earlier in the story, which accounts for the eagle men never flying from the crater. The boy asks them to break it for him. As he has rescued them from their enemies, they must come and fight his enemies. He describes an airplane. He says they must all be destroyed. With great sacks of hand bombs firmly tied to each side of their saddlebows, with our aviator in the lead, the hundreds of war eagles take off from their plateau and rise above the crater. The boy has rescued his compass from his airplane, and has fastened it to his saddle. He leads them towards New YOrk.

The enemy fleet is seen approaching New York, flying across the ocean. High in the air the great swarm of war eagles are also flying north. As the bombing planes just reach New York, the war eagles come swarming down out of the high clouds far above them and dive to the attack, hurling their hand bombs. In a terrific battle, the enemy air fleet is destroyed by the eagle riders.

Our aviator lands upon the Statue of Liberty, and with his great White Eagle beside him, looks over the city he has saved. He swings up his hand in a final salute, gathers his warriors about him, and flies back to the paradise he has left, and to the woman he loves.

****

END

There are no records of MGM management's reaction to Cooper's story pitch. No meeting notes or memos on the subject have ever surfaced. Likewise, neither *Daily Variety* nor *The Hollywood Reporter* carried any reports of Louis B. Mayer suffering a heart attack or crawling onto his office window ledge in the days following its delivery. All rather remarkable, given MGM's reputation as a rather conservative, even pacifist, provider of light, lavishly-produced escapist entertainment. What Cooper was proposing was not exactly up Mayer's alley, and it would likely cost a bundle. Thomas Schatz described Mayer's managerial and fiscal style best in his definitive account of the Studio era *The Genius of the System* when he wrote that Mayer *"...did not mind heavy spending so long as he knew exactly what he was getting for it—a standard Technicolor operetta with Jeanette MacDonald and Nelson Eddy, say, or a costume drama with Greta Garbo."*

Vikings riding giant eagles and battling Nazis with electricity-neutralizing rays over New York City was not some thing dreamt of in L.B. Mayer's philosophy. But somehow, miraculously, the project was green-lighted for development.

It could have been due to the considerable force of Cooper's own personality, selling a wary crew on the romantic promise of perilous voyage with untold riches awaiting them, much like his filmic alter-ego Carl Denham had. He was still a powerful persuader and an instinctive showman, as the proposal clearly shows. Or it could have been the studio's desire for a return to the heady days of Thalberg, who took risks, valued innovation and considered himself a filmmaker and not a bureaucrat like his erstwhile partner Mayer. Both are likely reasons, but the bottom line was probably *the* bottom line.

Something remarkable had begun to occur on American theater screens earlier that year: the return of horror and fantasy. RKO had re-released *King Kong* for the first time on January 1st, 1938, and the box office was strong. Emasculated by the Production Code Authority, it was shorn of several of its original scenes of bloodcurdling, close-up violence and also those that showcased Kong's obviously amorous interest in rearranging Fay Wray's underclothes. Hollywood had been on a more-or-less self-imposed moratorium on horror film production since June of '37, when the "H"–for "horrific"–film certificate levied by the British Board of Film Censors had restricted admission to such efforts to only those over 16. The importance of European revenues was still a huge concern of American film companies, and they had capitulated to complaints about content by the board. It had the result of also depriving US audiences of genre movies they had grown to love, and dealt a blow to Universal, whose new management had then busied themselves trying to emulate "classier" establishments like Paramount and MGM. Luckily, it was to be a short-lived stateside phenomenon, because, in another interesting development, an independent LA grindhouse began running a round-the-clock triple feature of *Dracula, Frankenstein* and *Son of Kong* to a packed house. The "new" Universal saw the returns and adjusted their philosophy accordingly, unleashing major 1938 re-releases of their two iconic monsters, and putting *Son of Frankenstein* into production as well. Money, the only reason Hollywood ever does anything, won out over propriety.

All of this activity had no doubt been noticed by MGM, and the fact that two of Cooper's productions had played a part in it was not something to be ignored. The stage was now set for something new, it seemed...

Most of this is largely speculation, some of it informed, on the author's part, and I made the statement in my introduction that such content would be clearly labeled. As nothing exists to confirm it except general Hollywood history, consider it marked. All we really have to go on are the existence of Mr. Cooper's document of September 20, 1938 and the scripts, art and imagery that exist in the following chapters.

Held up like a mirror to Cooper's face, the proposal can be read as a clear reflection of his life's pursuits and obsessions. From the dangerous journey of the young, rebellious aviator to the discovery of a lost world, teaming with prehistoric survivors, major events in his life are woven in. The bird people's migration in search of food reflects the subject of his first documentary film, 1925's *Grass*, wherein both Cooper and Schoedsack followed a "Forgotten People", the Bakhtiari, as they annually drove their herds into the Iranian highlands in search of better pastures. The struggle between the primitive and the advanced that runs like a thread through everything from *King Kong* to *She* is also here. Even the story's gigantic avian protagonist, White Eagle, is a thinly-disguised tribute to the mascot of the Polish Air Service, who Cooper flew with against the Russians in the years following WWI.

And there is war.

The world that Merian C. Cooper unveiled his concepts for *War Eagles* to was on the brink of it; America was trying hard to stay neutral while staring into the ugly face of it; and Hollywood, except for Jack and Harry Warner, was burying its head in the sand. As the escalation of violence and saber-rattling by Nazi Germany and its allies threatened all of Europe, the studios' eyes were still firmly fixed on the grosses and the aforementioned European market revenues. Looking back from this point in history, it is almost impossible to believe this situation could have existed, but it was still all business for most studios before the United States officially entered the fray in 1941. One of the arrangements that allowed for it was a handy clause in the Production Code handbook:

X. National Feelings
1. The use of the flag shall be consistently respectful.
2. The history, institutions, prominent people and citizenry of all nations shall be represented fairly.

So the official policy was "Hands off Hitler." in nearly every production office in Hollywood. Warner Brothers largely ignored it and formed the Warner Club to begin evacuating children out of Europe, and inside of a year would release *Confessions of a Nazi Spy*. They would be rewarded for their humanitarian actions with a senatorial investigation, and the PCA, led by its moralizing chief officer Will Hays, would ban any and all further production of anti-Nazi films.

If the motion picture industry was turning a blind eye towards what would shortly become the greatest evil ever perpetrated by modern man, the rest of the United States' popular media could not be accused of the doing the same. Radio, news magazines and pulps (alongside their newly-empowered offspring, the comic book) were all taking up arms against the looming Teutonic menace, and there is evidence that Cooper, always a voracious reader of both high and low literature, spotted something in the October 1938 issue of *Flying Aces* that inspired the climactic confrontation over New York in his synopsis. Traditionally, pulps were on the stands weeks *before* the dated month of publication, and the image of a German bomber with a bizarre electrical weapon cruising above an article tagline reading "Will Germany Hurl a 'Death Ray'?" could have caught his eye. The article, reproduced in this chapter, goes on to describe a neutralizing electrical field weapon identical to the one that would follow in Cooper's story and all subsequent scripts.

Merian C. Cooper had just set a story in motion that did everything but directly name the perpetrators of the coming world war, and finished off with a magnificent image that would look right at home under a "Buy War Bonds" banner.

Kristallnacht was less than two months away.

MGM, cruising into both unfamiliar territory and dangerous clouds, began looking for a seasoned pilot in the writer's building...

Will Germany Hurl a "Death Ray"?

THE SENSATIONAL STORY BEHIND OUR COVER PAINTING

○ ○ ○

WAR OFFICES the world over are trying to solve this question: "Have the Nazis actually perfected a silent, invisible weapon of destruction—an aero-engine-stopping 'death ray'?"

Well, it would seem that they have—for reports sifting through from key European capitals indicate that certain scientists of the Third Reich have developed a startling apparatus which throws piercing ultra short waves capable of choking off all electrical ignition engines within its range.

Such a terrible weapon—if really practical in form and if effective over a "fighting distance"—would virtually assure its owners mastery of the air! Other powers, even though they possess great air strength, as it is now reckoned in men and machines, would hardly be able to overcome such ray. Unless, of course, they are quickly able to devise some kind of a protective shield for their gas-fueled motors.

Now, it has been particularly noticeable in the past few years that German engineers have been feverishly at work developing new and more powerful aircraft Diesels. (See our article on page 8 titled "Has America Muffed the Diesel?"). These motors, being of the compression-ignition type, do not rely on electric sparks to fire the fuel vapor in their cylinders. And so, such engines would in no way be affected by any ray designed to blank out electrical ignition.

Thus, Germany already has planes capable of carrying ray devices. These craft likewise could be used against any country which developed similar "death ray" weapons.

We must point out, however, that this particular ignition-paralyzing ray is no new idea. For some years, electrical experts have been acquainted with the theory of ultra short waves which cut out ordinary electrical-current machines. Some time ago, motor cars were "stalled" along German roads in a test of a device which may have been the forerunner of the ray machine now reported in the Fatherland.

Word likewise has come through that Grindell Matthews, famed British inventor, has on several occasions successfully paralyzed auto engines by means of some electrical discharge system.

Heretofore, little has been achieved, however, in making these rays effective over any practical distance. But the new reports eminating from Germany very likely mean that this "bug" has been ironed out. And perhaps the British, too, have "gone along"—for we understand that a series of high latticed poles set up along England's north-east coast really is part of an electrical defense of some type.

Meanwhile, we are persistently told that the Nazis have mounted ray equipment on some of their new bombers and that they have also established ray transmitting

stations along their borders. It is said that the Reichmen are practicing diligently with this destructive apparatus—that they are ready to operate with deadly effect against any raiding planes which may approach the German frontier.

We grant, of course, that only the "inside engineers" know the real worth of the invention in its present form. But suppose that it *does* have an effective range of several hundred yards. And suppose that Germany decided to use the apparatus for *offense* rather than simply defense.

ON THIS month's cover, our artist, August Schomburg, has depicted a scene which may come true if the Nazis strike at France. He shows a dramatic engagement between ray machine equipped Diesel-powered German bombers and French fighters over the renowned Maginot Line, the Tricolor's concrete redoubts that frown across toward Germany.

Mr. Schomburg uses the striking Junkers Ju.86 planes for his Nazi raiders and the fleet Morane 275's for his defenders. (Some communications have it that Heinkel 60 bombers had been fitted with the ray apparatus, but this craft is obscure. More likely the real attack would see huge Jumo-Diesel machines in action.)

As for the "death ray" device itself, we have no idea as to how it would actually appear when mounted on a plane. It might be entirely concealed in the fuselage. For the purposes of "putting the idea over" on our cover, however, we "built up" an electrical discharge machine out of our own imagination—for we wished to provide something visible in our picture in order that the idea of this startling weapon might be grasped.

But now let us get back to our scene: The Germans, we take it, would carry a good supply of H.E. bombs in their Junkers. Thus they'd achieve double action—for while their "death rays" would repulse the onslaughts of the defending planes, "eggs" could be poured down to wipe out sections of the Maginot Line.

The 600-h.p. Gnome-Rhone powered Morane ships have rushed out of the south-west at the first roar of the Junkers Ju.86's. Quickly, the Tricolor flight leader has ordered his pilots to intercept the raiders. But suddenly the foremost Vee of Moranes flies into the invisible area commanded by the Nazis piercing rays! Immediately, without a single shot fired, their engines conk out, their props go dead—and down they spiral and spin, their pilots helpless!

Perhaps one or two of the young French flyers, uncertain what had happened, would take to the silk. Others would try to stay with their "paralyzed" planes, and maybe they would be able to get down "deadstick". Yet

> Reports persist that the Nazis have perfected an amazing device of destruction—a fearful, invisible weapon to paralyze opposing planes in mid-air and send them hurtling helplessly to the ground!

(Continued on page 67)

[15]

Will Germany Hurl a "Death Ray"?

(Continued from page 15)

crashes and deaths below could hardly be wholly evaded, especially if the terrain were decidedly unsuitable for "sit-downs."

Those that lived would witness the destruction of their forts without being able to raise a hand in defense. Thus the psychological effect—the blow to morale—would be far-reaching. Nothing is quite so unnerving as the unseen. If, as we inferred above, the "death ray" equipment were entirely concealed inside the Junkers, then many of the flyers would be wholly at loss as to what hit them.

No wonder the war experts of the world are on pins and needles. Germany may already have this fearful weapon in workable form—and a real defense against it has not, to our knowledge, yet been found.

HAS AMERICA MUFFED THE DIESEL? *See page 8*

FICTION MODEL BUILDING FACT

FLYING ACES

OCTOBER 15¢

WILL GERMANY HURL A "DEATH RAY"?

AUGUST SCHOMBURG

SOARING FEATURE: "ELMIRA LEADS THE WAY!"–PEPPY "CONROY" LESSON
PHIL STRANGE NOVEL, "COFFIN" KIRK YARN, PHINEAS MIRTHQUAKE
MODELS: NORTHROP XBT-1, $1-"DEMON" GAS JOB–NATIONAL MEET REVIEW

27

Dauntless pilot Jimmy Matthews and Professor Hiram P. Cobb are headed towards serious trouble in the opening act of Harold Lamb and James Creelman's draft of War Eagles. *Image courtesy of the Duncan Gleason Archives.*

A squadron of eagle-riders descend on their cave-dwelling enemies in the climactic Creelman Valley Sequence that was cut from the script when Cyril Hume took over writing chores in July of 1939. Image courtesy of a private collection.

The Plot is Hatched

Indiana Jones made a statement in 1981's *Raiders of the Lost Ark* about the dangers of archeology in which he listed *folklore* as one of the greatest. In my several years' quest for the facts behind the fate of *War Eagles*, I've found it to be the gospel truth. It's inevitable that something like an unproduced epic fantasy with a pedigree like *War Eagles* would generate quite a bit of mythology around its non-existence. For decades, there really wasn't that much around to actually *see*. Old stills and scraps of paper repeatedly printed and quoted in magazines and fairly esoteric books (like this one) tend to accumulate some odd ornamental details in the process of constant recycling, and before you know it, a sort of "alternate reality" account has taken on a life of its own, stalking around above-ground while the real remains still lie deeply buried.

Nowhere is this more true than in the tangled case of the authorship of *War Eagles* and its various screenplays. For decades there was a persistent belief among many film fans and academics that Willis O'Brien had actually conceived the idea and authored at least one draft of the script. Despite the fact that he had never actually written a feature—he was a man of many talents, and a good storyteller after his own fashion, but no scenarist— it was a fairly entrenched and unshakeable conviction on the part of many. Part of it was due to his well-deserved cult status as the man who breathed life into King Kong and so many other wonderful creations. I was, and still am, a card-carrying fanatic when it comes to Obie and his work, and having a fuller view of the difficulties he encountered has only made me admire him more. But there is sometimes a tendency in film circles to elevate personalities into realms they didn't occupy in life, and I think that began with O'Brien shortly after his death in 1962. He had truly become one of Hollywood's ultimate unsung heroes to many, and publications like FJA's *Famous Monsters of Filmland* began showing and telling his accomplishments to a new generation of fans. Gradually, *War Eagles* became Obie's great lost film project—and his alone. Merian C. Cooper took a back seat, and no one, Cooper included, really minded. It was all ancient history by then, rapidly fading into legend.

And there was also that script floating around with Obie's name on it.

Sometime in the early 1970's, an individual obtained a copy of a *War Eagles* script from Darlyne O'Brien, along with some attendant paperwork. It's not my place to go into the details of this event, or to address the fact that the material was never returned to Obie's widow, nor did she ever share in any profits. It's best to just say that theft is one of the other well known dangers of archeology and move on. Shortly afterwards, photocopies of the coverless draft

began to turn up and gradually circulate among fantasy film and animation enthusiasts. Naturally, this generated a *lot* of interest since a project that had been long considered truly lost now had a (nearly) fully-fleshed story to tell. A *body* had been found at last, and in the top right hand corner of the first page was the name W. H. O'Brien...

The paperwork that accompanied copies of the purloined script usually consisted of Cooper's September 1938 proposal, a set of technical notes describing effects setups for what would come to be known as the "Allosaur Capture Sequence", and another remarkable document entitled "Notes on the Great Eagles and Their People". Authorship of all but Cooper's proposal was quickly attributed to O'Brien since his name was on the first working page of the script, and a few rough sketches were to be found within, likely done in his hand. It was a mistake that would remain unchecked for many years, even finding its way into the file documentation of the Argosy Pictures Corporation at Brigham Young University, home of the Merian C. Cooper papers collection.

The supposition that Obie had actually written *War Eagles* had begun to unravel for me as far back as that first fateful phone call to Forry Ackerman back in 1977. One of the things he had told that breathless young fan on the other end of the line was that he had seen a script for the project that was being touted as Obie's work, but he had heard from someone at MGM years earlier that a writer named Cyril Hume had actually done the work. Even at that young age, I was familiar with the name since he had written MGM's highly regarded 1956 space opera *Forbidden Planet*, one of my favorite science fiction movies. Forry also told me that Hume had written several of the Tarzan films for MGM as well, and was employed by the studio for decades. He was hoping to maybe one day do a book or extensive article about *War Eagles* and some of Obie's other unproduced projects, and had recently acquired a number of sketches and stills, one of which was the image published in the issue of *FM* that had sparked my imagination and generated my call. I told him I couldn't wait to see more.

Forry eventually devoted a short section in his 1981 book *Mr. Monster's Movie Gold* to some of that tantalizing pre-production artwork and a few frames from the first *War Eagles* test sequence, but had not uncovered anything more to suggest Cyril Hume's proper credit be applied to the screenplay. He wrote "*When George Pal was working at the Studio* (MGM) *on* The Power, *I alerted him to* War Eagles. *He tried to find some trace of it. He was not successful.*" , so confirmation of Hume's involvement as a writer did not arrive till nearly a year later.

"WAR EAGLES"

1   FADE IN:
CLOSEUP - BRONZE PLAQUE "MISSING PERSONS
BUREAU" - INT. CENTRAL POLICE STATION -
NEW YORK CITY - DAY

A bronze plaque standing on a desk, reading
MISSING PERSONS BUREAU. Over the closeup
of plaque:

           Voice (spelling out slowly)
C-O-B-B. Hiram P. Cobb, eh?

CAMERA TILTS UP AND RETREATS to MED. CLOSE
SHOT disclosing a uniformed police sergeant
at the desk phone, a plainclothes man perched
in a chair beside him, reading a newspaper.

           Police Sergeant
        (hard-boiled, and busy, making notes)
How long's he been gone?....
        (writing)
Age? Fifty -- what? What's he look like?...
        (writing)
Five foot seven... heavy glasses. Stoop shouldered.
Say, who is this speaking?

2   MED. CLOSE SHOT
INT. NEW ENGLAND HOME - CORNER OF HALLWAY

A plump woman, with hard, thin-lipped face
and sharp eyes is perched on the edge of a
horse-hair sofa, talking excitedly into the
phone. Beside her, hanging over the phone
are two youngish-old men, pretentiously
dressed in a salesman-Rotarian manner.

           Woman (excitedly, into phone)
His cousin. His mother, Mary, was my mother,
Estelle's sister. Of course that makes me his
cousin. And I and my two brothers are Professor
Cobb's only heirs -- that is, his only living re-
latives.

           First Cousin (urgently)
Tell him about the money!

           Woman (into phone)
You see, officer, he's drawn out every cent of
his savings from the bank, and --

                        CONTINUED

The first fan-circulated page of a War Eagles *script and the source of much contention. Note that O'Brien's typed name does not appear in the conventional screenwriter's location. Courtesy of Gregory Kulon.*

Harold Lamb

I was born—New York-1892—with damaged eyes, ears, and speech and grew up so. For some twenty years it was an ordeal to meet people, and I am still uncomfortable in cities or crowds, although by now the damages of childhood have nearly righted themselves. "To build him up" I was sent from gymnasium in winter to the open country at other times; but all my free hours were spent in my grandfather's library.

School was torment and college—Columbia—worse. The hours that really counted were spent in the library of Columbia. There I dug into something gorgeous and new, chronicles of people in Asia. I wrote all the time—set up my stories in the attic at school and printed them on a hand press and then carried on with the Columbian literary magazine.

In 1914 my father broke down and I found a job as a make-up man on a motor trade weekly, then tried to do financial statistics for the New York Times and write stories at the same time. The stories were gleaned from the oriental digging and Adventure printed them. An understanding editor, Arthur Sullivan Hoffman, allowed me to write anything I wanted.

I wandered more than a bit, turned up at Plattsburg, 1919, and in the Seventh New York, later the 107 Infantry, in May 1917 as a private, but did not see any fighting. In June of that year I married Ruth Barbour, and I have wondered since then why men write books about unhappy marriages. We have a son and a daughter. We went out to the Pacific Coast soon after our marriage, accompanied by my father. Two years of that time were spent at Fort Bragg, in the forest along the Northern California coast.

I have had to gather together my own collection to work with—the medieval travelers, Persian and Russian chronicles, histories of elder China. I spend months in going through the scenes of a book in imagination until all details are clear. Then I try to put it all down in words. I shirk revising, which is an ordeal. When study oppresses I go straight to the Northern lumber camps or the decks of a schooner. My relaxations are chess, tennis, and gardening. I am six feet one inch in height, weigh 160 pounds and have prematurely gray hair.

Life is good, after all, when a man can go where he wants to, and write about what he likes best and know that other men find pleasure in his work.

—Harold Lamb, in his own words. Courtesy of his chief historian Howard Andrew Jones.

If Merian C. Cooper had been looking for a soul-mate as screenwriter, he couldn't have found a better candidate than Harold Lamb. Fellow Orientalists and adventurers, it's very likely that Cooper both knew his work well and specifically asked him to join the project. By that time, Lamb had already penned three large-scale adventures scripts, *The Crusades*, *The Plainsman* and *The Buccaneer* for no less a director than Cecil B. DeMille, and his sizeable body of quality pulp fiction and popular history volumes were widely read. No records exist that indicate he was employed on any other features being developed at MGM, and most of his output had been produced at Paramount, so the case can be made that he was sought out for this specific assignment by the producer.

Before we dig further into Lamb's history and sizable influence on *War Eagles*, I have an interesting story to relate. Both my own discovery of Lamb's role in the creation of *War Eagles* and my understanding of his larger influence as a writer occurred simultaneously over a two-day stretch in the spring of 2003. In addition to having an avid obsession with fantasy films of the 1930's and 40's, I've always loved the pulp fiction produced in the same era, the works of H.P. Lovecraft and Robert E. Howard, the creator of *Conan the Barbarian* and *Solomon Kane*, being my favorites. I shared this passion with several friends and we occasionally attended pulp conventions together and swapped stories and bits of history in conversation and emails. My friend and fellow Howard enthusiast Randy Fox had recently told me about a writer that had influenced *Conan*'s author enormously with tales of a wild Cossack warrior named Khlit, and dropped by my office one afternoon to deliver a collected volume of the stories entitled *The Curved Saber*. Apparently, Howard had found great inspiration for his brooding Cimmerian in the Khlit yarns and had acknowledged their creator, Harold Lamb, as one of the best adventure writers in the business. I was looking forward to reading them.

The next day I received an email from James D'Arc, the curator of the Arts and Communications Archives of Brigham Young University in Provo, Utah. I had messaged him as a result of a phone conversation I had recently had with Don Shay. Since Don had actually read a *War Eagles* script decades earlier for his exhaustive article on O'Brien—it had apparently been the copy once belonging to Darlyne, before it had disappeared— he had suggested I look for a university depository that might contain Merian C. Cooper's papers to see if any other drafts existed. A short internet search had led to the collections of the Harold B. Lee Library at BYU. They housed the largest accumulation of records, scripts and ephemera associated with Cooper, most of it directly donated by the man himself. I quickly emailed Mr. D'Arc with a request to locate any material labeled "War Eagles" and this was his response:

Dear Mr. Conover:

Here is what we have on WAR EAGLES:

1.   In the *Argosy Pictures Corporation Papers MSS 1849* (Box 19, Folder 2) there is a script by Harold Lamb, 17 April 1939, 135 pages.

2.   Script by Willis O'Brien, 1938, MGM, 134pp. pre-sented by M.C. Cooper, with script changes dated 17 April 1939, 20 April 1939, 22 May 1939; script has 7 full-page unnumbered sketches by O'Brien.

I still vividly remember the weird sensation that washed over me that morning as I looked back and forth between the computer monitor and the volume of stories that was still sitting on my desk from the previous day. I had heard the name Harold Lamb for the first time just a few weeks earlier and here it was again in relation to a cherished project I had just begun researching in earnest. They were one and the same.

Subsequent conversations and messages between James D'Arc and myself quickly confirmed that the two drafts were virtually identical and that the copy of the "O'Brien" script in the archives was exactly that—a photocopy. It was accompanied by the usual batch of paperwork and notes that circulated with it, and had been donated to the collection by O'Brien researcher Stephan Pickering a few years earlier. I had already obtained a copy of the draft attributed to O'Brien, along with his technical notes, from fellow collector Gregory Kulon, and within a few weeks received copies of the Cooper proposal and the "Notes on the Great Eagles and Their People" from Mr. Pickering.

It soon became apparent that the only thing Obie had authored was the set of technical notes, and that both the script and highly-developed cultural background material contained in the "Notes on the Great Eagles and Their People" had been crafted by Lamb. It was he (along with the yet-to-be-rediscovered James Creelman) who had taken Cooper's short proposal and expanded it into a full screenplay, employing much poetry and richly delivered dialogue that survived well into later drafts. While Cooper had simply suggested that the bird people were to be portrayed "after the type of Vikings", it was Lamb who had molded them into an actual lost Viking race, complete with a wonderfully authentic archaic English dialect. His detailed cultural background notes, which can be read as an appendix to this volume, bear all the marks of his intimate familiarity with groups as diverse as the Mongols and his beloved Cossacks, both of which are referenced on the first page.

I consider Harold Lamb to be the great unsung architect of *War Eagles*, and much credit should be given to his efforts to wrestle a gargantuan premise into a workable, if not entirely filmable, screenplay. By the time he had begun working as a screenwriter, Lamb had honed his storytelling abilities to a keen edge, and the only elements that seemed to still need refining involved the elaborate sequences involving the ape men and their blood-sport distractions in the Valley sequence. That section of the story would shortly become James Creelman's difficult task, and, as we will soon see, move *War Eagles* in another direction.

Most of the previously published accounts of *War Eagles*' short, troubled existence have used up an inordinate amount of their page-count in describing the action of the story.   I have dispensed with that approach in favor of vintage documentation.

What follows is a rare glimpse into the studio practice

of "script coverage" and an effective synopsis of the *War Eagles* storyline as penned by Lamb and Creelman. This report is an example of what a production executive at MGM could be expected to read in determining the viability and progress of a property, and covers the primary script being developed for the project at the time.

FILE COPY

WAR EAGLES
(Army Flier-Old Professor Line)
by Harold Lamb & James A. Creelman

4717

: Script No. 26102 :
: Dated 4/17/39 :

Hiram P. Cobb, an absent-minded professor of history, is so certain that the descendants of the Vikings are still alive in the Antarctic that--to the horror of his inheritance-hungry relatives-- he liquidates his entire fortune and embarks upon an expedition which strikes every normal-thinking person as being foolhardy. He gets Lt. Jimmy Mathews, a young, ambitious Texan, who has been grounded for stunting, to fly him to his destination beyond Tierra del Fuego. In the south polar regions their plane is sucked down into a volcanic district with an almost tropical climate. To the professor's delight they discover that this country is truly peopled by the descendants of the Vikings.

Naru, a beautiful young girl, is their first guide in this strange land which is not only inhabited by human beings but also by supposedly extinct reptiles and eagles the size of tremendous air-planes which the brave Vikings domesticate. Though he is at first regarded with suspicion by Atok, Naru's warrior brother, Jimmy estab-lishes himself as a hero and wins the affections of Nary by taming a hitherto untamable white eagle.

Atok's clan is summoned to the lush country of Skal, the chief of all the Vikings, to help in harvesting the crops. This work is interrupted by the appearance of tremendous man-eating monsters, alosauria, and of a brutish tribe of "earth-people", who live in caves and are the deadly enemies of the Vikings. There is a fierce battle with primitive weapons between the two forces, and in the course of this struggle the earth-people make away with Naru.

These beast-men plan to sacrifice the girl to an alosaurus which they have captured. They are thwarted by Jimmy and the prof-essor. The latter discovers a high explosive in a natural state and constructs a primitive though effective bomb that Jimmy uses to throw the brutes into panic. The aviator effects a thrilling rescue of Naru, who is being swung back and forth above the snapping jaws of the huge lizard. But the beast-men angrily take up the pursuit. The professor is transformed into a true Viking when Atok, who has been mortally wounded, entrusts him with his faithful sword. The otherwise so meek scientist goes berserk and stands off the brutes until the Vikings can rally their forces and complete the rout of their antagonists.

Skal orders a victory celebration in honor of Jimmy and the professor. During this feast Jimmy switches on the radio--one of the few things he rescued when his plane cracked up--and learns that a foreign power has issued a three-day ultimatum to the United States. It is rumored that the enemy is in possession of a neutralizing ray which will incapacitate all American planes. Jimmy is anxious to come to the defense of his country, and Skal places all his warriors and eagles at the disposal of his new friend. For two days the prof-essor works like mad to construct a sufficient number of his home-made bombs. On the third day hundreds of monstrous eagles set out for New York, carrying fighters and bombs.

Meanwhile, the enemy has paralyzed the United States's entire electrical system with its neutralizing ray. But the eagles meet the invading air force above Manhattan in a blood-curdling battle. Friend and foe alike are terrified by these huge birds which--aided by the professor's bombs, completely destroy the attacking force. Having saved his country, Jimmy flies back to the country of the Vikings with his beloved Naru.

33

Reader's reports like this one were, and still are, a backbone of the motion picture industry, and this anonymously-authored, single page summation seems to have impressed the writer enough to keep it on a positive, snappy level of delivery. One of the most interesting details of the document is the subtitled "Army Flier-Old Professor Line" that refers to the actual storyline. It 's a distinct indicator that more than one plot was being developed for *War Eagles* at this point, and this was confirmed when I made a research trip to Los Angeles in late summer of 2003.

If I can claim any credit at all for adding to the knowledge of *War Eagle*'s long-buried history, it's for the simple detective work I've done to clarify and untangle the screenplay credits and timeline for the doomed project. And, in one of those great strokes of serendipitous luck that have helped me out all along the way, I was able to accomplish nearly all of this by simply going where I was *told* to go. I had been planning on heading out west, to visit points in Las Vegas, Utah and LA to do interviews and research, when it became evident that the material at the Cooper archives at BYU was fairly limited in scope. Most of what was there I had already read or would shortly have access to, so I reluctantly marked Provo off of my list of destinations. But in a final phone conversation, James D'Arc had added, almost as an afterthought, that I should try to get in touch with archivist Ned Comstock at the University of Southern California's Cinematic Arts Library, because he had heard reports that there was some *War Eagles* material possibly located there as well.

The email I sent USC shortly afterwards eventually changed everything I thought I knew about *War Eagles*, and later that summer provided me with an opportunity to spend three days with what felt like the still-living spirits of the screenwriters. What the university had safely hidden in their basement archives were not script fragments or even period-produced mimeographs. The original manuscripts, straight from the writers' typewriters, were filed away there, with heavy hand-notations by the authors. In the long decades of their interment , no one had ever come calling before, and one of the first ghosts I met among those yellowing pages was the tragic shade of James A. Creelman.

The most startling thing about finding Creelman's name listed side by side with Lamb's in nearly half of the neatly organized and sequentially dated folders Ned Comstock wheeled out for me on August 11, 2003 was that it was so *logical* that he be there. Inevitable, really. JamesCreelman was a name that I and probably every other serious *King Kong* fan had been aware of for ages. He had been an established scenarist at RKO since the early 1920's and was well known as a "gag man"—a specialist in set-pieces or punchy ideas— with an especially wild imagination, and Cooper had hand-picked him as a writer to develop *Kong* into the non-stop thrill show he wanted. He had also penned *Kong*'s twin RKO production, *The Most Dangerous Game*, which was shot simultaneously and shared the same cast and many of the same sets. It was only natural that he'd be employed again by the same producer to perform exactly those duties he excelled at on a film that was supposed to

Just how immaculate the conception of a movie idea must be remains problematical. But the construction must be perfect–more perfect than even that of a play. Better talk to a playwright or read a good book on dramatic construction before you start. And the style must be pretty fair, too, or at least impressively florid. Movies are painted in strokes as broad as they are short. Don't be afraid to write the impossible. The camera has been developed to such an extent that it can, if necessary, reproduce any scene which Freud can conjure up...

James Ashmore Creelman, "*How to Stay Out of the Movies*", from *The Bookman*, November 1924

surpass *King Kong* on every level. Equally surprising, however, was that history had somehow forgotten Creelman's involvement.

He was Harold Lamb's partner throughout their entire run on *War Eagles*. While Lamb worked out the characters and interplay, Creelman was hard at work on the mechanics and spectacle Coop was after, and all indications seem to show it was a comfortable arrangement. They each took turns at individual drafts, altering the sequence of events from time to time to find the best story rhythm, and they both contributed to the earliest studio-commissioned work that still exists. Dated February 20, 1939, it is an 88-page treatment that pre-dates all of the previously known plotlines–including the "Army Flier-Old Professor Line"–and is a darker tale, containing some key character changes and plot elements with even closer ties to Cooper's wartime experience. The hand-written cover sheet by Creelman reads:

War Eagles
by
Harold Lamb and James A. Creelman
Revised Treatment, Adapted from Original Outline
By Merian C. Cooper

In this earliest of scenarios, the young pilot, Jack Matthews, is not hired by the amiable Professor Cobb, but instead by a mysterious older aviator, Victor Kovac, a wealthy and decorated war ace who apparently served with the younger man's late father in "the Polish-Soviet affair"—a direct reference to Cooper's own post-WWI Kosciusko squadron adventures. He invites him on the daring polar expedition, this time with the express intent of finding the legendary giant eagles and their Viking masters. The story unfolds more or less as described in Cooper's original treatment, but takes an intriguing turn after the chieftain's daughter, referred to as Maru instead of Naru, is rescued from the ape men by the two pilots. Having earlier smashed the radio, and now wounded and being feted as a hero by the bird people, Kovacs makes a startling confession:

Kovac waves away the boy's gratitude. "Stay here, always boy," he urges weakly. "With Maru... you've found the best in life. Keep it."

The boy nods, understanding. "I will..."

Kovac's voice rises, urgently. "Don't go back. Never go back."

Something in his tone catches Jack's attention. "What do you mean, Vic?"

"It's too late—you can't do anything."

Maru is watching Kovac's drawn face intently. Skal comes over to them, curiously.

"In three days your country will be destroyed." Kovac lifts his hand, as the boy starts to exclaim.

"No. No, I am not mad."

He raises himself with an effort. "Remember. I kept a calendar. You must—understand. The Dictators—my country—will gamble with war."

Maru echoes the word. The boy, incredulous, is staring at his friend. "What! You can't mean—"

"I know. I was sent to search for—air base."

Kovac takes a drinking horn from the nearest Viking and rouses himself to explain.

"I failed. So the attack will come over the Atlantic. Our planes will destroy New York. We have a new weapon—the attack will not fail." Kovac smiles. "I do not think the United States will accept any ultimatum."

The boy is thinking, his face set. "No, no they won't."

"I am glad—I failed. I hate this war."

Maru looks up, questioning. "Your country?"

Jack nods, his thoughts far off. "New York," he repeats. "Why, my squadron's there."

Kovac catches the note in the boy's voice, and grips his arm anxiously. "You can't—do anything."

Jack does not heed this. "Jim and his nobs will be there."

"Stay here. You are out of it—safe. Don't you understand? The whole of our world at war."

Maru withdraws from the two men, unnoticed.

Jack: "You knew this, and you brought me up here?"

Kovac nods, sinking back. "I wanted – to let you live. I saw your father die, behind our lines—years ago..."

A full script with these elements and characters seems to have been produced, but no copy exists in the archives. An interesting memo from Harold Lamb appears to confirm this, and something else:

3/24/39
3/28/39

Script Department:

The original name of the boy. "Barney Cochrane" in WAR EAGLES has been changed to JACK MATHEWS, and "Ivan Richtmeyer" to VICTOR KOVAC. We have endeavored to make these name changes all thru', but may have slipped up somewhere.

Thank You,

Harold Lamb

Harold Lamb

Was the change of names mandated by the studio? The shift from an obviously more Germanic surname to a Polish one certainly seems to indicate hesitation to engage in nationalist finger-pointing. This was the beginning of a trend that would dog the production until its final days, and by the next full draft dated April 17, 1939, Kovac and the spy-line were out and the more palatable Professor Hiram P. Cobb was in.

The late George Turner, in his groundbreaking *The Making of King Kong*, pointed out that James Creelman's strong suit as a writer was also his downfall at times. "*Creelman's fertile imagination provided good ideas, but he had difficulty keeping inside the bounds of financial and technical practicality.*" he wrote. While this may have been an issue on *Kong*, it appears that it may have been a key to Creelman's continued survival on *War Eagles*. Trouble had been brewing with a major sequence of the story since the beginning of the writing phase, and with a second major test for *War Eagles* being budgeted and scheduled, it was about to reach a critical point. Cooper's grand vision of the ape men's elaborate dinosaur capture and arena sequence was one of the most ambitious visuals ever conceived of at the time, and Creelman's abilities to construct fantastic gags were probably at their peak. But even he was having a hell of a time trying to figure out how to make it all work! His frustration is evident in some of his raw work pages at the time.

It was probably just beginning to dawn on Cooper that he may have overplayed his showman's hand by trying to do so much in one picture. When one reads even his original synopsis, the rescue of Naru from the clutches of the ape men and the dinosaur menace feels like the story's climax, and the wedding that follows the very happy ending.

But the protagonists *still* have to save New York!

181   INT. CAVERN   MED. SHOT NIGHT   *Moving Shot*

Jimmy knocks the apeman leader senseless against the
wall with a right to his jaw, and snatches his knife.
Just beyond, astonished apemen are holding Naru.
Jimmy dives into this group, knocks them away. As they
leap back to attack, he grabs Naru's rope with one hand,
knife ready in the other, and swings clear of the idol.
CAMERA FOLLOWS, as both swing out over the cavern floor
with the dinosaur leaping to attack. Jimmy meets the
beast's attack by stabbing the flint knife into his eye
as they swing past.

182   INT. CAVERN   MED. SHOT   NIGHT

Jimmy lands with the girl among the apemen ~~on the cage~~ *above the cavern mouth.*
~~by the stone stairs from the ledge above.~~ As He
swings up, he knocks ~~some of~~ them off the cage tops with
his feet. He drops himself and Naru to the top of the
cage.

183   INT. CAVERN   FULL SHOT   NIGHT

The apemen who have fallen to the cave floor are at once
attacked by the pain-maddened dinosaur.

~~INT. CAVERN   MED. SHOT   NIGHT~~

~~Jimmy knocks out the other apemen, then starts up the~~
~~steps~~
~~stone steps with Naru, but stops as they see~~ -

~~INT. CAVERN   LONG SHOT   NIGHT~~

running toward them from the ledge
~~- Apemen pouring down the adjacent stone steps from the~~
~~ledge above.   Also the apemen whom he knocked flat are~~
~~picking themselves up, ready to attack again. These~~
~~knocked-flat apemen are on the side of the stone steps~~ -

CONTINUED:

CONTINUED (2)

~~no one is on the other side. The road is open over the~~

~~cage tops.~~

184   INT. CAVERN   MED. SHOT   NIGHT

understands and

~~So~~ Jimmy, with Naru, ~~runs that way. The boy over the~~

drops to —

~~cage tops.~~

185   INT. CAVERN   *FULL* ~~LONG~~ SHOT   NIGHT

— the cavern floor. They shrink against the cages as they see

~~They climb over the cage tops toward the stone steps~~

~~leading to the cavern floor. This is beset with~~

~~difficulties, as the beasts within snap up through the~~

~~bars (full-size horns or claws protruding with~~

~~sound effects). Also because divisions between cages must~~

~~be climbed over.~~

INT. CAVERN   LONG SHOT   NIGHT

The apemen from the high ledge begin to descend

toward the cage tops along the handholds in the rock.

INT. CAVERN   FULL SHOT   NIGHT

Jimmy and Naru make their way across the cage tops.

Apemen, dropping from the handholds in the rock, begin

to make their way across the cage tops in pursuit.

CUT TO!

INT. CAVERN   MED. SHOT   NIGHT

~~Cobb is still~~ staring down through the hold in the roof,

stunned by the monstrous spectacle below. Now he sticks

Jimmy's broken sword in his belt, slips from the fissure

to the great volcanic fissure which adjoins it. He starts

making his way down the hand holds in this pillar. This starts

him toward the base of the pillar (which is just over the

closed cavern mouth).

(NOTE: We need another angle EXT. CAVERN at fissure to show him picking up the sword.)

INT. CAVERN   FULL SHOT   NIGHT

Jimmy and Naru, clambering over the cage tops, reach the far end of the cages and drop down upon the stone steps. They run down toward the cavern floor, and stop short as they see -

INT. CAVERN   FULL SHOT   NIGHT

- the dinosaur, finishing the destruction of the fallen apemen.

INT. CAVERN   MED. SHOT   NIGHT

Jimmy and Naru, at the foot of the stone steps, start to turn back and start up again to escape the dinosaur. They stop as they see -

INT. CAVERN   MED. OR FULL SHOT   NIGHT

- apemen arriving over the cages at the top of the lower stone stairs.

INT. CAVERN   MED. SHOT   NIGHT

Jimmy sees that they cannot go back. He notices the roaring of the triceretops in the cage beside him. Its latch is within reach. He looks back toward -

INT. CAVERN   FULL SHOT   NIGHT

- the dinosaur, which, having killed the apemen, is just turning back toward them. As it sees them -

INT. CAVERN   MED. SHOT   NIGHT

- Jimmy gets an idea and pulls the latch. The triceratops shoves the cage door open and rushes out on the cavern floor -

188   INT. CAVERN   FULL SHOT   NIGHT

- to attack the dinosaur.. A terrific battle ensues.

189   INT. CAVERN   MED SHOT   NIGHT

Jimmy sees his chance and, gripping Naru's hand, runs for

the ~~cave mouth.~~ *pillar with the hind holds.*

190   INT. CAVERN   FULL SOT   NIGHT

The fighting monsters block their path. The boy and girl,

blocked, have to flatten themselves momentarily against

the cages to escape destruction.

191   INT. CAVERN   LONG SHOT   NIGHT

The apemen foll w, pursuing the boy and girl, ~~down the~~

~~stone stairs from the cage tops to~~ *drop from above*

~~the cavern mouth to~~

192   INT. CAVERN   FULL SHOT   NIGHT

- the cavern floor. They run by the fighting monsters

toward the ~~cave mouth~~ *pillar*

193   INT. CAVERN   FULL SHOT   NIGHT

The fighting monsters move away from the cages, giving

the boy and girl, flattened against them, a chance to

run on toward the ~~cave mouth~~ *pillar*. Apemen, pursuing, are

caught by the dinosaur's tail and knocked flat.

194   INT. CAVERN   MED. SHOT   NIGHT

These apemen ~~They~~ are trampled by the tricer~~a~~tops.

195   INT. CAVERN   FULL SHOT   NIGHT
Start to climb the pillar by hand holds
The boy and girl ~~find themselves blocked by the drawbridge,~~

~~which, raised, closes the cavern mouth. Jimmy throws himself~~

~~against it, shoulder first, trying to break it down. It is~~

~~far too heavy to be smashed open that way. The ropes that~~

~~hold it are out of reach.~~

39

One spectacular sequence falls directly after another, and it makes for a huge shift in an audience's attention and expectations. Cooper had faced a similar situation, although on a much smaller scale, back in 1933 with *King Kong*: the notorious "Spider Pit" scene. Many fantasy fans know the legend of the film's most infamous missing sequence, but it bears repeating. After the scene involving Kong shaking many of his human pursuers off of a gigantic log and into a deep ravine, there was additional footage of some of the survivors being set upon and devoured by giant spiders, lizards and an assortment of other terrifying creatures. Accounts vary as to what prompted the scene's removal, with some saying that preview audiences were too horrified by the violence portrayed and others claiming it was simply cut due to time constraints. Cooper's own version is most likely the truth. He cut it out, he said "...*because it derailed the story. It took the audience's attention away from the chase after Ann and Kong and left them down there with other characters who were finished.*" It had to go. It was cut before the film's release, and, to this day, has never been seen or relocated. And it was probably the right thing to do.

Evidence that Cooper believed he was up against a new spider pit sequence of massive proportions appears in a telling note attached to the cover of James Creelman's script entitled VALLEY SEQUENCE, CREELMAN LINE dated May 11, 1939:

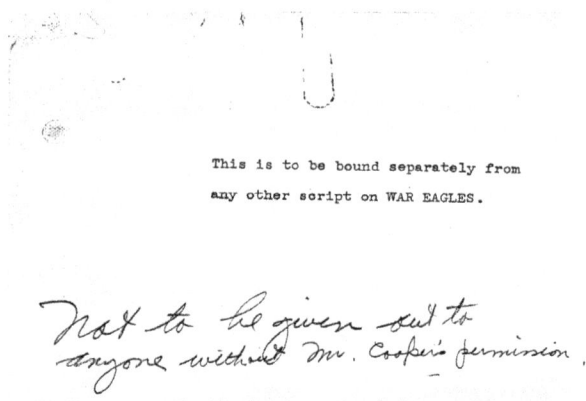

This is to be bound separately from any other script on WAR EAGLES.

Not to be given out to anyone without Mr. Cooper's permission.

Enormous amounts of conceptual work, artistic rendering and money had been expended in preparation for doing a Technicolor test sequence for portions of this storyline, with the intent of using them in the final film, just as Cooper and O'Brien had done for *King Kong*. But something broke down at this point. No memos or story notes exist to provide clear evidence of what happened. The studio may have intervened or Cooper may have come to the likely realization that this simply was too much, and the production had to be scaled back. He let Creelman continue to labor on the mechanics of the sequence, almost in quarantine, but within two months, both he and Lamb were off the picture.

As with almost every other facet of *War Eagles*' production, there are no records of the hiring, firing or reassigning of the writers on the project. Harold Lamb continued to work in the industry, most notably on *Samson and Delilah* and *The Golden Horde*. He wrote many more successful vol

umes of history and continued to publish steadily in magazines like *Collier's*, *The Saturday Evening Post* and *National Geographic*. His expertise in far and middle-eastern culture eventually led to his being selected for covert assignment overseas by the United States government during the coming war. His chosen life of adventure and intrigue continued to mirror Merian C. Cooper's, even after they parted company at MGM.

James Creelman was not so lucky. He had been nearing the end of his run in Hollywood by the time Cooper had brought him onboard the RKO productions and *War Eagles*, and his work on the film is his last recorded assignment of any kind. Largely successful until the widespread introduction of sound, Creelman had been a frustrated playwright for many years as well, and had seen virtually nothing produced. He entered what became a downwardly spiraling depression after his association with Cooper and Lamb dissolved, and it was probably close to the the the last straw.

His relative and family historian John E. Creelman spoke with me in 2006 about what he thought was key in Creelman's psychic make-up and how it may have led to his eventual demise:

"He seemed to always feel, from a very early age, that he had to somehow prove himself. He wanted to see action, something beyond what he wrote about, and was very frustrated when he didn't get into the scrap in World War One. His father had been a famous risk-taker and war correspondent for Hearst at the New York Herald *and Ashmore was the "second son" and always felt it. He was probably thrilled to be working with a man like Cooper, who had done and seen so much more, and to watch his luck run out afterwards must have been crushing. He became obsessed with getting into the armed forces prior to the next war, but by that time he was considered too old for service–or couldn't enlist for some reason– and that deeply depressed him, too..."*

On Tuesday, September 9, 1941, Creelman took an elevator to the roof of his sister's apartment building in New York and the following day's *Variety* told the rest of the story:

JAMES CREELMAN DIES IN N. Y. SUICIDE LEAP

James A. Creelman, who recently returned from Hollywood, where he was a scenarist, suicided by jumping from the roof garden of an 18-story apartment building on east 72d street, New York, early Tuesday (9). He was 40. Deceased had written several unproduced plays, but was little known on Broadway. Creelman was a brother of Eileen Creelman, film critic for the *N. Y. Sun*. Writer had been residing with his mother and sister for the past month. When he entered the apartment house Creelman asked the elevator operator to take him to the roof, rather than the apartment floor. Neither mother nor sister was at home when he jumped, the film reviewer being on her honeymoon after having recently been married. His father, who died in 1915, was James Creelman, war correspondent and editor.

Image courtesy of Tom Weaver

Harold Lamb and James A. Creelman worked on *War Eagles* from its inception in the fall of 1938 until July 15, 1939, when Creelman turned in his last set of script changes. The evidence seems to indicate that they were hand-picked by Cooper and created the original synopsis and at least 5 distinct drafts before leaving the project. The writer who took over the reigns after their departure was definitely MGM's choice. Wary of the project from the beginning, the studio heads brought in a specialist in taming out-of-control productions. Cyril Hume, veteran of many a celluloid jungle campaign, had been in tighter spots before...

Samuel Marx, writing in *A Gaudy Spree* , his funny, energetic memoir about his days as chief story editor for Irving Thalberg at MGM, best relates the tale of Cyril Hume's swift change of fortune at the studio—a series of events that would directly lead to his later employment on *War Eagles*. After confessing that he found Hume's first novel *Wife of the Centaur* the equal of F. Scott Fitzgerald's work, he goes on to write:

> *Cyril Hume had no special fame, although another book,* The Golden Dancer *had captured accolades from the critics. He was a virtually unknown writer whom I admired from afar.*

> *When I came to MGM, I discovered it wasn't so afar after all. In fact, he was perched just a few doors from me, in the writer's building, waiting out the final weeks of a three-month contract. He had failed at a couple of early assignments and the supervisors gave up on him as a screenwriter. He had survived the Saturday morning economy meeting because of the obligation of his contract but when it expired, he would be gone...*

> *At that time I became involved in seeking some sort of play doctor to administer to a very sick film.* Trader Horn *was to be the type of adventure film that audiences customarily loved, with animals and explorers, thrills and romance, all neatly packed into one exotic package. It was shot in Africa under the supervision of Bernie Hyman. It wasn't exactly shot—a better description would be "half-shot," and that could be taken literally and cynically...*

After considering a number of writers who he felt might be able to straighten out the jigsaw of jumbled celluloid, and being disappointed and turned down by many, Marx decided to make a gamble and see if Hume had any interest:

> *Hume was actually in the process of packing up his belongings when I walked into his office and told him why I was there. As we headed to Hyman's office, he mentioned that he knew of the* Trader Horn *mess (it was hardly a secret) and he had even taken it upon himself to read the book. But he made no offer to help. He felt that having sat for weeks without as much as a phone call, such volunteering would seem presumptuous. It was apparent that this serious-minded, white-haired author also had an un-Hollywood streak of shyness.*

> *I sat beside him in Hyman's office and left when the supervisor began explaining he would screen a sequence he felt contained the most important elements of the main theme. How Hume would write it would serve, in effect, to test his grasp of the story.*

> *Late that afternoon I returned and walked in on an extraordinary sight: both men weeping. Hyman thought Hume's scene exceeded his greatest expectations of how it should go, while Hume reacted to Hyman's exultant reaction so emotionally that both men had burst into tears.*

Cyril Hume
Portrait courtesy of David Hume

> *"I suppose," I stammered, "that like most huntsmen you chase adventure as much as anything else."*
> *"That's it!" he cried. "You might say it's really fine stories that I'm hunting."*
> *"What is better than a fine story?" I said.*
> *"Or what rarer?" he added.*
> *"One thing," I answered: "a human being fit to live one..."*
> *"Well now," he said slyly, "as a matter of fact, you strike me as a man who might very well take a good part in a good story."*

Cyril Hume, *Myself and the Young Bowman*, Doubleday, Doran & Company, 1932

That was a turning point in the life of Cyril Hume. His revised screenplay fused the disconnected sequences of Trader Horn into such a success the film went out as a roadshow attraction at raised admission prices... Hume was so good at depicting jungle life he was first choice thereafter on a whole string of movies the studio would make along that line.

His career saved, Hume went on to pen *Tarzan, the Ape Man* and most of its high-profile MGM sequels, his cache' at the studio no doubt increased by his personal discovery of the series' star Johnny Weissmuller while swimming at the Hollywood Athletic club. His expert handling of subject matter that had no relationship to his "lost generation" themed novels paid off very comfortably, and his reputation as a crack troubleshooter was made. It comes as no surprise then that he would be assigned to the juggernaut that *War Eagles* had become, and he delivered his first streamlined draft on July 31, 1939.

Gone were both the secondary protagonist Hiram P. Cobb *and* the secondary antagonists, the race of degenerate ape men. It was down to dinosaurs and faceless fascists. Hume whittled and worked the tale back down to its basics, and a form far more similar to Cooper's original proposal. All the while, he managed to maintain the beauty of language and clean flow of action that Lamb and Creelman had

labored hard on, and the best of both approaches survives in his final drafts. The menace in the Valley of the Ancients is reduced to the allosaurs that plague the bird people, and the studio's increasing unease with the implied Teutonic threat is somewhat diffused. The villains are clothed in uniforms of "no recognizable nation" and much is made of the concept of a rogue "Generalissimo" being the driving force behind the attack on New York. Of course, it's all rather transparent, and the shape of the swastika can still be defined in what goes on, especially in Hume's new choice for the villains' preferred mode of transport: a gigantic zeppelin.

FILE COPY! WAR EAGLES. Script No.22. 4717
Cyril Hume. Dated 10-10-39.

Lieutenant Slim Johansen, grounded and permitted to resign instead of being courtmartialed for stunting around the Statue of Liberty in the Army's newest plane, is immediately engaged by Laverock, owner of Bi-Car-Brome, an effervescent cure-all, to advertise his product by flying around the world from North to South instead of the more usual East to West way. Laverock's trademark shows Bi-Car-Brome encircling the earth, from pole to pole, so Slim is given the very latest thing in planes and told to fly this dangerous route, broadcasting as he goes.

Directly over the South Pole he runs into such a mountainous, fog covered stretch that he can see nothing. A huge shape, like a monstrous, pure white eagle, attacks the plane and Slim cracks up in a volcanic region of tremendous peaks and tropical vegetation. He saves nothing from the plane but his portable radio. A beautiful young girl, Naru, speaking English that sounds like a good translation of Beowulf, leads him to a settlement of what are evidently early Norsemen, somehow isolated for centuries in this strange, grim paradise.

Descendants of Vikings is what they turn out to be, whose leader Einar made them swear never to return to the unhappy continent of Europe. They have learned to tame and ride the eagles, large as airplanes, that inhabit their vast mountains. Slim, at first regarded with suspicion on account of his Box Of The Evil Voice, by Raud, Naru's brother and the leader of the clan, establishes himself as a hero and wins Naru's love, by taming the white eagle that attacked him.

Skal, Chief of all the Vikings, summons Raud's clan to help harvest the year's supply of fruit and fish upon which the clans, scattered through the mountains, must subsist all year. This harvest, the puny humans must wrest from the supposedly extinct prehistoric animals that still roam the lush lowlands. Slim falls foul of Skal who desires Naru. But he soon wins his respect and admiration by tracking the dinosaurs to their cave, breaking in the side of a crater and allowing the lava to pour in on the monsters and destroy them.

Their ancient enemy wiped out forever, Skal appoints Slim his successor and allows him to marry Naru. At the wedding feast, Slim switches on the radio and hears that a European power is about to attack the United States. The enemy possesses a neutralizing ray which kills all electrical devices. Slim, accompanied by Skal and all his warriors, flies to the rescue of his country on the gigantic eagles. Terrible scenes of the evacuation of New York, of the impotent defense squadron, paralyzed by the ray, shot from a dirigible, take place. Not a single power house, not a battery nor a magneto can function while the dirigible emits its terrible ray. New York lies defenseless until Slim and his warriors land on the dirigible's deck. With arrows, spears and battle-axes against machine guns, Slim and his Vikings drive the invaders to cover and then Slim, on his white eagle, wrecks the dirigible with one of its own bombs.

Immediately every plane on Long Island and in New Jersey starts up with a terrible roar and beats back the enemy bombers that have followed in the wake of the dirigible. From the outstretched arm of the Statue of Liberty, where he perches with his war bird and with Naru who has secretly followed him, Slim watches his Army friends finish the conquest he and his bird-men made possible.

A prophetic image from the October 1934 Modern Mechanix foreshadows Cyril Hume's magnificent aerial assault carrier from the final draft of War Eagles.

43

Much has been made of the use of the "dirigible"–even the German term *zeppelin* was expunged from the script–and how it was already an outmoded technology for warfare due to its volatile use of hydrogen to stay aloft. The truth is another matter. The German airship manufacturers had always entertained hopes of using non-flammable helium for their ships, but the United States had a vise-like grip on helium production, creating an artificially-inflated market for the gas, and no deals for large scale use were forthcoming, especially to potential enemies of the state. Combined with self-sealing gas-bags, the zeppelin *could* have become a very formidable high-altitude weapon in the 1930's, especially if it carried its own fleet of fighters and was packing a ray weapon like Hume had envisioned. Not only would it have been an incredibly cinematic image to behold, it would have also scooped the concept of the Death Star by 40 years!

The German air command had actually formulated a practical plan to bomb New York City during World War I using enormous, super-high- altitude airships called "height-climbers" that would have required the use of oxygen and heated cabins for the crews. As all other fighting aircraft of the period were open to exposure, there would have been very little chance to defend against them. Luckily they were destroyed in transit and on the ground before they could be deployed. Cooper was no doubt aware of this, having served during the period and dividing his contemporary interests equally between aviation and filmmaking.

Readers will at last have a chance to read the final draft of *War Eagles* in this book, complete with the last set of revisions delivered on February 24, 1940. This is very close to a shooting script and it is evident by some of the illustrations presented within the text that pre-production artist Duncan Gleason had meticulously illustrated at least a few of the major sequences. Hume's skillful streamlining of the action mixes well with the sweep of the previous scenarists' visuals, and a noticeably lighter touch with character relationships takes over. Hume had a playful side that extended from his largely fictitious "official" studio bio–he was the son of a successful New York tailoring family and not British *or* the brother of actress Benita Hume, as often claimed–to his often risqué poetry, and brought some laugh-out-loud moments to his work on *War Eagles*.

Cyril Hume's final draft was *the* final draft for *War Eagles*, but was probably already being viewed as impossible to produce when it was turned in. Within two months Germany would invade Poland and reality would rapidly outstrip fantasy. Cooper would eventually answer the siren's call to action that filmmaking could never compete with, and MGM would breathe a sigh of relief. Work on the script continued sporadically into early 1940, but Hume would soon be called away to many other assignments, and eventually, in 1956, to the stars and the golden age of science fiction films. *Forbidden Planet* would usurp Merian C. Cooper's lost dream as the most imaginative expression of his art, and bring Hume lasting fame.

A handwritten revision page by Hume that reveals his gift or creating lighter moments. From the collection of the author.

10-13-39
correctly numbered
pages + scenes to
correspond to new
script of 10-10-39

1 —

"WAR EAGLES"

N.B. Original from
[Lynd Aus]
10-13-39
This script completely
done over, except for
pages
98-99-100-102-105-106-107
108-110
111-112

SEQUENCE 1

FADE IN:
HIGH ANGLE (AIR) LONG SHOT NEW YORK CITY

The magnificent panorama wheels below. Finally the plane noses toward Bedloe's Island. As
the Statue of Liberty rushes rocking toward
CAMERA--

FULL SHOT BASE OF STATUE OF LIBERTY

At the approaching roar of a plane, the little
crowd of sight-seers ducks for cover. A pla-
toon of soldiers breaks ranks as the shadow
sweeps over.

**4 FULL SHOT STATUE OF LIBERTY
The plane
continues
to stunt.**

3 MED. SHOT INT. H.Q. FORT JAY BEDLOE'S ISLAND

As the plane sweeps past, an elderly officer
snatches up the telephone.

          Colonel (glaring up out window)
Get me Mitchell Field! --the Group Commander!

2. FULL SHOT STATUE OF LIBERTY

a wild Army pursuit plane stunting all around
it, horrifyingly close.

5 CLOSE SHOT INT. MILITARY H.Q. FORT JAY

The roar o.s. increases and diminishes.

          Colonel (ironically into phone)
Your boy is putting on an exhibition you'd be
proud of, Colonel.
          (suddenly exploding)
But if you don't get **him** away from here, I'm going
to turn out the A.A. batteries, and shoot **the idiot**
down in self-defense!

the idiot

him

He ducks as the plane dives past the window,
blowing all the papers off the desk...

          QUICK DISSOLVE:

45

Ray Harryhausen and his trusty Mitchell animation camera, circa early 1970's.

A Visit to the Aerie
Ray Harryhausen Interviewed

Ray Harryhausen and "Jennifer", his favorite animation model of Mighty Joe Young. Taken nearly ten years after his first meeting with Obie, the film would be his first professional credit as an animator. From the author's collection.

Ray Harryhausen holds many unique positions in the filmmaking world. From being an Academy Award-winning innovator in the realm of stop-motion animation and special effects, to serving as an authentic hero and creative inspiration to legions of fans and professionals now working in the movie industry, to finding himself considered the true auteur of the many science fiction and fantasy titles he helped create—an honor usually reserved for a very short list of directors or producers. I have been a lifelong fan of his work since catching my first glimpses of the massive "sextopus" menacing the Golden Gate Bridge in *It Came From Beneath the Sea* and the titular *Beast From 20,000 Fathoms* on afternoon television at the age of four. I grew up and matured as a moviegoer in the 1970's watching reissues of *The 7th Voyage of Sinbad* and *Jason and the Argonauts*, as well as new releases like *The Golden Voyage of Sinbad* and *Clash of the Titans* and they enriched my own childhood imagination and artistic ambitions. The same can probably be said for nearly everyone holding this book in their hands.

But he also holds another distinction, unique in the history of *War Eagles*.

While still attending Manual Arts High School in Los Angeles in 1938, he lucked into the meeting that would forever define his career direction and eventually produce the body of work he is so well known and loved for today:

He spent an afternoon with Willis O'Brien in the production office of *War Eagles*.

He is apparently the only living person with direct experience of the pre-production phase of the project, and has maintained a lifelong interest in seeing it documented and possibly completed one day. As such, that makes Ray the only actual "eyewitness" in this examination of its history, and it makes me a very lucky man to have been able to talk to him about it several times over the years.

Within a year of the start of my serious research into *War Eagles*, we were very pleased to have Ray and his wife Diana as guests at WonderFest, the annual model, film and FX expo that I program, and, as they found themselves between a film festival in Seattle and the ceremony dedicating Ray's star on Hollywood's Walk of Fame, they were able to spend a week relaxing in Louisville, Ky, before the show. It was a truly unforgettable time. We have met several times in subsequent years, mostly in Los Angeles, and it was there, in the home of Ray's longtime friend and agent Arnold Kunert, that we conducted the final interview for this book in 2008.

What follows is an account, drawn from transcripts of our conversations, about the day Ray met Obie, and the role *War Eagles* played in both of their lives.

47

DC: *I know it's touched on in nearly every extensive interview you've ever done about your career, but given my very specific interest, I'd like to talk as much as we can about the day you met Willis O'Brien and what lead up to it.*

RH: So it's to be the Third degree, eh?

DC: *I'm afraid so.*

RH: Well, I suppose I can't get away with "I have nothing to say." since it's been documented already. But, yes, even though it's been such a very long time ago, it's one of those days that will always be with me, just like that first viewing of *King Kong*. Obie had been such a hero of mine already, ever since seeing *Kong*, so the day that began our friendship really remains one of the highlights of my life. An event.

DC: *And you had already been doing animation at home by this time, making your own films and tests?*

RH: Yes, but I'd never really considered actually trying to contact him yet. Even though we were both living in the same city. I still felt very much like a kid with an obsessive hobby, you know. Very wet behind the ears. And I also felt that what went on behind the studio fence was a very different world. And it was, to a degree. I wasn't really prepared for the level of preparation that I was to see.

DC: *This tale actually begins, like a lot of interesting ones, with a woman, doesn't it?*

RH: Yes, it does. I was in my senior year at high school, and I met this girl— or rather *saw* this girl— in my social studies class, reading a big bound book with what looked like *King Kong* illustrations in it! Well, of course I was intrigued, so I walked up to her at recess and introduced myself and asked to see it and it turned out to be a leather bound *Kong* script that belonged to her father.

HARRYHAUSEN, RAY
Publicity Club 4
Masquers' Club 3, 4
Movie Club 1, 2
Cartoon Club 2, 3, 4

Mighty Young Ray: Harryhausen's 1939 graduating class yearbook photo from Manual Arts High School

DC: *But this was not Willis O'Brien's niece, as has been reported...*

RH: No! No, I don't know where that story ever came from. Her name was Redmond. And it happened that her father had worked with Obie on a couple of films. The only one that I definitely remember was *The Last Days of Pompeii*. So I told her all about my fanatical love for *Kong* and my animation experiments and it turned out that she actually knew O'Brien and that she thought he was a very kind, very understanding man and said "You should just call him up!" She knew he was currently working on a picture at MGM.

DC: *Was her father working with him there?*

RH: No, I don't believe he was. He and Obie were apparently good friends and kept in touch, so that must have been how she knew.

DC: *So you called him up...when? At home?*

RH: At his office, there at MGM. I was naturally a little hesitant because he was such a heroic figure to me and I put it off a few days, and she kept encouraging me to call, so I finally looked up the number and called and Obie answered the phone himself. I was dumb-struck, but managed to get some words out and luckily he was able to understand them and said I should visit him there at the studio where he was preparing this new, big fantasy picture called *War Eagles*.

DC: *And that's when you first heard the title? Did he tell you it was another Cooper production?*

RH: He told me the name of the picture, but I don't remember if he mentioned Cooper on the phone. I don't think so. But I certainly knew it was Cooper's production by the time I left the lot that day. So, yes, he was very nice, very pleasant on the phone, and I told him I had been making my own models and things and he said he'd be happy to take a look at them and that I should "Bring 'em over." We set a day and I packed up a bunch of my creatures in a suitcase and brought them with me.

DC: *And this was around... when? Do you recall a date or time of year?*

RH: No, I can't clearly recall any date since so many years have passed. I can't remember what I had for breakfast this morning! It was my last year of high school, and I graduated in '39. It was a typical day in sunny California, I believe, and I did drive out to MGM myself as I already had a car by that time.

DC: *Some of the accounts I have read say that no testing had been done yet and when you were there they were primarily doing the pre-production artwork, etc., and others say the tests were under way. In other words, you didn't see any models or filming on a set or anything like that?*

RH: No, there were no models in the offices—there were three rooms, connected as I recall—and Obie said they were just getting started on their test film. I wasn't on any stage during my visit. After we got to know each other much later, Obie told me quite a bit about how things didn't go well at MGM. That there was a lot of opposition to "outsiders" and that he ended up having to shoot his experiments and tests in a tent outside the soundstages.

DC: *I've read that, and since there's no paperwork available on specifics like sets or any time set aside for Technicolor tests on that first shoot, it's hard to say what happened. If they were doing that first test in three-strip Technicolor, and shooting animation with an expensive rented camera locked down, I somehow doubt they were doing it in a tent. That's why I believe the first test might not have been in color.* (**When I conducted this portion of the interview, that was indeed my belief, but subsequent evidence indicates the first test was filmed in color- DC**) *The dates I have on set construction and shooting the first test seem to indicate you were there sometime between mid-October and late November of 1938.*

RH: That's entirely possible.

DC: *But we've gotten way too far ahead in the story, so you arrived at MGM and...?*

48

RH: ...And I went over to Obie's office and knocked on the door and when it opened I was just stunned by what I saw! The walls were *covered* with artwork—probably two or three hundred drawings and watercolors and charcoal renderings. My jaw actually dropped. I remember some of the watercolors like these you've found, and there were two very large oil paintings. One was an enormous picture of the Statue of Liberty with the eagles perching on the spikes of her helmet and there was another of a large dirigible flying over New York with giant eagles wheeling around it.

DC: *That's interesting, the dirigible painting, because that wasn't being mentioned in the scripts around that period—not yet at least.* (Note: Neither of these large paintings seems to have survived, although another FX animator, Jim Aupperle, recalls seeing a photograph of the Statue of Liberty painting sometime in the early 1970's.)

RH: Well, it was one of the stand-out pieces that I strongly remember seeing. I'm not sure who painted it, but Obie had at least three artists working for him on the film at the time. There was Duncan Gleason, who did a lot of those sketches that have survived, and the other artist, the one who did the paintings for the polar expeditions. He was hired to do the big background landscapes for the glass shots...

DC: *Leland Curtis?*

RH: Yes, Curtis. I have one of his oil paintings and it used to hang in my dining room in Los Angeles. It wasn't from *War Eagles*, but it was from one of the arctic expeditions, so it's very similar to the work he was doing on the film. And there was another artist whose name, I believe, was Schmidt. He did illustrations for the *Saturday Evening Post* and other magazines.

One of Leland Curtis' lost valley landscapes for War Eagles.
Image courtesy of Bob Burns.)

DC: *Harold von Schmidt may be the man. When you first mentioned him, I looked into it and found that he had actually worked on posters for John Ford's westerns. That's a pretty strong link to Cooper, so it's likely he could have done some work on War Eagles. I haven't been able to find anything by him so far, but his son is helping me look. Were any of the artists there that day?*

RH: I don't recall seeing or meeting any of them. There were people in and out of the office and Obie spent quite a bit of time telling me about the production. That helped to settle me down a bit because I was just overwhelmed by all that I was seeing. It really was a dream come true for me to be there and he was very encouraging to me since so few people were even aware of stop-motion work. So I reluctantly started showing him some of the models I'd brought with me and he studied them carefully while I fidgeted. He

liked my mammoth and pointed out some things I might improve on, and when he got to my stegosaurus—probably the one I was proudest of, since I'd won an award in a contest for it—he paused, and then said "The legs look like sausages." Now he said all of this in a very kind and constructive way, and when I looked at them I realized he was completely right. He said "You've got to get more character into your work and study anatomy." So I took his advice and later enrolled in some classes. I think what was most important to me that day was to "meet my maker" and have him see my work and have it appraised. Being in the studio while they were preparing for *War Eagles* was certainly a thrill, but I never got back to see him there.

DC: *That was my next question. When did you see Obie next?*

RH: We stayed in touch and about six months later my parents and I went over to visit Obie and Darlyne at their house. By then I was confident enough to bring along some of my own films and he was just as constructive a critic of my animation. He showed me where improvements could be made and was very positive about the things I did right. It meant so much to both me and my parents to hear this as they'd been supportive of me and helped me with so much of what I'd done. I can't underestimate how important that can be. There was literally no one else pursuing this at the time, so I guess Obie felt he could begin to mentor me a bit. He began calling me "Young Harry" and we kept in touch on a regular basis from then on.

DC: *So this was probably in mid-1939 and he was still on War Eagles. Did he say anything about how the production was going at this time.*

RH: No, I don't recall anything specific about it, other than it was still in preparation. It wasn't until a few years later that he actually opened up about all that had happened at MGM and his frustrations there.

DC: *This was when you went to work for him on Mighty Joe Young?*

RH: Yes. We'd stayed in touch throughout the war years and I got a call from him around the end of 1945 about this new Merian Cooper project - at the time it was called *Mr. Joseph Young of Africa*—and he asked if I wanted to assist him on it. Well, I didn't hesitate at all to agree, and went to work with him at his home on preparing all the artwork for it. Obie was very pleased to be back with "Coop" after such a dry spell and felt that, despite the collapse of *War Eagles*, it was going to be a big step forward. We worked for a little less than a year before it was given a go-ahead and we moved to RKO.

DC: *And Obie started talking about what had happened at MGM around this time?*

RH: Yes, it began to come out. He said that he had faced an *enormous* amount of opposition from some of the people at MGM, some of it even insulting. He said that Cedric Gibbons, who was the head of the Art Department there (And would no doubt have eventually received full credit as art director on the picture- DC) had stopped in to see the preparation work on the picture one day and then just looked down his nose at Obie and said "We only make Cadillacs. We don't make Fords." and walked away.

DC: *Which is kind of a ridiculous statement if he's refer-ring to* War Eagles *as a B-picture. They were being kept afloat by their Tarzan and Andy Hardy movies, which were pretty much "B's in A clothing"!*

RH: Exactly. Obie felt it was mainly the fact that he and his crew were brought in from outside by Cooper, and that the powers-that-be at MGM really resented that—even though they couldn't have produced anything like the animation that was required! I believe Cooper had talked MGM into financing the writing and preparation for *War Eagles* and that was one of the reasons for the resentment. There weren't many independent production companies around back then, so it simply wasn't done.

DC: *Did Obie ever mention any specific objections by anyone on the MGM effects staff? Buddy Gillespie ran the department back then and is referenced in the final draft as a provider of certain visuals.*

RH: No, nothing of that sort. I think the creative people all got along fine, but that it was, typically, the man-agement that had issues with the arrangements. Obie had hired Marcel Delgado to construct the models and Harry Cunningham machined all of the armatures. I know that Obie first met George Lofgren at MGM, and he ended up working with Marcel on the eagles. I've heard that Marcel was going to use his usual build-up techniques on the eagles and then attach feathers, but George protested and said they would never look realistic enough, so he developed a way to use real bird skins to cover the bodies. He was an ingenious taxidermist and later came up with the rubberized fur for the Mighty Joe puppets.

DC: *Yes, I believe they did use real bird skins: Crows, actually. And he may have employed his rubber under-skin method then, too. One of the only good stills of the models seems to confirm the crow theory and it might explain why the armatures are on the smallish side for the period. They scaled everything to the birds. Lofgren was an MGM staffer who never got the credit he deserved, I think, until he started working with you on later projects.* **(For an intriguing account of Lofgren's rubberized skin techniques, see the artists' section.)**

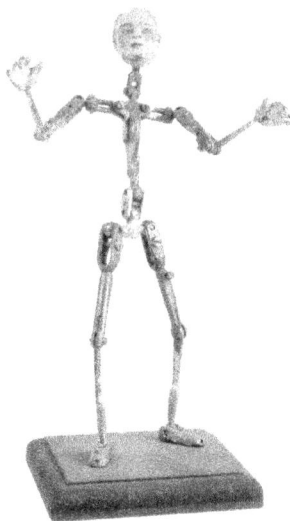

The only remaining Viking animation armature from War Eagles. *From the collection of Ray Harryhausen.*

RH: George was a wonderfully talented man, and worked with Charles (Schneer) and myself on our later pictures, too. I do have one of the human armatures that was built for the Viking eagle riders and it is was in scale with the eagle. About six inches tall. Obie brought both an eagle and the human armature in when we were working on *Mighty Joe Young* and we actually used the little human figure for the long shots of Terry Moore playing the piano. I still have it.

DC: *Did Obie ever mention the test footage or how he felt about the results? Or anything about shooting in Technicolor? I would imagine that would have taken some adaptation, given the light requirements and all.*

RH: Nothing specific, other than to say it *was* in color and ran about 400 feet. I think they were all pleased with it and it had been difficult, given all the wire work, but I've only seen some stills from it over the years. Everyone be-lieves it's lost. I'm sure we would have screened it endlessly if Obie had had a copy of his own, but I can only assume that it stayed at MGM, since they paid for it. I wouldn't be surprised to learn that they burned it or threw it out at some point. (Miklos) Rozsa told me that they had burned all of his original scores when they shut down. Just tossed them into the furnace.

DC: *That seems to have been the designated fate of a lot of the material I've been provided with. If it hadn't been for the ac-tions of a couple of folks being told to gather up what they wanted or pulling something out of a trash can, it all would have vanished after the 1970 MGM auctions. I've had no luck in turning up any footage, but I would be very surprised if Cooper did not keep a copy.*

RH: Yes, especially since it was his concept, his story. I think he was determined—like everything else he did—to see it completed, but the war began while they were working and he went back into the air corps. I believe he had two or three projects working at once and abandoned them all. After the war, he moved on.

DC: *Yes, while MGM was footing the bill for* War Eagles, *he also had Schoedsack and Korda developing* Jungle Book *and Walter Wanger on* Eagle Squadron *for Pioneer. He left both of those productions, too, but they did eventually get made. I get the feeling that without Merian C. Cooper to push,* War Eagles *didn't stand a chance. Any views on that, or Cooper?*

RH: He was a bulldozer! But an amiable one, and I liked him. I think he was loyal to his friends, and if he hadn't been there when he was, Obie's career might have ended before it began. And of course my own would never have come about without *Kong*. And he remembered his friends, which certainly made a difference later in Obie's life, and in mine. If he had stayed with fantasy pictures after the war, things might have turned out differently for everyone, but he was also loyal to John Ford and went back to work with him, producing some great films.

DC: *Did you ever hear Cooper say anything about* War Eagles, *or did he or Obie give a definite date of when things shut down?*

RH: No, nothing beyond he'd wished they had made it. Cooper never struck me as a man who dwelt on past events much, but Obie felt defeated at times. For the most part, though, Obie was a very "happy-go-lucky" kind of guy. When he was working, he was happy. All he ever said was that they had to stop work on War Eagles when the war broke out. And, as I said, Coop just moved on to what he had to do next.

DC: *He didn't stand still, that's for certain. And neither does time. I have heard you tried to get War Eagles back into production yourself?*

RH: Well, I think a few people have tried over the years, with little success. Forry (Ackerman) was always rather obsessed with the picture and he tried to get George Pal interested in reviving it during his time at MGM, but that didn't come to pass. I know Jim Danforth had some discussions with MGM after that, but probably got the same response as Charles and I did when we approached them after the success of *Clash of the Titans*. It had done quite well financially and we were asked "What's Next? What would you like to do?" by the studio people. We told them that they already had a property called *War Eagles* that we'd been interested in doing for a long time and they took one look at the script and pronounced it "Old hat." They didn't think anyone would want to see a period picture with prehistoric creatures fighting Nazis or anything like that, and it would have cost so much to update it to modern standards that it became pointless to pursue.

DC: *Which is all very ironic since the other big hit of 1981 was Raiders of the Lost Ark. A big-budget fantasy adventure with Nazis as villains...*

RH: Everything old is new again, but in this case only if you want it to be, I suppose. I'm glad there's still so much interest in it and I'm *amazed* with what you've managed to turn up! Really, since I never expected to see many of these pictures again or learn anything more about the production. How *did* you find all of this?

DC: *It was nearly all a matter of being in the right place at the right time, and by that I mean meeting the right people, who shared my love and interest in it. Of course, your meeting with Obie is a reflection of that same kind of thing, otherwise we wouldn't be having this talk. So I have to thank you for being at the right place at the right time as well.*

RH: You're very welcome!

One of the most intriguing details to come out of my last interview with Ray in 2008 was the actual name of the girl he met at Manual Arts High School in his senior year, and how she became his contact point for meeting Willis O'Brien. In past interviews, both with myself and others, he had left out that detail, and since she happened to be the daughter of an effects artist who had worked with both O'Brien and Cooper, I thought her history, no matter how obscure it might turn out to be, would be worth pursuing.

My first stop in any biographical query on genre film history is always Mr. Bob Burns, the legendary cinema archivist, raconteur, and dear friend of nearly 20 years. I asked him if the name "Redmond" rang any bells and he replied that it certainly did: Harry Redmond. He had apparently been an effects man during the 1950's and 60's and later a television producer. The only issue was, despite his apparently advanced age—Redmond was pushing 100 if still alive— he would have been just a little too young to have had a high-school-aged daughter in 1938. It was an odd situation as the name and history fit, but a quick check of the Internet Movie Database revealed that there was often a "Jr." placed behind Harry's name. His father was Harry A. Redmond, and they had *both* been effects artists working at RKO!

And they had worked on every Cooper picture made there... including *King Kong*.

I could find no obit for Harry Jr., so I searched for a phone number and, to my surprise, two listings turned up. Despite my doubts that a man who had actually worked on *Kong* was still alive, I dialed the first number and it was answered by a very perky, energetic older man. I asked the inevitable question and he answered "That's me!" and I soon learned that I was speaking to a 99-year-old survivor of the golden era with a perfect memory for detail. We talked for a bit about his days working with his father, O'Brien and Merian C. Cooper, and then I confessed that I was actually calling with a question about his sister.

"My *sister?*" he said, "Margie?"

And then I related the story of how she had attended school with Ray and put him in touch with the man who would give him his first job. Harry was tickled to learn of the connection, but had been unaware of how many links existed between his family and Ray's chosen path. He confirmed that Margie— her proper name being Margaret— had indeed attended Manual Arts, and that Obie had given his father the bound *Kong* script as a gift of thanks after the film's completion. Margie had later married and moved to another part of California, and was, unfortunately, now deceased. But Harry was very happy to hear that her pivotal role in this story was now going to be remembered. His own career in special effects was such an amazing account of working on so many genre classics that it cried out to be documented. My friend Mark F. Berry took up the challenge, contacted Harry, and produced a wonderful career-spanning article about his family's work that was published in the December/January 2009 issue of *Video Watchdog*.

As of publication, Harry is still going strong at over 100 years of age, and I will never forget the words we parted with on that first remarkable phone conversation. I confessed "I have to be honest here, Harry, and admit that I am amazed that you're still around."

To which he replied "So am I!"

Two very early pre-production paintings possibly executed by Stanley Johnson. Part of a series of original studio stills preserved by William Cappa, a worker in MGM's Matte Department in the 1960's. Images courtesy of Mark Berry.

Taking Flight

One of the surviving War Eagles eagle animation armatures machined and built by Harry Cunnigham. Image courtesy of Bob Burns.

While *War Eagles* never approached completion in any sense of the word, it did provide employment for a sizeable number of workers and artisans for over a year. No payroll accounts have been recovered, but if Forry Ackerman's estimate in *Mr. Monster's Movie Gold* is anywhere near correct, over $135,000.00 had been expended on the project before the fall of 1941. I suspect the totals may have run considerably higher. *War Eagles* did go into a fairly large-scale form of limited production, however, due to Merian Cooper's plan to completely replicate his experiences creating *King Kong* for RKO. He and O'Brien had already been well into two elaborate test sequences— Kong's exciting fight with the tyrannosaurus and the log sequence, where the giant ape sent men spiraling to their doom in the later-excised spider pit— as a sort of "proof-of-concept" effort, before the execs had completely green-lit the show. When they saw the "tests", which were later simply cut into the rest of the film, they went wild with anticipation, and Cooper literally killed two

birds with one stone.

By the time he delivered his *War Eagles* proposal to the MGM brass, similar plans were underway to dazzle the money men upstairs, this time in Coop's beloved Technicolor.

For years, the only evidence that a *War Eagles* test sequence was filmed existed in a handful of black-and-white stills and the limited testimony, given decades after the event, by some of those involved. When I began serious research, a few more tantalizing images were unearthed, and a larger, clearer picture of what had, and hadn't, been shot began to slowly emerge. It happened, as good things often do, because of a linked chain of friendships. I wrote previously of my belief that Forry Ackerman had always wanted to write about *War Eagles* and that was part of what brought our paths together nearly 30 years ago. He had begun to collect and publish images from the film at around that time and it seems to have coincided with the

Another possible Stanley Johnson pre-production painting depicting the deleted ape men arena sequence. From the author's collection.

appearance of vintage production material at the legendary Larry Edmunds Bookshop in downtown Hollywood. No one can assign a date or exact year, but sometime in the mid-to-late 1970's a notebook full of vintage studio photographs of artwork and test setups passed through the store.

Large-format negatives were made of the material and new stills began to move among collectors. Forry bought copies of everything available.

I have a theory—and it is *just* a theory—that these events may be tied to the death of *War Eagles'* art director Howard W. Campbell on July 1, 1978. Some accounts place the appearance of the material in earlier years, and some later. Something else may have fallen into Ackerman's hands around this time as well, and it quietly disappeared into his voluminous files for decades before it came into the possession of one of the most passionate collectors of *King Kong* and Willis O'Brien there is: director Peter Jackson. A longtime friend and fan of Forry's , Jackson had begun to purchase items from Ackerman's collection to help contribute to his support. In his later years, Forry's health and fortunes had taken quite a beating in a series of legal battles with unscrupulous former partners that had become a well-

known and devisive issue in film circles. He was in the process of arranging the sale of many of his beloved props and possessions when he made a deal with Peter that would both aid one of fandom's most beloved figures and shed new light on one of *War Eagle's* most abiding mysteries.

In 2005 Jackson purchased several of the *Kong* props and animation models that had been part of Forry's famous "Ackermansion" collection for many years. The remains of the stop-motion models of the stegosaurus, styracosaurus and pteranodon, as well as the practical effects miniature of the brontosaurus were the primary elements of the sale, but smaller items and attendant paperwork were also included. In one slim folder were found all that remained of Howard W. Campbell's art direction paperwork for *War Eagles*. I am deeply indebted to Peter Jackson and our mutual friend Bob Burns, as well as animator and FX expert Chris Endicott, for providing this material to the reader.

For the first time, a truly forensic approach can be taken while exmining the details of what took place between September of 1938 and February of 1939. Evidence and testimony begin with the following:

Frank O'Neil

TEST SEQUENCE

SCENE 1:

(A) Miniature set. Scale 1" to 1'. Small birds flying left to right to be done by animation.

(B) The large birds seen at first in the distance will also be done by animation.

Out —

(C) Test of one large bird in flight with the thought that we may be able to print this into previous animated scene. Also purpose is to show us what we can expect of miniature birds in final bombing of New York.

(D) Bird that leaves the flock and dives over camera and then out of picture and then returning again and alighting, to be done in animation.

Where the rider gets off, is a combination of animation and full-sized man. The method is miniature projection - that is, we have already shot the bird and man landing and bird landing with man beginning to dismount. Now then, we make a process plate for a man swinging from behind bird. We project this against our animated bird from in back of our animated bird. This covers all of scene one. Approximate time 4 days.

+ E - ADD. F.S. L.S. of man AS 1st LEAP: FROM BILL

SCENE 2:

(A) Plate of man against full-sized background with rope tied off scene to be projected against foreground scene of animated bird.

(B) This method is - animated bird foreground, man on miniature process plate.

(C) Where the javelin is pulled from the scabbard - done on full-sized set with man getting javelin from stand which is covered on the projection screen by the body of the bird.

SCENE 3:

Man throws spear from right to left of scene and the bird getting more nervous and jumping away with man clasping to rope which is attached to the ring in the birds nose. It is done in the same method as the last scene.

SCENE 3 (cont'd)

(A) Set full sized - man for spear throwing.

(B) Allosaurus entrance and large birds' entrance in animation. Miniature foreground set. 3 days.

(C) Full-sized man for miniature projection plate as man begins to mount bird.

(D) Animated bird. Combining the above.two in miniature projection. 4 days.

(E) For the entrance of the large birds with some of them banking in the immediate foreground and diving. Riders throw spears into the Allosaurus in passing. Entirely animation. 3 days.

(F) Where Allosaurus grabs bird, and man is thrown to the ground.

(1) Man #2 on full-sized set.
(2) The action of the Allosaurus leaping into the air and bringing the eagle down and tearing it to pieces. The fight done in animation. Time included in above.

SCENE 4:

(A) Animated background of fight between eagle and Allosaurus. See birds circling overhead. 1 day.

(B) Full-sized foreground set with man #2.

SCENE 5:

(A) Full-sized man and full-sized set. Man #2 crawls to the left of picture.

(B) Back to original long shot miniature set of Allosaurus struggling with bird. Bird and riders swooping down on animal, throwing spears and shooting arrows.
As one bird is on the ground wounded, we now have left 2 birds swooping around. 2 days.

SCENE 6:

    (A) Zoom shot of Allosaurus in distance - man prone in bushes. Animation. 3 days.

ROCK

    (B) Full-sized portion of bird built for airplane mount, with man #3 on bird. ½ day.

    (C) Additional zoom shots. Time 2 days.

SCENE 7:

    (A) Complete animation. 3 days.

SCENE 8:

    (A) Full-sized shot of man on full-sized set.

        (1) Wounded man on ground.
        (2) The men who have landed for the matador business.

    (B) The rest is all miniature. Animated foreground of the Allosaurus and his killed bird...The Allosaurus as he attacks the wounded man...Rider and bird landing in foreground attracting the Allosaurus...The landing of the birds...The weakening Allosaurus...The charging of the birds...and the landing of the birds.

    And in this scene we will need three miniature projection machines which is all we expect to need for any of the following scenes...and 4 stop-motion machines. 6 days.

SCENE 8A:

    (A) Men on ground full sized.

    (B) Animated birds with rear projection of full-sized men.

    (C) Foreground full-sized men with rear projection of miniature. Total for above 2 days.

SCENE 9:

    (A) Full-sized men on full-sized set.

    (B) Animated birds - rear miniature projection.
4 days.

SCENE 10:

    (A) Full-sized men. Swords for their maneuvering
to pull out wounded man.

        (1) Men with swords entering scene to pull out
wounded man.

        (2) Where two men attack Allosaurus - one from
the side and one from the rear.

        (3) Exit of men.

    (B) Animation of Allosaurus in a wounded condition
when he is ham-strung and when he is in his death
struggle - miniature rear projection. 4 days.

SCENE 10A

    Additional footage of scene 9. Time included
in above.

    NOTE: Allow two weeks' testing time, Mr. O'Brien,
before we shoot any of the above.

This detailed, four-page breakdown of the Test Sequence is so full of technical detail, including shot descriptions and estimates of time, that one would assume Willis O'Brien was its author. But the final note *"Allow two weeks' testing time, Mr. O'Brien, before we shoot any of the above."* indicates he wasn't, and strongly implies that Technicolor tests were going to be conducted. While the writer is unknown, the handwriting in the notes is definitely Howard Campbell's. Also of interest is the name written in the top-hand left corner: Frank O'Neill. O'Neill was a scenarist at MGM with a limited number of credits, 1939's *On Borrowed Time*, being his most well-known. Is it possible he was being considered as a writer? The only certainty in that department is that at this stage— the paperwork was delivered on the same date as Cooper's proposal—they were operating without a script of any kind. The sequence is obviously constructed to be shot without major characters or important dialogue, with any details, including close-ups, easily cut in ordubbedlater.

Three days later, on September 23, 1939, the first budget estimate arrived.

SETS AND PROPS

Mr. Horning
September 23, 1938

"COOPER TESTS" - JOB 102

5 Large Eagles	1" Scale	$300.00 Each	$1,500.00
4 Eagles	1/2 " Scale	200.00 Each	800.00
4 Eagles	1/4 " Scale	100.00 Each	400.00
4 Men	1 " Scale	200.00 Each	800.00
4 Men	1/2" Scale	50.00 Each	200.00
4 Men	1/4" Scale	25.00 Each	100.00
1 Large Eagle	1 " Scale: Operating model for normal speed:		500.00
1 Allasaurus	1 " Scale		600.00
Assortment Props			400.00
Equipment for operating birds			*Out to 5* 1,200.00
1 Miniature Set			1,50.
2 Miniature Sets-Small Section			*Out -* 600.00
Track for Zoom Shot			300.00
1 Full Size Set Sections			1,000.00
1 Full Size Section of Bird - For Airplane Mount-Process			3,000.00
Daily Operating Crew: 56 Days (Not Including O'Brien) *30*		150.00 Per Day	7,500.00
Foreground Matte Set			500.00
(2)French Plate Glass 7' x 9' (2)			75.00
" " 5' x 7' (2)			40.00
" " 9' x 12'(1)			70.00

Greenwald
rented of all...
to 12/... 2309.

13,585

59

The "Mr. Horning" indicated as the author in the upper right hand corner is no doubt William A. Horning, one of MGM's most talented and effective art directors. At the time of this estimate, he was engaged in the design and construction of all sets for *The Wizard of Oz* and an apparent technical expert on difficult assignments. Interviewed for Aljean Harmetz's *The Making of the Wizard of Oz*, his assistant Jack Martin Smith said "It was the lunchtime game among the art directors to try to ask Horning a question he couldn't answer....You couldn't stump him."

It is a fascinating document for animation fans, as it lays out expenditure for all of the animation models. Provision is made for the construction of 14 eagle models in varying scales, as well as human figures and an Allosaurus. A 50-day work schedule is remarked to 30 days with an adjusted payroll (not including O'Brien) for 50 workers of $4500.00, and for the first time the terms "Cooper Tests" and "Job 102" appear. It is possible that Campbell wasn't assigned as art director yet, but another budget breakdown sheet created just three days later lists him in the position and O'Brien (misspelled as "O'Brian") as the director.

FORM 202

5 tons

TOTAL AREA_____ EST. COST / SQ. FT._____ ESTIMAT$1014

Quantity	Unit	ITEM	L	M	Labor	Material	Total
		711-3-11 MILL & CARP.					
240	s.f	Table	40	15	100	15	115
~		Screen frames large	$20	$5	20	−5	25
72	s.f	Zoom runway	150	25	150	25	175
		3 ply wall for paint backing					
					SUB.		
		711-6 PAINT & SIGNS					
		Misc. paint	23	2	23	2	25
					SUB.	23	2	25
		711-14 SCENIC PAINT					
224	s.f	Backing scenic	35	02	79	4	83
96	s.f	Staff modeling	15	02	14	2	16
					SUB.	93	6	99
		711-5 STAFF SHOP					
96	s.f	Staff modeling	$263	$25	275	40	315
					SUB.	275	40	315
		711-13 GRIP					
					SUB.			
		711-2 LABOR					
					SUB.			
		711-4 METAL & ELEC.					
		Oscillating gag			55	20	75
					SUB.	55	20	75
		711-10 PLUMBING					
					SUB.			
		711-15 PROP. SHOP					
150	s.f	Glass (----------) & set CLEAR 1/4" PLATE	$35	$2	35	300	335
					SUB.			
		711-7 NURSERY					
		Trees & dressing					
					SUB.			
		MISC.					

ESTIMATED BY___Frost___ APPROVED_____ TOTALS | | | 621 | 393 | $1014 |

DATE ___9-26-38.___ DATE_____

ART DIRECTOR___Campbell___ DIRECTOR___O'Brian___

TITLE OF SET_____ PROD. No.___JOB 102 SET No._____

Howard H. Campbell is a bit of a mystery. An art director with a long and successful career at MGM, but a man almost completely lacking in biography. He had worked as an associate art director (as almost everyone was credited, the egocentric Cedric Gibbons taking co-credit on every associate's pictures) on many second string productions until he hit his stride with the succesful *Tarzan* series. His selection as *War Eagle's* art director seems to confirm that management was wisely moving work on the film to the *Tarzan* unit and his preliminary list of locations includes mention of standing backlot locations, including the "Tarzan rocks" and "Tarzan river".

Howard's career reached its peak in the television era, when he provided art direction for a number of hit TV shows like *Maverick*, *The Beverly Hillbillies* and *The Andy Griffith Show*. His son W. Stewart Campbell followed in his footsteps and became an art director on later high-profile features like *Chinatown* and *The Right Stuff*. When I interviewed him in 2004, he could not provide much information on his father, despite their parallel career paths, since his parents had divorced when he was quite young and contact with his father had been very limited after that.

The above still from 1932's Tarzan the Ape Man *shows the Tarzan rocks standing set on MGM Lot #2 and the Duncan Gleason rendering of the eagle men's harvest camp mirrors the placement of the large rock on the left. The background camp and terrain would have been completed by a "Newcombe Shot"– MGM's in-house term for matte photography. Both images from the author's collection.*

Duncan Gleason at work on one of his magnificent War Eagles *production paintings. Image courtesy of the Duncan Gleason Archives..*

Obie and his crew were deep into concept work and preparation for shooting by this time, and without the services of his usual production illustrators Mario Larrinaga and Byron Crabbe (MGM insisted on their in-house artistic staff), Obie and Campbell turned to Duncan Gleason, a seasoned illustrator who had worked at both Warners and MGM, and another intriguing artist with no other recorded history of film work, Leland Curtis. Both artists were popular California painters who subsidized their incomes by working at the studios. Gleason specialized in nautical subjects and Curtis was an outstanding landscape artist who specialized in mountainous regions like the Sierras. He was actually one of the founding members of the Sierra Club, and may have known Cooper through his associations there. While Gleason concentrated on designing much of the picture, Curtis was assigned primarily to depicting the details of the multi-tiered environments of *War Eagles'* lost world setting. It would turn out to be a prophetic assignment, for within a year Leland Curtis would be with Admiral Byrd at the South Pole as a team member of the US Antarctic Service Expedition.

O'Brien's long-time collaborator and model builder Marcel Delgado was hired to create the numerous animation puppets and the armatures for them were machined by Harry Cunningham, who also doubled as the designer and builder of many of O'Brien's miniature projection systems and animation cameras, created the animation armatures. Delgado was interviewed on a number of occasions later in life, and he is the only artisan involved with *War Eagle's* production to ever go on record with any recollections:

About 1939 I worked for Obie at MGM on War Eagles, *which Cooper was going to make. I made a spearman riding a giant eagle and throwing a spear at a tyrannosaurus. It could have been a hell of a good picture. I don't know exactly why they didn't finish it; they spent a hell of a lot of time and money on it. The film is lost now. George Pal has been searching for it. MGM was going to start on it again after the war, but they didn't.*

From an interview conducted by George Turner, circa 1968. Delgado expanded a bit more on his experiences in a letter and interview with Don Shay, presented in Steve Archer's book *Willis O'Brien, Special Effects Genius:*

Cooper was a funny guy. When we were working on War Eagles, we made a sequence on it. I never saw it... I don't know whatever happened to it, but Cooper wanted the Chief of the tribe in a costume especially designed for this fellow. He had a room full of sketches from different artists for this particular costume. Well, I found out that he was trying to find a costume for this tribesman, so one day I didn't have anything to do—and out of what I had on my table—scraps of chamois and rubber, I started making a costume for the little man—I had a little dummy. So I left the doll sitting on my table. Well, one day, Cooper comes looking around and sees the little doll sitting on the table and he picks it up and looks at it and says "That's just the thing I've been looking for—who did this?" He asked everybody. "Well Marcel did it I guess. I've been spending a lot of money and this is just what I want." Too bad we didn't make the picture. I made some little natives and a couple of eagles about the size of a crow, and we made a short sequence with about four or five giant eagles with native warriors fully dressed in their native costumes, riding on the eagles' backs, fully equipped with spears, clubs, stone-hewn instruments, etc. soaring at high altitudes and diving toward the gigantic dinosaurs and spearing them, using a 1-inch scale. The animation of the eagles was on very fine, invisible wires, and some stills were made of these settings. It would have been a tremendous spectacle.

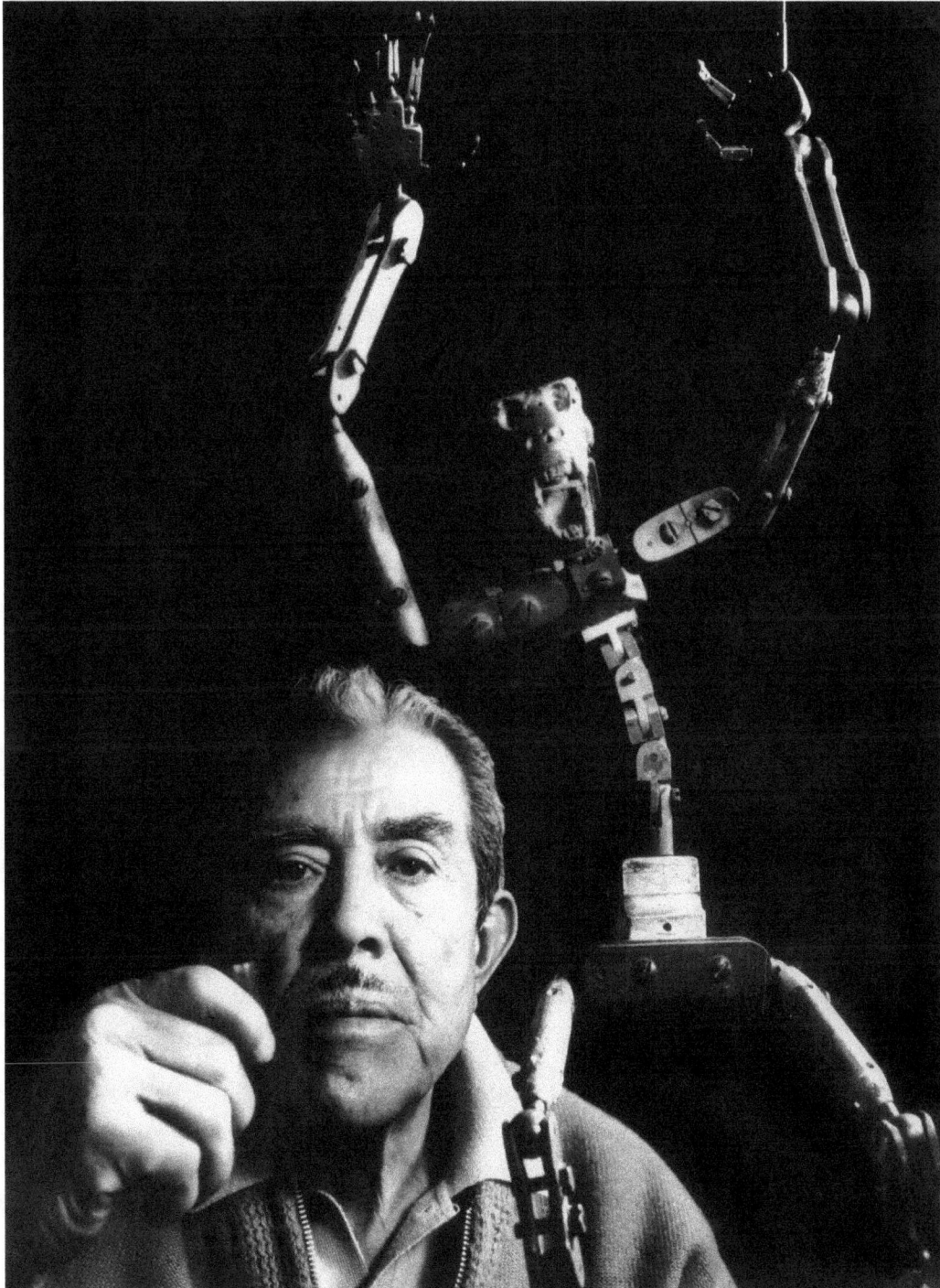

Marcel Delgado and a famous friend. Image courtesy of Gregory Kulon.

When Delgado experienced difficulty trying to attach real bird feathers to his eagle animation models, MGM staffer George Lofgren was called in to help. Lofgren was a British-born taxidermist by trade who specialized in movie work and had recently created the Cowardly Lion's costume for *The Wizard of Oz* and had been creating special animal props, from oversized rubber crocodiles to fake horses for rear-screen cowboy rider setups. He had patented a technique for rubberizing animal furs for durability and ease of construction, and it was likely that he used this process to treat crow skins—birds had notoriously thin hides that cannot be tanned—to be attached to Delgado's puppets. Don Shay explains the process further in *Cinefex #7*:

To begin with, the Lofgren process called for a non-tanned hide from a freshly slaughtered animal.

The fur would be carefully combed out so it would lie properly and then covered over with a thick coating of wallpaper paste or some other water-soluble adhesive. Thus treated, the hide would be placed in a sealed vat filled with dermestes beetles. In its larval stage, particularly, the dermestes is a voracious scavenger that will eat nearly any dried animal material. As a result, within a short period of time, the exposed skin would be completely eaten away, leaving the unpalatable glue and hair behind. Without the skin, the hair roots would be exposed and over these could be brushed several layers of liquid latex, dyed brown or black. The final step was then to dissolve out the glue, leaving the original fur implanted in a rubber skin that was both durable and easily affixed to the animation puppets.

George Lofgren prepares an animation setup for RKO's Mighty Joe Young, *his second collaboration with Cooper and O'Brien. Image courtesy of Gregory Kulon.*

Lofgren's technique was his ace-in-the-hole in a competitive studio filled with specialists, and he guarded his niche carefully. Animator Jon Berg got to know Lofgren quite well after his retirement to Northern California and told me a little about him in an interview conducted on September 29, 2003:

I remember George telling me that L.B. Mayer and some of the other studio bigwigs called him up to the executive offices and tried to intimidate him into giving the studio his patent for his rubberized fur system. He was very proud of his work and would not cave for them...

George and Lyla had no kids, but from what she told me after George passed away, they both felt very paternal towards Ray (Harryhausen). She also told me that when George and Ray were

working on the stop-mo for 7ᵗʰ Voyage of Sinbad in an old market somewhere in LA, during a hot summer day, Ray asked him if he'd mind working at night, so that they could have Lyla make a picnic lunch and go to the beach. Who could say no to that?

With the conceptual artists and effects technicians working away, and nothing resembling an actual script to appear until the following spring, the unconventional production barreled towards its first Technicolor test sequence. On October 7, 1938, a streamlined Test memo, describing the action to be portrayed by the live actors on the full-sized sets for the sequence was released. At some point between the date of this document and December 15, 1939, the test was shot and edited, and the only completed scene ever lensed for *War Eagles* was in the can.

10/7/38

TEST

(Full size sets, which will be used in the
miniatures as process plates. There will
be four major sets, referred to as a,b,c,
and d.)

SET C   Man #1 enters from right to left, swinging into scene holding onto a
rope. He takes spear from rack (which is built on set), throws it from
right to left. Rope jerks and man swings up in the air out of scene.
Take several feet after he exits.

Man #2 enters scene, swinging in on rope, takes two spears from rack,
throws them from right to left (but more towards camera). Rope jerks and
man swings up out of scene.

Man #3 and #4 enter scene, repeat this action, throwing their spears from
right to left.

SET B   Man #1 comes crawling into scene. He will be looking to his left, and he
will crawl as if he is trying to get out of the way of the rock rolling
towards him, which will be put in later with miniature. After 25 or 30 feet
have been taken, lay full size rock up against his leg. Shoot approximately
400 feet of him registering horror and agony, etc.

After this is shot, man #2 and #3 enter scene from left to right, release
man #1 from under rock. Man #2 is equipped with a spear, and man #3 is
equipped with a large sword.

The crippled man (#1) is taken out of scene from right to left by man #2.

Man #3 remains, slashes with his sword at a piece of 2x4, which will be set
up later and covered by the allosaurs' leg.

SET A   Man #1 and #2 enter scene from right to left. Man #2 puts crippled man (#1)
down, takes his spear and stabs it through, leaving spear in body of allosaurs,
which will be covered by the allosaurs later on. Allosaurs struggles, and
man pulls spear out again.

Man #3 enters from right to left, and man #2 and #3 both jump up on a two
step, which will be covered by allosaurs later.

SET D   Man #2 swings into scene from left to right, holding onto rope, and throws
spear from right to left, to attract animal from Set B.

Man #3 and #4 repeat this action with slight variations. Exit to left.

SET B & C (redressed). Three men swing down from ropes. One man holds the three ropes
while men #2 and #3 exit right. Man #4 mounts bird, and they all exit.

The only two "behind the scenes" images from the production. Above is a shot of the tabletop Valley of the Ancients miniature set with two miniature projection frames set up, but not yet integrated into the scenery. The worker in the background is possibly scenic painter Jack Shaw. Below is a test of the miniature rear-screen setup with an over-exposed frame of the live actor holding a spear as he faces the miniature allosaur on the tabletop set. All scenic and background elements are completed. Both images courtesy of Ronald V. Borst.

Above: The allosaur menaces a miniature eagle and rider to the left of the frame while another eagle, with markings like a Bald eagle, rushes into attack from the right. The blacked-out portion of the lower frame is for later insertion of foreground action or scenic elements. Below: The most commonly printed image from War Eagles. *The eagle and rider engage the allosaur in combat as what appears to be a rear-projected live actor cowers in the lower left of the frame. Both images courtesy of Ronald V. Borst.*

The allosaur takes down and kills the eagle, while another rider and eagle are seen facing the camera to its left. Below: In closeup, the allosaur turns to face another attacker. Both images from the collection of the author.

The most impressive surviving image from the first War Eagles test. A live actor is flawlessly composited with a model eagle. Details of the animation puppet can be made out, with its saddle and spear holster most prominent. Note that the model does not match the Bald eagle coloration from an animal in the same position in an earlier frame and that its crow-like origins are more evident. The rope that the actor swings in from disappears at the top of the rear-projection frame, but was likely going to be continued into the miniature setup as an animated wire. To the right is a small frame blowup that shows the same unknown actor without the model inserted into the scene. The large image is courtesy of Bob Burns and the smaller image is courtesy of Douglas Turner.

69

Speared in the throat by the attacking rider in the previous frame, the allosaur veers away. Image courtesy of Gregory Kulon. Below: The allosaur is finished off in another composite shot with a live actor wielding a larger bladed weapon on the miniature dinosaur. This is the final known frame from the short sequence. Image courtesy of Bob Burns.

Lost in the Clouds?

One of Duncan Gleason's early small gouache thumbnail paintings depicting a rider about to mount up. From the collection of artist and collector Russell Shears, whose father was a friend and colleague of Gleason.

One of the most enduring mysteries in the case of *War Eagles* is the status of the test footage: Is it truly lost?

Maybe. Maybe not.

On the negative side of the argument lies the fact that none of the principals involved in the production ever owned or produced a copy for viewing in subsequent years. Not even Marcel Delgado, who was one of the chief technicians on the project, ever saw it. As Ray Harryhausen noted in our interview, never, in his long years of association with O'Brien, was it never screened. Obie didn't have a copy himself. There is also no copy in the Merian C. Cooper archives. This "disappearing act" seems to indicate that MGM alone exercised control over the footage and that it went into storage or was destroyed after the production was abandoned.

On the positive side, the fact that it was shot in Technicolor may mean something may still exist, possibly unlabeled as *War Eagles*, hidden away in an archival vault. Various appellations appear for the project in MGM files—from "Cooper Tests" and "Cooper Show" to "Merian C. Cooper Job #102" and "Merian C. Cooper—Prod. 1635"—and the production appears to have been rarely referred to by its actual title. There are even two separate production numbers commonly listed: 1134 and 1635.   For years I

believed that the first test footage may have actually been shot in black & white, due to the lack of color stills surfacing. When the nitrate color frames did appear, and were apparently from an unrelated sequence that was just beginning to be uncovered, I took it as further confirmation.

That all changed with the document that follows. The "Allosaur Capture Sequence" meeting notes are probably the most important papers rediscovered about the project, and, once again, I am indebted to Peter Jackson and Chris Endicott for their use here, along with the other documents in this chapter. Dated December 15, 1938, they confirm that the first test was shot and edited, and that the producer wished to use the footage in the finished film. That meant Technicolor was employed. The Technicolor Corporation does not have a reputation for throwing much away, and there is indeed strong evidence that some elements of the *second* planned *War Eagles* test survived. The images found in the nitrate frames preserved by Bob Burns (and a duplicate set in the possession of the Duncan Gleason Archives) are from animation setups and tests from this second sequence, and in 2004 I located an entry in the Technicolor Collection stock shot card index on file at the Margaret Herrick Library of the Academy of Motion Picture Arts and Sciences that matched the images.

The index is filed by subject matter and under "Dinosaur" there was one card labeled "NEWCOMBE TESTS (MGM) Dinosaurs & Cavemen in woods; dinosaurs in woods alone."

The footage, which meant a *motion picture* of stop-motion animation, had been kept for possible sale to later productions, like everything else listed in the catalog. Those elements may still exist, but so far no search has relocated them. The evidence continues, with the following:

ALLOSAURS CAPTURE SEQUENCE

(Notes taken in conference between Mr. Cooper, Mr. Lamb, Mr. O'Brien, Mr. Campbell, Mr. Johnson and Mr. Shaw, December 15, 1938.)

In order to keep our crew together, we are immediately going into a sequence in which the ape people capture the allosaurs and carry it down into their cave home.

This is going to be a heaven to hell sort of thing, with a common ground between. Heaven is where the bird people live; hell is the caves of the ape people; and the common ground between is where the bird people, the ape people, and the prehistoric animals all have to come to get their food. Here on the common ground all the inhabitants of our world come together in combat. It is like a great amiptheatre, into which everyone and everything is drawn by one common need - the search for food.

This sequence will be in color, and every single shot, every conception, every gag must be one that color enhances -- something that black and white couldn't compare with. In this sequence we are going to try to sell color, and we must have really good color effects for everything. Every shot must be exciting.

We will have the ape people dragging the giant cart, digging the trap, baiting it with one of the bird men, enticing the allosaurs to the trap, and inveigling the allosaurs into leaping for the birdman; the allosaurs falls into the trap, the ape people rope and drag him out, load him into the cart, and drag him down to the arena, which is the arena of sacrifice down in the caves of the ape people.

The first thing we need to do is to decide what the country looks like. What is the geographical formation of the common ground between the heaven of the bird people and the hell of the ape people?

The most important thing right now is to get a map of that country. Mr. Campbell is to work with Mr. O'Brien and get this out right away.

Mr. Johnson's job is to make a series of gags, each of which will be a knockout as a gag possibility, from the capture of the allosaurs through the carrying of the animal back into the caves. These sketches should be carried through right into the caves, giving particular attention to the caves themselves, as they will bear a lot of relation to what is outside.

For story purposes, and for suspense, this should be intercut with the girl being prepared for the sacrifice, the other animals being prepared for the arena, with the allosaurs the only thing missing for the ceremony. We cut back and forth from the sacrifice preparations to the capture and hauling back of the allosaurs.

Mr. Cooper's suggestions regarding appearance of this country:

The country is a big circular bowl, at least 20 miles across. The top should be just as beautiful as we can possibly make it, Swiss Alps in effect, with snowcapped mountains in the background, but also with green things growing -- a picture postcard effect. Water pours down from the snow, and all these waterfalls and streams flow into one great main river, which in turn flows into a lake. From that lake the water goes down into the ape people's country in the caves below. Way down below the water from the river will end in mist and steam from the heat of the subterranean volcano. The water flows in a torrent until it reaches the lake. From the lake it will flow more sluggishly.

(Mr. Lamb suggested the ancient river tradition, such as the river in Asia where from the lake it seemingly drops down into the bowls of the earth.)

HELL. This will develop as a series of strata -- graduating from great beauty down into something that is fairly natural, then down into a lower strata, then down into the great caverns. Way down below will be fires burning, the volcanic fires that give heat to this valley, - volcanic fires that have kept this place alive and green in the polar regions. We must have the feeling that these ape people live in hell.

Physically, there is only one _must_ that we have to have for action. There has to be some real reason why the bird people can't get in these caves and get at the ape people in their home, until our hero finally finds a way to break through. There must be some blockade that keeps the bird people out. Maybe there is a water gate, or a tremendous cavern with fires burning below that has to be crossed, perhaps by a swinging cage. Whatever it is, it must be something that will keep a man on foot out, and keep the birds from flying in. It has to be some enormous obstacle that all the bird people's efforts can't overcome.

We have talked about floating the giant cart down the river, but Mr. Cooper is not sure that this is the right gag. Just using the river will probably be too much like a travelogue. However, Mr. Cooper either doesn't want to use the river at all, or he wants to use the river entirely. How can the river be made exciting? Perhaps there are big animals to attack the barge as it floats down stream, and the ape people have a method of defending themselves. Or maybe they have to cross over natural stone bridges, with the fires of hell burning below. Perhaps they swing over a great chasm onto a natural rock bridge. Mr. Cooper feels that this has not been worked out satisfactorily yet.

Mr. Cooper does not want to make any shots that involve the use of the full size glasses unless the effect will be very spectacular visually, or a very spectacular complete sequence.

In this test we have just finished, Mr. Cooper feels that it is too much like a desert. Perhaps we can work that strata so that we come right off the desert into some other part. We want to use this sequence if possible. Also, there isn't enough feeling of altitude. It is a good set, but it hasn't enough of a feeling of towering sides.

Another thing we must watch is distance, haze, mist. It was very difficult to cut this present sequence, and it was necessary to cheat in cutting it in order to really get a look at the birds coming down.

This striking painting is production illustrator Leland Curtis' only known contribution to story development. It depicts the capture of the allosaur in a rockier environment than other renderings and is one of the images saved from destruction by Wiliam Cappa. From the author's collection.

75

The list of attendees present indicates most of the creative crew were involved. Cooper, O'Brien, Harold Lamb and art director Howard Campbell are listed. Jack Shaw was an MGM staff matte painter, and there is also a "Mr. Johnson" on the roster. As his duties were to conceive of a series of "gags" through sketch work, it is possible that it was Stanley Johnson, a concept artist whose only other known credit is on Cooper's RKO production of *She*. His style seems to match several of the cruder concept pieces that surfaced in the 1990's and depicts the subject matter of the meeting notes, which the reader will note mirrors the events that James Creelman later wrote in the abandoned

"Creelman Valley Sequence" months later. Once again, as of the date of this document, they were working without a solid screenplay of any kind, and were shooting for an even more ambitious and visually impressive sequence than before. It also lacked any intelligible dialogue, which made it an easy "drop in" scene for editors.

The notes also indicate that Cooper was not entirely happy with the environment as depicted in the first test, and changes needed to be made to graduate the more arid landscapes into a lusher, jungle-like setting. Some interesting modifications of existing artwork resulted, as well as a new large-scale tabletop set.

An entirely reworked miniature environment resulted from the "Allosaur Capture Sequence" notes. Stand-in models of the allosaur and humans sit in new, more forested surroundings, with a river in the foreground and a revised mountain range in the distance. An airborne eagle and rider–probably a rear-projected image–can be glimpsed in the circled area of the frame, between two jagged peaks. From the collection of the author.

Above is Duncan Gleason's original concept painting of the allosaur cart being pulled into place by the ape men, and below is the revised version. New, denser growth and forests– and a modification of the mountain range–have been painted over the original. From the collection of the author.

The tone of the meeting notes indicates that time was becoming a factor in the production. The opening sentence declares that *"In order to keep our crew together, we are immediately going into a sequence in which the ape people capture the allosaurs (sic) and carry it down into their cave home."* and Cooper seems to mean business. Within two days Howard Campbell received a somewhat terse inter-office memo (the only one I've ever located for *War Eagles*) that indicates things weren't moving along as quickly as the producer desired.

By December 19th, Campbell had delivered a finalized budget of $19,325.00 for test #2. His typed budget report and several handwritten sheets survive. Of interest is the mention, under Special Equipment, of new projectors and repair of "Stop Motion Machines" that account for almost half of the projected budget. This could have been an attempt by Cooper and O'Brien to subsidize replacement and repair of Obie's personal production equipment by MGM,

and would certainly have introduced some friction into the relationship. This is only a theory, but it could possibly help to explain the subsequent standstill in production of this test. There were many studio-based animation divisions in Hollywood, including MGM's own, which was just getting off the ground at this stage. But there were no other units quite like O'Brien's in operation, and no one seemed to have the desire, patience or ingenuity to copy his methods yet. The documents, notes, art and film frames that fill this chapter relate the rest of the story, and represent the last recorded efforts on the part of the artists, planners and technicians to create a truly unique and innovative fantasy film. Most of what is displayed came to light due to happenstance, luck and misfiling

The single notation to be found in the surviving files of MGM's Art Department regarding *War Eagles* is *"abandoned."*

INTER-OFFICE COMMUNICATION

To MR. HOWARD CAMPBELL

Subject JOB #156

From Merian C. Cooper   Date Dec. 17, 1938

I wish to have a meeting with you every afternoon at 5:20, to discuss the progress of the work.

I have not yet received the sketches on the wigs, makeup, masks, costumes, and weapons for the ape people. I would like to have these as soon as possible.

The only official MGM memo that the author has recovered from War Eagles *seems to indicate that Mr. Cooper was in a bit of a hurry to get filming of the second test sequence underway. From the author's collection.*

COOPER TEST
MINIATURE & FULL SIZE SETS, DROPS
AND MISCELLANEOUS EQUIPMENT.

	Scene Numbers	Estimate
1. MATTE SHOT (Newcombe)		
One Miniature Set Appx. 4 x 8		225.00
One Full size Rock Set with Road on 4° Platform		950.00
		1,175.00
2. PROCESS- Two 5 x 7 Painted Glasses		
One Painted Backing Appx. 3 x 4		450.00
One Full Size set with Foliage & Mountain Bkg. on Platform		1,000.00
One Full Size Tree Trunk		175.00
One Fore Ground Rock		75.00
One Fore Ground Tree with Foliage		225.00
		1,925.00
3. TWO 5 x 7 Painted Glasses		
One Painted Backing Appx 6 x 8		450.00
Redress Full Size Set #1 (Built for Set #1)		75.00
Repaint Full Size Set (Built for Set #1)		75.00
		600.00
4. PROCESS		
One Miniature Set		150.00
One Full Size Foreground Tree OUT		50.00
		200.00
5. PROCESS		
One Full Size Foreground Tree Limb		225.00
6. PROCESS		
One Full Size Foreground Set		150.00
7. PROCESS		
Full Size Set (Portion of Cart) (Note - use same in set #8)		500.00
7A. PROCESS		
Full Size Set (Portion of Cart & Pit)		1,200.00
8. PROCESS		
Use Full Size Portion of Cart from #7 — FS. TAIL ?		?
9. TWO 5 x 7 Painted Glass & one Painted Backing Appx. 5 x 7		450.00
10. PROCESS		
Two 5 x 7 Painted Glasses & one Painted Backing		450.00
One Miniature Set (Roadway)		75.00
One Full Size Foreground Set		250.00
		775.00
11. ONE Miniature Set		300.00
One Painted 5 x 7 Glass		100.00
Miniature Cart & Men		200.00
Miniature Operations		200.00
Electric		150.00
		600.00

Estimate

12 MATTE
    One Miniature Set   350.00
    Repaint Full Size Set   75.00
                                                     425.00

13. ONE Full Size set - Painted Backing   175.00
    One Miniature Set   50.00
    Two 5 x 7 Painted Glasses & Backing   450.00
                                                       675.00

                          TOTAL SETS   8,900.00

SPECIAL PROPS
    Two Allosaurs   750.00
    Two 3 x 4 Plate Glasses   30.00
    Miscellaneous Equipment   350.00
    One Miniature Cart   75.00
                                                 1,205.00

SPECIAL EQUIPMENT
    New Projectors   8,120.00
    Repair Stop Motion Machines   850.00
    New Stop Motion Machine   250.00
                                                 9,220.00

A quickly-rendered concept painting, presumably by Stanley Johnson, depicts the last sequence (Scene 23, Set 9) planned and budgeted for War Eagles. *It was only partially shot before the production was abandoned. Image courtesy of Mark Berry.*

MINIATURES

x √ #1 - MINIATURE WAGON ———————— 75°°
        SIX DAYS TO BUILD

x #2 - PORTION OF ROAD ———————— 150°°
  √ SET UP #1
      THREE DAYS TO BUILD & PAINT.

x #3 - UPPER PORTION OF PIT. — 75°°
  √ SET UP #2
      THREE DAYS TO BUILD & DRESS.
  √ SET UP #6
      NO TIME NECESSARY

x #4 - LOWER PORTION OF PIT — 85°°
  √ SET UP # 7A.
      THREE DAYS TO BUILD & PAINT

x #5 - PORTION OF ROAD & CLIFF. — 100°°
  √ SET UP # 10
      THREE DAYS TO BUILD & PAINT

x #6 - CRATER ———————— 2050°°
  √ SET UP #11
      SIX DAYS TO BUILD & PAINT.

x #7 - PORTION OF FORE GROUND — 75°°
  √ SET UP # 13
      TWO DAYS TO BUILD, PAINT & DRESS

NOTE
THIS ESTIMATE DOES NOT INCLUDE
TIME FOR TECHNICOLOR TESTS
        HWC

Campbell's notation at the bottom of his miniatures estimate list: "This estimate does not include time for Technicolor tests" falls into line with the language used on the first test's breakdown about "allowing two weeks' testing time" before shooting and that is the approximate length of time that passed before the next document appeared. It is a detailed, and, for stop-motion photography, rather fast-paced breakdown of the action for the sequence. It is dated December 29, 1938.

ALLOSAURS CAPTURE SEQUENCE

Scene 1   Set 1.   LONG SHOT, showing portion of the plateau at left, and at the right can be seen the valley many thousand feet below. A crude natural roadway leads to the plateau. On this roadway, near to the plateau, is a huge cart pulled by many men. We truck in until we come to these men, then pan left until we show a portion of the plateau where the men are finishing a pit to trap the allosaurs. For this we will require two 9x12 glasses; one back drop 9x12; one miniature cart; miniature roadway and pit; one full size jungle set about 30'x10' high, with 25 feet foreground; two full size sets with rock backing, 30 feet wide by 10 feet high; one full size tree trunk as per sketch, to be used as foreground miniature projection; distant fire and smoke to be projected in. Cart to be animated. This shot to be panned from right to left.   2 days animation.

Scene 2   Set 1. Full size set. A closer shot, with mat, showing men coming out of the pit and covering it, and showing primitive type men tying up a birdman whom they have captured.

Scene 3   Set 1. Same as above, except closer shot with mat. In this will be the completion of the action in scene 2, so that the two may be intercut.

Scene 4.   Set 1 (lefthand part). Same as above, with the exception that the full size set of pit has been replaced by miniature. In this we will show men throwing ropes over tree and hoisting birdman into the air, head down. This will be a miniature man.   1 days animation.

Scene 5   Set 1. Close shot of right hand full size set, at tree trunk. Men
           pulling on rope, hoisting. Straight shot.

Scene 6   Set 2. This should be a wooded scene where the man calls the
           allosaurs with a peculiar horn. The allosaurs can be seen in b.g.
           coming through the trees. Man exits left to right, and allosaurs
           pursues him out of set. This will require two 5x7 glasses, one
           back drop 4x5, a small piece of miniature, and a full size
           set for miniature projection.   2 days animation.

Scene 7   Set 3. Man being pursued by allosaurs. This will require two 5x7
           glasses, one back drop 8x4. F.g. miniature and about 30 feet of
           full size set for b.g. projection. This will be at a much lower
           camera angle than sketch.   2 days animation.

Scene 8   Set 4. Full size projection shot. Man hanging head down over pit.
           Man being pursued by allosaurs enters, followed by allosaurs. Two
           5x7 glasses, miniature, and one 8x4 back drop.   1 days animation.

Scene 9   Set 1. Allosaurs enters scene. Springs at captive man hanging above
           pit. Men jerk birdman out of allosaurs' way. Allosaurs just misses
           pit, and walks around it still trying to reach man above. The men
           lower birdman, tempting allosaurs again. Allosaurs jumps, misses
           footing and falls in pit.   4 days animation.

Scene 10   Set 5. Full size projection. Men in tree, swinging man above allosaurs
           before it falls in pit. Allosaurs reaching to get man. Small
           miniature.   1 days animation.

Scene 11   Set 1. Full size projection and miniature projection. Closer shot,

allosaurs in pit, men tying him up.   2 days animation.

Scene 12   Set 1. Extreme long shot, men pulling allosaurs into air.

Miniature projection.   2 days animation.

Scene 13   Set 1 (full size sets already used), showing men pulling on ropes,
  "   14
  "   15   winding them around trees, and some pulling ropes with aid of

crude windlass.

Scene 16   Set 1. Extreme long shot. Man pushing huge cart under allosaurs,

which is suspended in air. Miniature projection. 1 days animation.

Scene 17   Set 1-A. Closer shot of allosaurs in the cart, men binding logs

to hold him in. Miniature and full size projection. (Full size

section of cart.)   1 days animation.

Scene 18   Set 1. Extreme long shot, using entire set. Men are pulling

cart out of picture. Miniature projection.   1 days animation.

Scene 19   Set 1. Closeup of huge wheel of cart, with men prying at it to

get it started (full size). Also full size projection with

miniature projection showing tail or leg of allosaurs. 1 days animation.

Scene 20   Set 6. Looking down the valley towards hell, showing the border

of trees. Men pulling cart. Miniature projection. Two 5x7

glasses; miniature cart.   2 days animation.

Scene 21   Set 7. Medium close shot of the huge cart crossing a natural
           bridge. Below is a river of molten lava. Cart exits from scene.
           Full size wheel, projected vapor, two miniature projections, and
           miniature.   1 days animation.

Scene 22   Set 8. Miniature and glass. Miniature cart and miniature men.
           Projected vapor, around circle of lava. Lava to be projected.
                                                         2 days animation.

Scene 23   Set 9. Long shot, looking down into the valley below. In the
           right foreground a birdman is standing beside his eagle. We see
           the procession far below him. He mounts eagle and flies away.
           This scene will have vaporous smoke coming up from below.
           Miniature projection, two glasses 9x12, one back drop 8x9,
           miniature eagle, full size set with rock backing. Projected
           vapor.   2 days animation.

The great irony of this second test sequence, and all of the related documents and artwork that have been recovered, is that the entire plot thread was eventually dropped from the storyline. The probable reasons for this were discussed in the script chapter, but the timeline suggests this test was scheduled to be filmed any time between late January and the end of February, 1939— which was still *months* before a full script was completed. And it would not be until mid-July of that year that the thread was completely written out of *War Eagles*. Were there already serious doubts at this

relatively early stage? It seems likely, but Obie was characteristically soldiering on with his plans to shoot the large-scale scene. What follows are the technical notes long attributed to Willis O'Brien. They may have been created by some other member of the production team, but I am following the traditional assumption that since they accompanied his personal copy of the script over so long a span, he probably authored them. They bear close resemblance to a Technical Supplement prepared in 1941 for his other ill-fated project, *Gwangi*, that is commonly associated with him.

This preliminary sketch by Duncan Gleason shows the full frame action described in Scene #1 below. It was the basis for his full painting of the same sequence that was later modified to bring the visuals into line with the more jungle-like environment described in the "Allosaurs (sic) Capture Sequence" meeting notes of December 15, 1938. Image from the author's collection.

Set #1

1 miniature 4'x 8'.
1 miniature cart 1/12th full size.
1 full size rock set to be shot from 2 angles.
This becomes a matte shot, Newcomb doing everything except
center portion of picture where cart, men and pit work.
Men are rear projected on 2 miniature screens. Plates shot
on above full size set. Lava and smoke to be dubbed in
afterward.

Scene #1

Extreme long shot showing portion of plateau at left and at the right can

be seen valley many thousand feet below. Smoke, vapor and lava in extreme

lower right hand corner of picture. A crude natural roadway leads up to

wooded plateau. On this roadway in the center of our picture is a huge cart

pulled by many men right to left.

Scene #4.

Same set up as Scene #1. Men are pushing cart into pit.

Scene#18.

Extreme long shot same as Scene #1. Men are pulling cart out of pit. Two

projectors working.

Artwork depicting events as described in Scene #9 below. The artist is unknown, but it could possibly have been produced by Willis O'Brien himself as the dinosaur anatomy shows more familiarity and precision—a rarity for War Eagles pre-production art! It is one of a series of original stills salvaged from the MGM Matte Department building by William Cappa before demolition. Image from the author's collection.

Set #2.

2 - 5 x 7 painted glasses.
1 - 3 ¼ 4 painted backing
1 miniature set approximately 3' x 4' with pit.
1 full size set built with forced perspective approximately
    25' x 10' and 20' deep to painted drop.
2 miniature screens, plates for same shot on right hand and
    left hand side of above full sized set.

Scene #2

MED. LONG SHOT - full sized PROCESS. This becomes a plate or full sized
projection with full sized limb and real men in front of 16' screen. Men
are tying up birdmen and finishing covering of pit.

Scene #3.

CLOSEUP shot of above full sized shot. Men tying up birdmen.

Scene #7.

Same as Scene #2 f.g. men hoisting on rope. Birdman rises on rope. Birdman
now becomes a miniature.

Scene #6.

Men putting rocks under wheels of cart in pit.

Scene #9.

Same set up as Scene #2. Allosaurs enters left to right. Springs at bait
above. Man jerks bait out of reach. Allosaurs just misses bait and walks
around it. Man lowers bait, tempting Allosaurs. Allosaurs jumps again, misses
footing and falls into pit.

87

SET·3-   SCENE 7

A storyboard sketch, probably by Duncan Gleason, depicting action described in Scene #5 below. The set number is correct, but the scene number is revised. As noted, the sequence was actually shot from a lower angle than pictured in the sketch and a later production sketch by Harry Stevenson and a surviving color nitrate film frame actually depict this scene. Image courtesy of Gregory Kulon.

Set #3.

2 painted glasses 5' x 7'.
1 painted drop 2' x 3'.

Scene #5.

Men rear – projected on two miniature screens. Plates for same shot on full sized set in Set #1. Projected man blows horn to call Allosaurs. The Allosaurs can be seen in the b.g. coming through the trees. Man runs left to right as Allosaurs pursues him out of picture.

(NOTE: This will be shot from a much lower angle than shown in sketch.)

Action as depicted in Scene #8 below. Another Gleason storyboard sketch that depicts a captured eagle rider being used as bait for the allosaur pit trap. In this version the ape man being pursued is using a bullroarer-type instrument to excite the dinosaur. In other drafts and artwork it is sometimes pictured as horn, and the live human bait is replaced by a straw dummy. There are many variants connected to this ambitious sequence which was ultimately cut from the film. Image courtesy of Ronald V. Borst.

Set #4.

2 - 5' x 7' painted glasses.
1 - 3' x 6' painted backing.

Scene #8.

Shot with real man hanging head down in front of process screen. Plate of

Allosaurs pursuing man to be made on miniature set used in set #1, using one

projector and miniature screen. Man in rear projection on miniature screen.

Plate for same made on full sized set of set #2.

A Gleason storyboard sketch depicting elements in Scene #10, with the allosaur leaping up to grab the live captive bait before falling into the pit. The sequence was to vary between medium shots involving live actors with projected animation backgrounds and long shots showing the action in full stop-motion with miniature rear-screen projection inserts. O'Brien specialized in such shots, whose complicated nature soon led to their abandonment. Image courtesy of Ronald V. Borst.

Set #5

Full sized process.

Scene #10.

Real man on full sized tree limb in front of projection screen.
Plate for same made on set with miniature Allosaurs and miniature
man hanging head down.

O'Brien's technical notes are a wonderful glimpse into the process of translation from artistic imagery into practical effects setups and this Duncan Gleason sketch illustrates the overall look of what is described, with live ape-men swarming over and around the pit and subdued allosaur, here seen with the application of a log 'gag'. Image from the author's collection.

SET #6

One full foreground set.

∗∗∗

Scene 11   Full Size set and men in front of projection screen.
Plate for same made on Set (1, using miniature pit and
Allosaurs in front of miniature screen, plate for same
made on Full Size set (#1-C).

∗∗∗

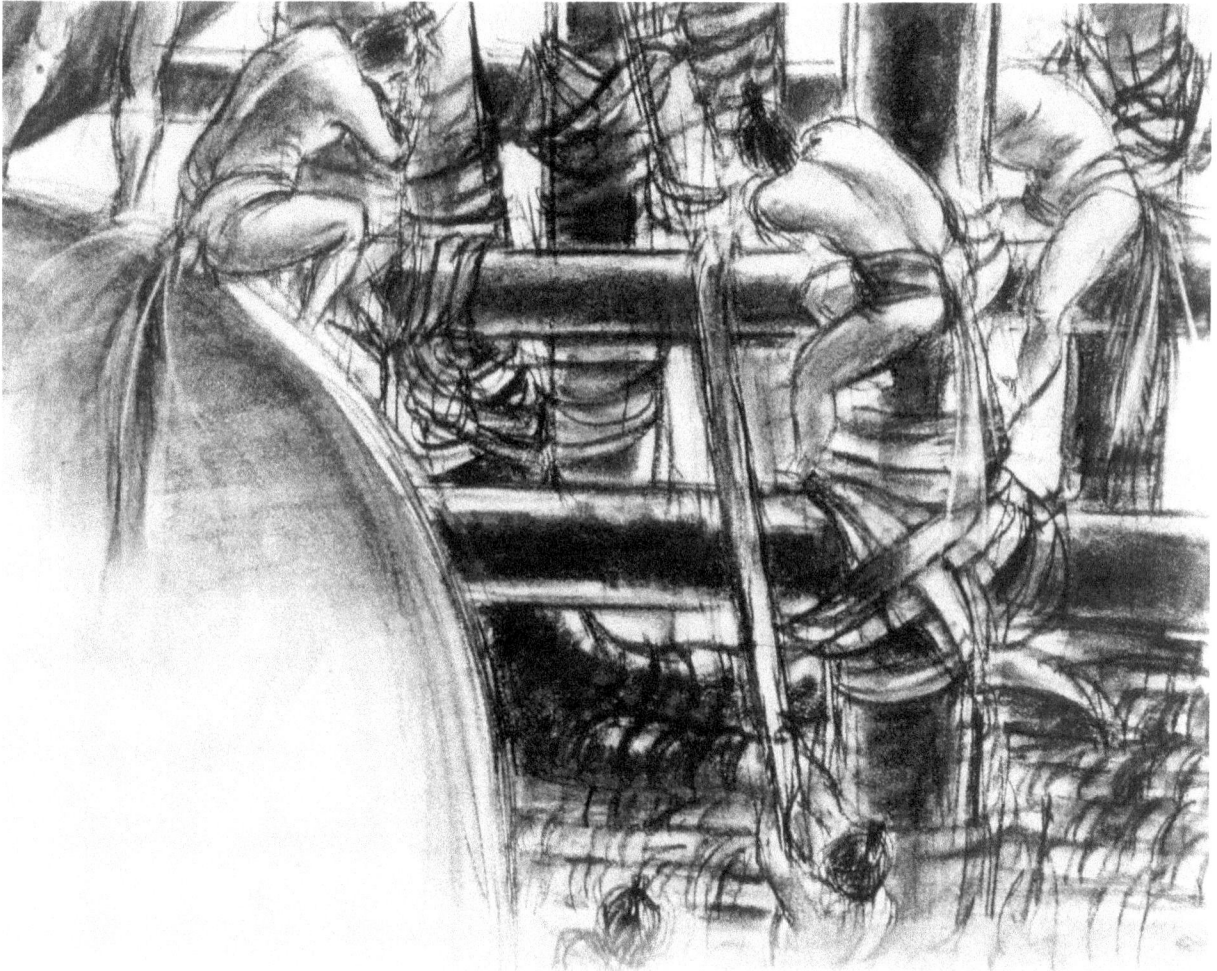

The full-sized portion of Set #7 as described in the notes below, in a sketch by Gleason. Live actors and the partial wheel and cart would appear in the foreground, with the action of the struggling animated dinosaur and opposite side of the miniature cart appearing as elements in the background. Sometimes these shots would be accomplished by on-set rear-projection and other times by early optical printing techniques. Image courtesy of Douglas Turner.

Set #7.

1 full sized f.g. set.
(Portion of camera side of cart and wheel)
Full size process.

Scene #17.

Men in front of process screen. Plate for same made in pit on set 2
with miniature Allosaurs in cart with camera side of cart and wheel
removed.

Another sketch depicting the full-sized set and scenic elements for the capture sequence. Only a partial full-sized cart was to be built, so any scene involving a full view of the allosaur and cart would have been accomplished in miniature and projected behind the real men in front of process screens as described in the notes. Image courtesy of Ronald V. Borst.

Set #7A

A full sized set approximately 34' x 24' and 8' deep.
Full sized process of cart.

Scene #17A

Real man on set in front of process screen. Plate for same to be shot

on miniature set #2 in pit using Allosaurs and cart with camera side of

cart removed.

Nean projection, men ... ...
cage of pit.

(Handwritten notation: "rear projection men running around edge of pit.)

More action that would have taken place on full-sized Set #8 with live actors working with a prop cart wheel. In this case, the ape men appear to be levering the rear wheels of the cart into motion while their compatriots form a human pull-team on the opposite end of the captured allosaur. The concept of a captured and cart-bound dinosaur would late find its way into 1969's The Valley of Gwangi, with the complicated issues of dinosaur wrangling wisely eliminated by a crossfade! Image courtesy of Douglas Turner.

Set #8.

Full size f.g. set.
(Portion of wheel. Use same from set #7.)

Scene #19.

Full sized process. Full sized wheel in front of process screen. Plate
for same made on Set #2, using miniature cart and Allosaurs working in
front of miniature screen. Plate for same to be made on full sized set #7A.

A rough Gleason sketch depicting the full sequence action described in Scene #20, with stop-motion elements, glass mattes of the descent into the ape men's lair in "the Hell" and no less than three miniature projectors working. The hand notation of "#9 OUT" seems to indicate that this miniature set was pulled and the complicated shot abandoned early in the planning for Test #2. Image courtesy of Douglas Turner.

Set #9

2 - 5 x 7 glasses painted.
1 - 3 x 4 backing painted.
1 miniature set approximately 2' x 5' in between glasses.

Scene #20

Looking down the valley toward the Hell showing men pulling cart with Allosaurs from right to left on miniature between glasses. Plates for same to be shot on full sized set used in set #1. Molten lava and smoke in b.g. projected in from front. Three projectors working.

Continuing the harrowing trip down the narrow cliffside to "the Hell", this rough shows the foreground foliage set specified in Set #10 below, as well as the live and projected elements that would have made up the scene. The fallen rock that the hand notation refers to can be seen to the left and beneath the large rear cart wheel. Image courtesy of Douglas Turner.

Set #10.

2 - 5 x 7 painted glasses.
1 - 3 x 4 painted backing.
1 miniature set approximately 3' x 4' between glasses.
1 full sized f.g. set with foliage.

Scene #21

Full sized process. Foliage set and men in front of process screen. Plate
for same to be made with Allosaurs in miniature cart, minus front wheels.
Wheel and man to rear projected on miniature screen. Plate for same to be
made on full sized set used in set #1. With full size wheels used in set #8 A
Molten lava to rear projected on miniature screen. Smoke and vapor varied
in with front projection.

(NOTE: There will be no falling rock as indicated in sketch.)

no falling Rock ——

#/0

An impressive Duncan Gleason production painting of the master shot of Set # 11, depicting the huge volcanic crater that heats the lost valley and the procession of ape men and captured allosaur in the lower right. No less than three different pre-production artists created images of this scene, with Gleason's being the most refined effort. It is very likely that he and matte painter Jack Shaw would have produced them on glass for the actual filming. Image courtesy of Bob Burns.

SET #11

~~One 5 x 4 lava.~~
One Miniature set (small portion of rim).
One miniature cart and Allosaurs with
    procession of men - Appr. 1/60 F.S.
One miniature crater (Appr. 6 ft. Dia.)
    with lava.

* * *

(RIM OF CRATER)

Scene 22   RIM OF CRATER painted on glass around miniature rim set
            with cart and miniature men moving R. to l. In front of
            miniature screen. Plate for same shot of 6 fot. minia-
            ture of crater with boiling lava. Smoke and vapor to
            shoot and burned in by front projection as in Scene 1.

97

This simple, uncredited pre-production painting depicts the action specified in Scene #23 below. It is part of the collection of studio stills preserved by William Cappa and may have been executed by Stanley Johnson, an illustrator who had worked with Merian C. Cooper previously on She, and referenced in the meeting notes of December 15, 1938 as "Mr. Johnson". Image courtesy of Mark Berry.

SET #12

One miniature set appx. 5 x 4. (lower
portion matted off)

∗∗∗

(MEDIUM LONG SHOT)

Scene 23   MEDIUM LONG SHOT shooting across crater at men pulling
cart (#1-I) with captured Allosaurs from R. to L. Men
projected from rear on miniature screen, use same plate
made in P.G. set (#1-F) for Scene 1. Moving matte foreground by Reis to be shot on 6 ft. miniature in Set #11.
Smoke and vapor to be burned in by front projection as
in Scene 1.

A detailed drawing of Scene #24, probably executed by Harry Stevenson, that depicts a lone eagle rider and his mount spying on the activities of the ape men in the valley below. The procession and cart can just barely be seen in the lower left of the image. Further sketches and actual production matte paintings were created and filmed for this scene, but there is no evidence that it was completed. Image courtesy of Douglas Turner

SET #13

  Two 5 x 7 glasses.
  One 3 x 4 backing.
  One full size set with painted backing,
   appx. 10 x 10.
  One miniature foreground set, appx. 3 x 3.

    •••

   (MINIATURE EAGLE)
Scene 24 MINIATURE EAGLE on foreground set. Man projected in from
    rear on miniature screen, plate shot on full size set.
    Procession in lower left hand corner projected from rear
    onto miniature screen. Plate to be made on Set #1. From
    high set up, shooting down. Plate for Set #1 made on full
    size set (#1-F) likewise shot from high angle. Molten
    lava in background, rear projector on miniature screen.
    Use plate from Scene 1. Smoke and vapor to be front pro-
    jected, burning in as in previous scenes.

Despite all of this intensive preparation, and the construction of at least some of the miniature sets and backgrounds, the sequence was never shot. The Technicolor tests *for* the scene were, and the two sets of nitrate color frames that have survived consist of color test images only. There is evidence of model animation utilizing human and allosaur models, and the Technicolor stock shot index listing found at the Academy Library would, once again, tend to suggest that a certain amount of motion picture footage was shot. These images are rarest extant elements of *War Eagles*, and I thank both Bob Burns and the family of Duncan Gleason for the opportunity to have them digitally scanned for inclusion in this work.

Despite the densely-packed and rich, multi-matted image, this is not a frame from a story sequence. The most telling evidence is the appearance of the animation models. Above: The small human figure is dressed in the garb of an eagle rider, complete with headband, as seen in production art and stills from the first test. It is not an ape man figure. Below: The same figure flees across a miniature set from the allosaur, but the allosaur is the static "stand-in" model used for lighting tests. Both images courtesy of Bob Burns.

A different tabletop setup that conforms to the action described as the allosaur chases the ape man through the jungle. Above: The same eagle rider figure posed in a reaction shot. Below: What he is reacting to: an animation model of an allosaur. It is a distinctly different model from the stand-in version and indicates stop-motion was being tested. It is a slightly overexposed and softer shot than the one above it, also making it appear to be a motion picture frame. Both images courtesy of Bob Burns

A comparison of one of Duncan Gleason's sketches to the frame shows just how close the shooting emulated the pre-production art-work. Since Gleason was also employed by the "Newcombe Unit"–MGM's matte-painting division–he probably executed the background and "glasses" himself. The allosaur stand-in model reappers in the frame, accompanied by the same animation model of the eagle rider. Both images courtesy of Bob Burns.

The "beauty shot" of Marcel Delgado's allosaurus model, which appears to be animated in this frame. The model has the smoother appearance of having been sculpted and cast in foam rubber, rather than Delgado's earlier technique of build-up. He generally shied away from this method, but there is evidence he was going to use it for O'Brien's later project Gwangi. The armature depicted at right is associated with Gwangi, and many believe it may have originated for use on War Eagles. The author believes there are scale issues involved and that it may have been too large to have been used for the models in the tests. Frame image courtesy of Bob Burns. Armature image courtesy of Gregory Kulon.

103

The Script

Confabulation is defined as *"...the spontaneous narrative report of events that never happened, consisting of the creation of false memories, perceptions, or beliefs."*

For decades, students of fantasy film history and animation enthusiasts alike have inadvertently practiced a form of confabulation by assigning incorrect authorship to the various drafts and treatments of *War Eagles*. It was no one's fault, really. A very spotty history was all we had to work with and the more-or-less complete picture that now exists only came about within the last 5 years. It's been an exciting ride, playing a small role in the process of uncovering the truth, and you are about to read the best part. This script is the final draft, written by Cyril Hume and dated October 10, 1939, and includes revisions up to the end of the project's active life. It is the closest thing to a shooting script that exists. Hume did a masterful job in wrestling an out-of-control story back down to Merian C. Cooper's original concept, all the while adding humor and dazzling visuals of his own invention. Sacrifices were made along the way, including the plucky Professor Hiram P. Cobb, but the end result still easily qualifies it as one of the greatest movies *never* made.

You are going to enjoy *War Eagles*.

"WAR EAGLES"

by

Cyril Hume

Oct. 10, 1939
With Changes
FEB 16 1940

105

Duncan Gleason's costume concept sketch for the Viking eagle warriors. Image courtesy of a private collection.

WAR EAGLES

SEQUENCE ONE

1   FADE IN:
          HIGH ANGLE (AIR) LONG SHOT - NEW YORK CITY

          The magnificent panorama wheels below.
          Finally the plane noses toward Beldoe's Island.

1-X1   ZOOM SHOT

          as the Statue of Liberty rushes rocking toward
          CAMERA.

1-X2   INT. PLANE (PROCESS) B.G. STATUE OF LIBERTY

          As the plane rushes toward Statue of Liberty.

2   FULL SHOT - STATUE OF LIBERTY (MINIATURE)

          A wild Army pursuit plane stunting all around
          it, horrifyingly close.

3   MED. SHOT - INT. H.Q. FORT WOOD, BEDLOE
          ISLAND

          An elderly colonel stands at the window with
          his adjutant, the CAMERA so placed that we do
          not see what is happening outside. We HEAR
          the roar of a motor.

                 Colonel (glaring up out window)
    Get me Mitchell Field! - - the Group Commander!

          As the adjutant jumps to obey -

4   FULL SHOT - STATUE OF LIBERTY (MINIATURE)

          The plane continues to stunt.

5   CLOSE SHOT - INT MILITARY H.Q. FORT WOOD

          The adjutant hands the colonel the telephone.

                        CONTINUED

The roar o.s. increases and diminishes.

                    Colonel
                (ironically into phone)
Your boy in D-75 is putting on another exhibition
you'd be proud of, Colonel.
                (suddenly exploding, his bark worse
                than his bite)
But if you don't get the idiot away from here, I'm
going to turn out the A.A. batteries, and shoot
him down in self-defense!

        As a tremendous roar comes by window, and a
        shadow momentarily cuts off the light, all
        the papers are blown off the desk. We do not
        see the airplane.

5-X1   FULL SHOT - STATUE OF LIBERTY (MINIATURE)

        Plane continues to stunt.

                                QUICK DISSOLVE:

6   MED. SHOT - INT. H.Q. OFFICER MITCHELL FIELD

        Colonel Haslip, the very impressive
        Commanding officer, is shaken with chagrin

                    Col. Haslip (grimly into phone)
        Colonel, the matter will be attended to directly.

        He carefully hangs up, stands, hands clasped
        behind, staring out over the air field, and
        struggling awfully for composure. Suddenly
        he leaps convulsively for the dictophone.

7   MED. SHOT - INT. FOURTH PURSUIT SQUADRON
                OFFICE

        The telephone is ringing. Major Aving, a
        serious officer of forty answers.

                    Major Aving
        Fourth Pursuit Squadron - -   -
                (wincing, respectful, as receiver pops)
        Major Aving speaking, sir.

                                CONTINUED:

          Major Aving (continued)
        (his face growing longer and longer)
Yes, sir! -- of course, sir! -- at once, sir!

    He hangs up softly, turns slowly, discovers
    Capt. Lang in the doorway, still wearing his
    flying clothes. Lang glances anxiously at
    Aving's face, softly closes the door.

          Major Aving
        (avoiding Lang's eyes)
Your flight came in shy one of the new ships,
didn't it, Lang?

          Capt. Lang (nervously improvising)
Oh, the ship's safe, sir! You see we -- we sort
of flew into a cloud and -- and --

          Major Aving
        (grimly finishing for him)
And when you came out of it, that pet screwball
of yours had flown himself right into the Group
commander's hair!

          Capt. Lang (almost wailing)
The one thing in skirts that guy don't run from
has to be the Statue of Liberty!

          Major Aving (ruefully grinning)
The old girl has seemed to need a dusting-off
recently -- but your boy's in a jam.

          Capt. Lang
        (throwing his helmet down)
Hang it! Slim Johansen's the best pilot in the
Flight!

          Major Aving (sober, regretful)
And the worst soldier in the Squadron --

                DISSOLVE:

The young pilots of the Second Flight looking
off anxiously into the air. Some have removed
their flying suits, and are in uniform.

First Pilot (gloomily)
Why did he have to do it in one of the new ships!

Second Pilot (ruefully reminiscing)
Remember the West Coast maneuvers when he went
hedge-hopping, trying to spot Hedy Lamarr's back-
yard?

As all grin involuntarily - -

Third Pilot (suddenly pointing o.s.)
Here he is!

9   LONG SHOT A SINGLE PURSUIT SHIP (MINIATURE)

coming in upside-down toward CAMERA, and
whimsically stunting.

10   FULL SHOT GROUP

All are watching with disapproving appreciation.

Second Pilot (sadly)
Yeah, that's the Swede, all right!
Fourth (shaking his head)
Sure ain't anybody but!

11   LONG SHOT THE PLANE (MINIATURE)

At the last moment it flips over right-side-
up, lands, and skids to a flashy stop.

11-A   EXT. SLIM'S ARMY PLANE MED. SHOT PORTION
           OF PLANE

A long, lanky, mildly cheerful individual in
a flying suit (Lt. "Slim" Johansen) climbs
out joint by joint. As the other pilots walk
into the SHOT in a funereal group - -

Slim (hitting the ground)
Hi, fellers!
Second (reproachfully eyeing him)
Hi, Slim!
Fifth (darkly)
Hi, old man.

Slim looks them over puzzled, smiles

Slim (to his particular friend)
What's eatin' these guys, Tex? - - they sick?

              Third (sadly nodding)
Reckon we're all kind of sick, feller.

Slim looks from face to face, uncomprehending.

              First (at last, hopelessly)
Commander's been on Cap's neck about you.

              Slim
Yeah?
        (with a despondent, bewildered sigh)
Then I guess they're all mad at me again.

              Third (lugubriously shaking his head)
Sounds like a court-martial this time sure enough!

              Slim
Court-martial!?
        (his voice cracking with indignation)
What have I done?
        (deeply wronged)
Haven't been drunk on duty - - or absent without
leave - - or cracked up any Government property!
        (blustering, defiant)
They can't court-martial me!
        (then slowly, uncertainly, as all continue
           watching him with funereal mournfulness)
Can they?

Slowly and in unison, all nod affirmatively.

              LAP DISSOLVE:

12   MED. SHOT INT. GROUP H.Q.

          Col. Haslip is seated behind a table with
          papers in his hands, Aving on his right, and
          Lang on his left. Slim, shoes shined, uniform
          comparatively neat, hair slicked down at least
          in front, stands at attention before them,
          anxious and bewildered. As Haslip looks up
          from the papers, Slim breaks into a sweat.

          Col. Haslip (not unkindly)
Under the circumstances, Lt. Johansen, I must
require an explanation of your most recent - - and
flagrant - - breach of regulations.

          slim swallows, glances appealingly toward
          Land and Aving.

          Maj. Aving (awkwardly cueing Slim)
About - -hm - - -about the Statue of Liberty - -
               CONTINUED:

          Slim (nervously improvising)
Sir! I was just trying to learn my ship - - you
know! - -under real combat conditions - -
         (with an air of sweet reasonableness)
- - wanted to see if the wings would come off - -

     At this, Aving and Lang, who have been
     pulling for him, wince and close their
     eyes.

          Col. Haslip (altogether official)
All ships are thoroughly tested before being
issued to the pilots.
         (a note of conclusion)
Is that all?

          Slim (with sudden impulsive
           sincerity)
I don't really know now why I did it, sir! But
up there in that new single-seater job, something
happened to me. All of a sudden I - -I just had
to let go, and fly the pants off her!

          Haslip (starting to fold up papers)
Explanation inadequate.

          Slim (desperate, inarticulate)
I had to, sir! With all that speed and power
under me, I felt like I wasn't just only a man
any more - - it was like I finally had wings of
my own!

     The officers glance sharply at him, in
     their eyes a hint of sympathy.

          Cap. Lang (urgent, hopeful)
We can all understand that feeling sir!

     Haslip's face slowly sets. All the humor
     leaves his eyes. He folds his hands.

          Col. Haslip (cold, grim)
At the moment, Captain Lang, our personal feelings are irrelevant. Half the world is at war.
We may not overlook any item of our own pre-
paredness.
         (wistful a moment, then hard again)
The days of single combat are as dead as those
of knight erranty - -and any pilot - -no matter
what his individual qualifications! - -who cannot
conform to an iron discipline, must be eliminated
while there is yet time. Technically, Lt.
Johansen, I have now no alternative but to pro-
ceed to your court-martial.

The faces of all the men are held expression-
less. The final decision has been reached.

            Col. Haslip (dubious, hesitant)
However, both your immediate superiors have so
urged your high personal character and outstanding
ability as a pilot that I am prepared in this case
to stretch a point in your favor.
            (picking up the final remaining type
sheet, handing it to Slim)
Sign this, and proceedings against you will be
dropped here.

      Slim studies the paper for a long time.
      His lip starts to tremble.

            Slim (shakily, looking up)
But it's a resignation!
            (indignantly tossing the paper down)
I can't give my commission up!

            Col. Haslip (soberly)
You don't seem to realize that a court-martial
could result in your dishonorable discharge.

            Slim (bursting out at them)
You don't seem to realize this is my whole life!

            Maj. Aving (urgent, leaning forward)
Even without a conviction you'd be grounded.

            Cap. Lang (returning the paper)
Sign it, Slim! This way you'll at least have your
reserve commission if there's a war!

            Slim (unwillingly, taking paper)
But it's like pulling your ship out of a fight!

            Col. Haslip (whimsical, sympathetic)
Why not just consider yourself - -shot down.

      Slim looks wretchedly from one to another
      at last takes the pen, bends over the paper.

            Maj. Aving (watching him sign)
There's bound to be plenty of other flying jobs
for a man like you.

            Slim (smiling wistfully)
Do you know of any other armies like this one, sir?

      Not seeing the three extended hands, Slim
      turns, walks quickly o.s.
            Col. Haslip (calling after him)
Good luck, young man!   CONTINUED

Maj. Aving (regretful, rising)
Goodbye, Johansen!

Capt. Lang (warmly moved)
So long Slim!

13   BIG CLOSEUP SLIM IN DOORWAY

Slim (looking back, tears in eyes)
Thanks! - - I know I got a break!

As the door closes - -

14   FULL SHOT THE THREE OFFICERS

Capt. Lang (bitterly, turning away)
The Flight is going to miss that big Swede!

Col. Haslip stands frowning at his desk,
hating what he has had to do. Aving follows
Lang to the window. TRUCK AFTER THEM INTO A
TWO SHOT as they stand looking out. (We do not
see anything outside the window).

Maj. Aving (musing, regretful)
That boy is caught in the wrong century. He ought
to have been born back there where every man
fought for himself - - like his Viking ancestors.

15   CLOSEUP COLONEL HASLIP

Col. Haslip (still frowning at desk)
Happen to listen in on the short wave at two o'clock
this morning?

16   FULL SHOT ROOM

as Aving and Lang turn from window, and the
men move together, TRUCK THREE SHOT.

Maj. Aving (ironical, resentful)
Yes, it seems they don't think much of the Monroe
Doctrine.
Capt. Lang (with sarcastic laugh)
Ain't that too bad!

Aving starts to join the laugh, then sees
that Haslip's face is still grave.

Maj. Aving (shocked, breathless)
Col. Haslip! You surely don't doubt the Air Force!?

CONTINUED:

                    Col. Haslip (wearily irritable)
I've no doubt at all that when the day comes
every man and ship will be in its place - -
                    (with measured serious meaning)
- - even though that place may be on the ground,
unable to take off!

                    Maj. Aving (slowly, appalled)
You actually think they may have something Really
Big?

                    Col. Haslip (avoiding his eye)
I mean that Jeliffe of Langly Field tells me it's
technically possible.

                    Capt. Lang (advancing, anxious)
Excuse me - - I don't understand, sir!

          Haslip and Aving exchange a glance. At last
          Haslip nods dubiously, turns away.

                    Maj. Aving (quietly to Lang)
Suppose, Lang, an attacking air forces carries with
it some sort of super electric ray - -
                    (watching the effect of his words)
- - tuned not to interfere with its own bombers, but
powerful enough to hold every engine in the defend-
in air force absolutely dead.

                    Lang (startled)
Why, they could bomb New York!

                    Col. Haslip (grumpy, worried)
Probably just some more confounded blackmail, Lang.
But I wouldn't talk of it among the men. Might
take the edge off their self-confidence - -

          Very slowly Lang takes in. When he speaks
          again, there is an undercurrent of bitter-
          ness and tension in his voice.

                    Capt. Lang (ironical, mocking)
Lucky thing you got rid of Johansen, Colonel! While
all of us good little soldiers were dying at out
posts, he'd disgrace the Group by shinning up a radio
mast and trying to knock down an enemy bomber with a
monkey-wrench!

          Neither of the others smile. They are staring
          blindly at the frightful picture which has
          taken shape in their minds. DISSOLVE TO:

17   HIGH ANGLE LONG SHOT NIGHT BROADWAY

          dominated by a big animated electric sign,
          representing the earth, with an airplane
          circling it. And the words: BI-CAR-BROME - -
          FROM POLE TO POLE.

                              DISSOLVE TO:

At the desk is a dauntingly beautiful and
efficient young woman. As Slim enters
cautiously and dubiously, consulting a slip
of paper in his hand - -

                 Girl (severely into telephone)
Mr. Laverock is in conference.

                 Slim (clearing his throat)
Excuse me - -

                 Girl (into telephone)
Mr. Laverock is in conference.

                 Slim (uncertainly consulting paper)
Bi - -
              (trying again, syllable by syllable)
- -Bi-Car-Brome?

                 Girl (briskly)
Your business please?

                 Slim (apologetically)
Well, I'm a flyer. My name is- -

                 Girl (reacting sharply)
You're a flyer!?

                 Slim (guiltily)
Yes. My name - -

                 Girl (rising with suppressed ex-
                 citement)
Have a seat please!
              (then crossing hurriedly to one of the
              office doors behind her which is
              slightly ajar)
Mr. Petty - - !

As Slim sits down gingerly in one of the
still chairs, the girl is seen through the
open door talking excitedly but inaudibly to
Mr. Petty, a smallish, baldish, fussy little
man magnifying eye-glasses. As they exchange
a few remarks in a tense undertone, their
eyes are fixed solemnly on Slim - -which
makes Slim very uncomfortable. As Mr. Petty
comes bustling out, followed by the girl
Slim rises with anxious respect.

                 Petty (sharply, hurrying over)
You say you're an aviator, young man?

                     CONTINUED:

                  Slim (doubtful of the word)
Well, I'm a- -
        (then wretchedly producing a wad of
        credentials from his inner pocket, and
        handing them to Petty)
Maybe you better look at these.

        With a piercingly appraising look at Slim,
        Petty accepts the papers and begins thumbing
        through them. After a moment or two he
        starts reacting with a visibly sharpened
        interest to what he reads.

                  Petty (brightening over each
                    successive paper)
Hm.... hm!....hm!
                  (then sharply, glancing up at Slim)
This is you?!

                  Slim (dubiously after a peek at
                    his own credentials)
Well, yes!

                  Petty (consulting the papers again,
                    disguising his eagerness)
You're willing to undertake a round-the-world
flight?

                  Slim ((Just so it isn't Mars)
Round-the-world?
              (heartily)
Sure!

                  Petty (his eyes still popping at
                    the credentials)
Solo?

                  Slim (anxious to please)
Well, of course I wouldn't object to a passenger.

        Petty looks at slim for a moment almost
        reverently, the collects himself with a
        start, and moves rapidly toward the inner
        office, still holding the papers.

                  Petty (firmly as he goes)
Wait right here! - -right here!
                  (with a significant glance as Slim
                  resumes his seat)
Miss Lafarge, keep this young man entertained - -
        As the door closes on Petty - -
                  Girl (with dazzling smile)
Stranger in town?
         Slim starts violently, and gives her a
         wretched helpless look.

22   FULL SHOT LAVEROCK'S OFFICE

Big and imposing - -rather too much so. On
one corner of the enormous desk is a small-
scale model of the big sign on the roof.
Mr. Laverock, an eccentric middle-aged man,
is tumultuously pacing the floor as Petty
respectfully but excitedly enters with Slim's
papers in his hand.

        Laverock (turning on him)

Well, Hasn't Airways called. Hasn't the Pilots'
Club called? Hasn't anybody called?

        Petty (soothingly)
All of them called, sir, but none of them wanted
to assume the responsibility.
          (complacently handling the papers)
However, I personally - -

        Laverock (tragically interrupting)
The enormous pity of it, Petty! Here we've built
up a fifty million dollar business on the hangover
alone! But now when Bi-Car-Brome's ready to take
in sour stomach and the common cold, you're not
capable of producing a common aviator!

        Petty (starting to protest)
But, Mr. Laverock- -!

        Laverock (pacing with extravagant
          gestures)
That magnificent sign on the roof just running to
waste! - -my greatest idea! - -the most brilliant
selling-trademark in history! Only sign like it
in the universe! Stead of going - -
          (illustrating with a vertical motion)
- -goes this way! "Bi-Car-Brome! - -zzzzzzzzzzzzzzz!
- -From pole to pole!"

        Petty (plaintively trying to get
          a word in)
Mr. Laverock - -!

        Laverock (bitterly, throwing him-
          self down in his desk chair)
But here I am! - -the world my province! - -and my
hands are tied like a half-wit!

        Petty (eyes closed, very firm and
          loud)
Mr. Laverock - -!
                      CONTINUED:

                    Laverock (mildly, taking notice)
Yes?

                    Petty (with modest pride, gesturing
                    toward the outer door with Slim's papers)
I'm trying to tell you sir! - -I've got a man
waiting! - - been through Kelly Field! - -high bracket
test pilot! - -magnificent constitution! - -good
habits - -
                    (triumphantly lowering his voice to
                    a whisper)
 - -and single!

                    Laverock (cynically illustrating)
Want to go this way, I dare say! - -None of 'em
want to go like the sign.

                    Petty (knowing, self satisfied)
If I know the symptom of pressing emotional and
financial difficulties, Mr. Laverock, this one'll
go any way!

                    Laverock (jumping up, illustrating)
Jingo! - -Bring him in! Don't waste my time!

                    Petty (hurrying toward the door)
I'll check his credentials on the telephone while
you're interviewing him, sir.

22-X1   CLOSE SHOT LAVEROCK

                    Laverock (muttering distrustfully
                    to himself)
Two to one he still wants to go this way- -

22-X2   MED. SHOT SLIM

               waiting in the outer office. Miss Lafarge is
               favoring him with a series of languishing
               smiles. Slim, deeply anxious, and acutely
               uncomfortable, sits with his knees pressed
               together, determinedly pretending not to
               notice. When Petty appears in the door and
               beckons, Slim jumps up in eager relief.
               PAN HIM OVER INTO A TWO SHOT with Petty.

                    Petty (aside, leading Slim toward
                    Laverock's door by the arm)
It might be wise to make some appreciative reference to the sign.

               Slim nods solemnly, his eyes on Laverock o.s.
               As Petty shoves him reluctantly through the
               door - -

pacing the floor.

    Laverock (turning as Slim enters)
Well, young man! young man! understand the terms?
- -Pole to pole!
    (anxious, illustrating)
None of this!
    (whipping a contract out of his desk
    as Slim nods solemnly)
And fifty grand on the line the day you get back
in New York!

    Slim (staring, wide-eyed)
Fifty - -thousand - -dollars!? Mr. Laverock! what
do I got to do?

    Laverock (startled, staring)
Fift- -!   - -Do?
    (then smoothly, thinking fast)
Just once around! And of course, twice a day some
little word over the radio - -

    Slim   (startled, balking)
Me talk over the radio?

   During the above, the outer door has opened
   behind Slim's back, and Petty has appeared,
   beaming, and wig-wagging to Laverock that
   credentials are splendidly authentic.
   Laverock gets it instantly, takes out his
   fountain pen, and as he replies to Slim,
   begins altering the financial terms of the
   contract.

    Laverock (brushing Slim's objection
   aside)
Just tell 'em how you feel - -where you are - - and
what your chances look like. Signing off with
some dignified reference to the Product.
    (sliding across contract and pen)
Twenty-five grand the minute your wheels touch New
York! Initial here - -sign here- -

    Slim (harshly, refusing the pen)
Wait a minute!
    (then knowingly, as Laverock starts
   with nervous guilt)
- -what kind of a ship do I fly?

    Laverock (hearty, relieved)
Glad you asked! Glad you asked! Does everything
but cook your breakfast for you! - -Lampson-Osprey
N 74
    Slim (reluctantly taking pen)
But suppose I don't make it?

CONTINUED:

Laverock looks deeply pained and shocked.

                    Laverock (darkly suspicious)
Oh! - -You've been letting those old women down at
the Explorers' Club tell you it can't be done.
                    (coldly turning away)
Of course, if you can't even be loyal to the
Corporation- -

                    Slim (anxious, protesting)
Mister! I never even been in the Explorers' Club!

                    Laverock (turning to Petty,
                         irritated)
What the dickens is the matter with him then! I
can't have my time wasted by incompetents!

                    Petty (with quiet reproach)
Mr. Laverock!
                    (a benevolent, encouraging smile at Slim)
The young man's just a trifle shy.

     Laverock looks startled, incredulous, laughs.

                    Laverock (slapping Slim's back)
Well! you'll have to get over that if you're going
to work for me!

                    Slim (gloomy, doubtful)
I don't know, Mr. Laverock - -I've always been like
that. It's practically a disease.

                    Laverock (hearty, insinuating)
Nonsense! I'll have the Rockettes pour tea for
you the day you get back.
                    (genially philosophical)
Nothing like a 150 or so perfectly matched girls to
get a man over his natural diffidence.
                    (then inspirationally as Slim is about
                         to make another startled protest)
Of course you'll make it!
                    (pointing toward the ceiling)
The sign makes it, don't it?

                    Slim (out-thought two-to-one)
Well, sure! But - -
                    (helplessly signing)
Gosh! I never signed so many papers in my life!

     Laverock snatches the contract, blots it.

                    Laverock (handing it to Petty)
File this in the safe, Petty!
                    (sailing toward the door)
Come on, young man - -we'll have a look at the N 74!

as Slim is swept towards the door.

> Laverock (exuberantly continuing)
> Where's your hat? --What's your name? --When can
> you start?

> Slim (struggling to answer)
> Well, Slim Johansen! --Right away!
> (with a sudden warm grin at Laverock)
> No hat!

DISSOLVE:

23   NIGHT - CLOSE SHOT - LOUD SPEAKER HORNS

at the top of a mast.

> Announcer's Voice
> Will the police ask those people on the runway to
> stand back?

24   FULL SHOT   NIGHT (STOCK) AIRPORT

A large crowd pressing round a dimly seen
airplane. Searchlights on the packed heads.
Noise and excitement.

> Loudspeaker (continuing o.s.)
> Lt. Johansen will be taking off very shortly now,
> folks. This is the great Bi-Car-Brome Flight,
> in the new Lampson-Osprey N 74--

25   DARK MED. SHOT UNDER PLANE'S WING

Photographers are steadily shooting flash-
light pictures. The crowd is held back by
police lines. Everybody is laughing. Slim,
in flying clothes, stands helpless and
horrified in the vigorous embrace of a
strange young woman who is planting rapturous
kisses on both his cheeks.

> Slim (wailing, feebly struggling)
> Hey! --look out! --Oh please, Miss, for Heaven's
> sake!
> (then relieved but with an odd wistful-
> ness as she finally lets him go)
> Gee!

As the laughter continues --

CONTINUED:

          Girl (turning cheerfully to crows)
Well I thought somebody ought to kiss him goodbye!
        (giving his cheek a final pinch)
You sweet thing!

    As she runs off, laughing, into the crowd,
Slim observes one of the photographers re-
moving a camera plate which he has just exposed.

          Slim (starting forward, dismayed)
Here! you can't publish that!

    The photographer ducks out of reach, laughing.
His friends block Slim's way.

          Photographer (calling back)
'Fraid your wife won't like it, Lieutenant?

          Slim (stopping, appalled)

My wife!
        (appealing to the crowd)
Why I'm a bachelor!

          A reporter (with mock incredulity,
        as the crowd laughs)
Go on!

          Slim (with deep sincerity)
No fooling!

    Laverock comes bustling in.

          Laverock (reproachful, drawing
        Slim aside)
Come, come Johansen! --this is no time for dilly-
dallying!

          Slim (very much upset)
Honest, Mr. Laverock, I never saw that girl before
in my whole life!

          Laverock (with a ribald look and
        inflection)
And you say you're shy!?
        (then quickly recovering his dignity)
Never mind --
        (drawing Slim closer toward the plane)
Now listen --you'll be on the air twice daily over
station WQZA --11:30 a.m. and 7:30 p.m. Eastern
Standard Time --

    During the above Slim has observed another man
with a small suitcase, standing beside the   CONTINUED:

plane, and watching him with ironical amuse-
ment. As the man climbs aboard the plane--

          Slim (interrupting Laverock)
Wait a minute! Who's that guy?

          Laverock (surprised)
That's Enright--didn't I tell you? Lampson-
Osprey technician who laid out your itinerary.

          Slim (a little sulky)
I thought this was a solo flight.

          Laverock (giggling reassuringly)
Enright? Cross the poles? Knows too much!
          (quickly covering his break)
--Hrrr! brr! You'll drop him at Quito! Quito!
after you're familiar with the ship--

          Loud Speaker (imperious o.s.)
All right, Lt. Johansen!--the runway is clear--

As Slim moves slowly towards the ship--

          Laverock (excited, keeping step)
Got everything? Got everything? Well--see you
this day week!--Bar-Car-Brome is the name of the
product!--zzzzzzz--! Pole to pole!--Bi-Car-
Brome--!

He is still talking as Slim enters the ship.

          QUICK DISSOLVE:

26   FULL SHOT (STOCK) CROWD, CHEERING CRANING

           as the ship takes off into the dark.

27   MED. SHOT LAVEROCK'S LIMOUSINE

           hemmed in by the roaring crowd. Laverock and
           Petty have their heads out the window.

          Laverock (estatically)
Listen to that! Listen to that! Publicity's paid
for itself now even if he cracks up in Jersey!
          (then turning upon Petty, shocked)
Don't say that! Don't say that!

DISSOLVE TO:

MONTAGE to show it has traversed the Gulf,
Texas, and Mexico.

29   MED. SHOT (PROCESS) INSIDE THE CABIN

The very latest thing in equipment. Slim sits
relaxed, adjusting the controls now and then.

        Enright (with grudging approval)
You sure have caught on to this ship.

        Slim (indifferently)
She flies herself.

        Enright (coldly watching him)
That's' what you'll want over Antarctica. - -Hundred-
mile winds over those mountains down there - -nothing
but stone and ice - -and temperatures that knock the
bottom out of the thermometer!

        Slim (cheerful, unaffected)
That's what I'm getting paid for.

Enright shrugs, turns on the radio.

        Enright (turning the dial
Let's check on the radio again- -

        Radio (a News Program)
"In spite of growing European tension, the State
Department today reasserted its intention of en-
forcing the Monroe Doctrine. The Battle Fleet is
at present - -"

        Slim (wincing, turning it off)
That's a lot of bunk!

        Enright (eyeing him curiously)
Hope you're right.
        (then indicating a little portable radio
        behind a seat)
This Alpine portable receiving set is in case you're
- -forced down. If you know what's being done to
locate you, you may be able to cooperate.

        Slim (turning, a little mocking)
You boys think of everything!

MONTAGE showing the plan's progress over Panama, and down across Venezuela. (This sequence might be built up by INTERCUTS, showing landings and take-offs.)

31   MED. SHOT INT. CABIN (PROCESS)

Slim and Enright are bent over a map of Southern South America, and the Coast of Antarctica in the same longitude. Slim's course has been drawn on it. INTERCUT WITH INSERTS when necessary.

          Enright (indicating a tiny island
            off Cape Horn)
This island is your last fueling stop before the big hop down under. There's a good landing beach, and we have a ship there. If you come in after dark, send up a rocket, and they'll light flares--

          Slim (listening, business-like)
O.K.

          Enright (glancing at him)
We chose South America because it gives this line as the shortest hop you can make over the Pole.

A slight change comes into Slim's face.

          Slim (quietly touching the map
            between the Antarctic coast and the
            Pole)
Along in here - -isn't there something about a "Blind Spot"?

          Enright (rather too casual)
Well, that's what they've been calling it lately.

          Slim (meeting his eye)
Ever since Jerry Trailer disappeared into it?

          Enright (avoiding question)
Seems to be a permanent area of fog.

          Slim (incredulous)
Fog! --in that cold?

          Enright (studying the map)
Maybe there's a volcanic formation under it.
          (then unwillingly, deprecating)
After all Jerry was only a stunt man. And he didn't have anything like this equipment

                  CONTINUED:

                    Slim (steady, watching him)
Those Argentine Army flyers last year had everything
didn't they?

                    Enright (cold, indifferent
Of course, it's optional with yourself whether
you follow this course, or skirt the whole area.

        Slim stares incredulously for a moment.

                    Slim (exploding into laughter)
Optional!? --whether I add eight or ten hours to
my flying time over your "stone and ice" mountains?
                    (then thoughtful, half to himself)
I'll trust the instruments to get me through
--whatever it is--

32   LONG SHOT N 74

                Continuing MONTAGE over Ecuador.

33   MED. SHOT INT CABIN (PROCESS)

                Outside, (STOCK a magnificent panorama of
                the Andes --condors in flight. Enright has
                his little satchel ready to leave the ship.

                    Enright (now trying to be friendly)
You'll be following the regular airlines from here
down along the Andes.
                    (an afterthought)
By the way --the commercial pilots always warn
newcomers to watch the condors!
                    (thoughtful, looking out)
All the birds of prey seem to get bigger the farther
south you go along the continental backbone --

                    Slim (cutting him off)
I'll watch it.
                    (then with a hint of mockery,
                    pointing forward)
Beautiful city, Quito.

                    Enright (at last, evenly)
Looks all right to me.

        As Slim noses the ship down --

                              DISSOLVE:

A corner of the operations office. Enright,
satchel in hand, stands looking up into the
air, watching plane, which we do not see.
The roar of a motor comes over the SHOT. A
few customs officials, a mechanic or two,
and a few natives are in the SHOT.

DISSOLVE TO:

35   FULL SHOT - NIGHT N 74

MONTAGE showing the course has continued
south along the Andes and the coast of Chili.

36   CLOSE SHOT NIGHT SLIM AT THE CONTROLS
(PROCESS)

He is tense and serious now that he is alone,
keeps anxiously checking his position, looking
down into the darkness below. Finally, with
visible nervousness and reluctance, he tunes
himself in on the radio.

                    Slim (taking a deep breath)
N74 coming on! - -N74 - -Bi-Car-Brome Flight - -
Pilot Johansen speaking.
                    (a weak imitation of the radio manner)
Well, folks, we're still heading South from civi-
lization. Pacific Ocean's keeping us company to
the right. But off there to the left the Andes
Mountains have petered out considerable since this
afternoon.
                    (anxiously peering down)
Before long we ought to pick up that last filling
station before I start to curve in under toward
the pole. If we don't spot her pretty soon, I - -
                    (checking with manuscript beside him
                    and continuing very lamely)
- - I'm going to have one of the Bi-Car-Brome cap-
sules in a glass of water and start thinking fast - -
                    (suddenly, excitedly, peering down)
Wait a minute! There's something down there now.
                    (as he noses the ship over)
Yes! - -it's the ship all right!

37   LONG SHOT (MINIATURE, PROCESS AND ANIMATION)   18
              AN OLD SAILING SHIP

              Lying at anchor off a forbidding dark beach.
              Airplane is circling.

38   OUT

39   CLOSE SHOT SLIM AT THE CONTROLS (PROCESS)

              His whole manner expresses tremendous relief.

                    Slim
They're lighting flares along the beach.
          (hastily signing off)
Bi-Car-Brome - -N74 - -Slim Johansen signing off
for now! - -I'm going to try a landing.

40   HIGH ANGLE LONG SHOT (FROM PLANE)
              (MINIATURE, PROCESS PLATE, AND PROCESS)

              A line of flares, burning at the foot of the
              cliffs along the beach, rush towards the
              CAMERA. As Slim levels off - -

41   FULL SHOT (MINIATURE) N 74
              taxi-ing on beach, coming to stop. To the
              left is the old sailing ship. (Sketch #4).

42   MED. SHOT ALONG BEACH TOWARD OCEAN (PROCESS
              BACKGROUND), (BACKGROUND TO BE SHOT ON
              LOCATION)

              Flares still burning. In f.g. an old row-
              boat is drawn up on the beach. Standing be-
              side it, a huge, bearded man (Captain Erick-
              sen) and a dozen of his sinister crew. As
              the N74 coasts in and outs its motors, TRUCK
              THE GROUP FORWARD. As Slim emerges stiffly - -

                Ericksen (entering, effusive)
              (smiling as they shake hands)
It seems there is no part of the world where
Scandinavian names have not reached.

               Slim (looking absent-minded)
Your ship sure looked pretty from up there!

                    LAP DISSOLVE:

               Part of the crew is piling gasoline tins be-
               side it, others ready to start fueling, Slim
               reaching inside for something.

                     Slim (emerging, filters in hand)
Here - -we'll use my filters.

                     Ericksen (genially restraining him)
The gasoline is clean. We are very careful.

                     Slim (eyeing other's matted beard)
I'm not risking a plugged feed-line over in there
past the pole.

               He stands supervising while the men begin
               silently fueling the ship. Ericksen watches,
               hesitant, uneasy.

                     Ericksen (apologetically coming up)
You will then make this flight?

                     Slim (surprised, glancing over)
What are we here for!

                     Ericksen (slowly shaking his head)
It cannot be done.

                     Slim (incisive, turning on him)
What you mean is, it hasn't been done - -yet!

                     Ericksen
You do not know this continent of Antarctica that
you would cross - -cruel and empty like the moon!
- -such a place where the biggest land animal is a
spider not so big as the end of my thumb!

                     Slim (turning away)
Not planning to land.

                     Ericksen
What you plan and what you will do is maybe two
things, young man.
               (pointing ominously toward the dark south)
Off there in the Blind Spot under the world - -

                     Slim (eager, wheeling round)
What do you know about the Blind Spot?

                     Ericksen (uneasy, shaking his head)
Know? I know nothing!
               (then hesitant, impressive)
Once when I am a boy our whale-ship is held in the
ice, and I crawl inland against the wind, looking
for food - -for some little bugs even - -Maybe then

Erickson (continued)
I see it. Far away against the dawn - -fog rising
up into the sky like mountains on top of mountains.

Slim (interrupting, resentful)
What does a ship with these instruments care for
fog!
(passionate, indignant)
Is there suddenly not going to be any more air to
fly her in? Is some big hand going to reach up
from the earth and grab me down - -?

Under Ericksen's eye, Slim falters.

Ericksen (soft, regretful, admiring)
Yah! You have the Viking heart!
(then drawing attention to the group
fueling the plane, as they watch Slim
sidelong, muttering together)
But, see! My men know what we speak of.
(lowering his voice, watching Slim)
Some of them are Terra-del-Fuegans, natives of this
terrible country where we stand. At home they live
in misery - -yet through their suffering they feel
the magnetic currents of the earth, and at night
they read the runes of the auroras across the sky.
(suddenly turning, calling roughly)
Geng-bek! Where the blind spot - -show! - -this
man - -show!

44   REVERSE ANGLE FULL SHOT GROUP

As the man addressed turns away in sullen
silence, they all mutter resentfully.

45   TWO SHOT SLIM AND ERICKSEN

Ericksen (gently, anxiously)
You see, my friend? They will not even look toward
the South!

Slim (hoarsely calling o.s.)
All right, you guys - -what's on your minds?

Ericksen (smiling, shaking his head)
If you ask them all night and all week and all year,
they will say only that it is not good to enter the
Blind Spot.
(his manner almost like that of his crew)
In the fog is something of death - -something which
does not wish one to pass through.

CONTINUED:

                    Ericksen (continued)
              (then suddenly vehement and urgent)
Young man! turn your propellers now toward those
cliffs! Let your machine run at them alone - -!

                  Slim (startled, horrified)
Crash my ship!?
                Ericksen (taking Slim's arm)
Who is there but myself to say it was not a bad
landing? - -I will put you off at some port of
civilization! Back in your own country, you will
get your old job, and see your girl again - -

    Slim's face has set into a harsh, bitter
    expression. He slowly withdraws his arm.

                  Slim (somberly thinking)
I haven't got a job - -or a girl - -or a country.
I'm Slim Johansen - -and I like to fly 'em.
              (then turning suddenly in blazing anger
              to one of the men who is pouring gaso-
              line, with his chin hanging in the
              funnel)
You! - -take your greasy whiskers out of that gas!

    As all stand looking at him in awe - -

                         LAP DISSOLVE:

46   LONG SHOT N74 (MINIATURE)

    reeling, wind-shaken in a dark sky.

47   CLOSE SHOT SLIM AT CONTROLS (PROCESS) (STOCK)

    He is tense, making constant adjustments.

                  Slim (with forced cheerfulness)
Folks, the open water's behind us. We've crossed
the pack-ice of the Antarctic Coast. Making good
time through a ninety-mile cross-wind)
              (constantly checking instruments)
The mountains are starting to pile up down below.
In a few hours we ought to have crossed the pole.
All my heaters are on full, but inside this cabin
it's cold - -

                         DISSOLVE TO:

48   MED. LONG SHOT N74 (MINIATURE)

    with dim mountains sweeping past below.

          Slim (quietly, looking ahead)
This is a very lonely place.
          (frowning, peering forward)
As the sky begins to brighten, there's something
off there, dead ahead, like a black wall standing
up between me and the dawn. No way around it or
over it that I can see - -and it looks solid.
          (slowly, dubiously)
But I guess it's fog - -so I'll be going through.

                    DISSOLVE TO:

50   LONG SHOT THE N74 (MINIATURE)

disappearing into a huge dark bank of fog.

51   CLOSE SHOT SLIM AT THE CONTROLS (PROCESS)

Outside, nothing but pearly, opaque mist.

          Slim (gravely checking dials)
The wind has dropped. I seem to be just floating
up here - -as though there wasn't any more real
world or time or force of gravity- -
          (down to business with an effort)
My altimeter tells me that the mountains are
steadily rising under me. I've just lifted her
to twenty-six thousand feet.
          (with a significant inflection)
According to anything I know about, I ought to be
just about freezing now, but five minutes ago I
was able to shut off all but one heater- -

                    DISSOLVE TO:

52   MED. SHOT N74 SPEEDING THROUGH MIST
        (MINIATURE)

53   CLOSE SHOT SLIM AT THE CONTROLS (PROCESS)

His face begins to be a little drawn.

          Slim (with a forced satisfaction)
There's just no ceiling to the ship! If this
wasn't a pressure cabin, I'd be using the respi-
rator now. Those mountains down there have boosted
us up to twenty-nine thousand feet- -!

                    DISSOLVE TO:

VERY LONG SHOT N74 VANISHING INTO MIST
(MINIATURE)

55   CLOSE SHOT SLIM AT THE CONTROLS (PROCESS)

The motors are laboring audibly.

                    Slim (carefully casual)
At thirty-two thousand feel we're having a little
heavier going, but for the last five minutes- -
              (suddenly startled, reading altimeter)
Wait a minute! all that geography must be starting to fall away down there!
              (exultantly laughing)
The old girl's over the hump! Folks! this N 74
ship is the triumph of science over wild nature- -
              (dazzled by his own inspiration)
- -just like Bi-Car-Brome!
              (sober, as the ship bucks violently)
Little bumpier now in the up-drafts. Did I say
those mountains were falling away from under me?
              (incredulous, reading the altimeter)
It must be like the Grand Canyon under this fog!
              (suddenly doubtful, shaken)
If - -if my altimeter's right, the only slopes like
these are inside the craters of the moon! And it's
really warm now! I've turned off all the heat- -

    His words end in a gasp.

56   NEW ANGLE CLOSE SHOT SLIM (PROCESS)

    He is staring out, incredulous, wide-eyed- -

                    Slim (weak, swallowing hard)
You'll have to excuse me, folks. I - -I thought I
just saw something.
              (puzzled, groping for words)
A - -a kind of white thing, making a wonderful banking turn off into the mist!
          As he is speaking, a huge shape sweeps past
          outside - -wide, white, moving very fast.

                    Slim (with a catch in his voice)
Believe it or not - -!
              (then grinning, shaking his head)
No - -I guess it's the altitude.
              (feebly plugging Bi-Car-Brome)
Or maybe my stomach's a little acid - -

    His words die away as the thing passes
    again, very close.
                    Slim (in blank amazement
Why there it is! It crossed right off my wing-tip!
- -sort of a big white glider, circling all around   CONTINUED:

134

                    Slim (continued)

me like I was standing still! And --and bigger
than the ship!
               (leaning back groggily, grinning)
Folks, I guess I got a ghost on my tail.

Suddenly he stiffens, looking forward.

57   NEW ANGLE LONG SHOT THROUGH WINDOW (PROCESS)

          As the thing rushes toward CAMERA.

                    Slim (ducking, with a yell)

HEY! --here it comes - -

There is a crash and a shock as tremendous
talons shatter the cabin roof, tear out great
sections, throwing debris into the propellers
which break with a tremendous roar, and start
shaking the ship to pieces. Slim cuts the
motors, and grabs the controls as the ship
noses over crazily- -

58   LONG SHOT (MINIATURE)

          Plane falling into mist, and dim figure of
          gigantic white bird soaring off into the
          mist, and disappearing.

58-A   CLOSE SHOT CAMERA SHOOTING TOWARDS SLIM'S
          face.

          Slim his plane in slow spin, struggling to
          right it.

59   HIGH ANGLE FULL SHOT N74 SPINNING
          (MINIATURE)

          down and down only partially in control.
          HOLD THE SAME ANGLE until it disappears into
          the mist below. ON A SUDDENLY SPINNING
          CAMERA- -

                              DISSOLVE TO:

As the SHOT settles down right side up,
Laverock is shadow-boxing away from the radio.

                    Laverock
               (ducking, waving his arms)
Get away! What is it!?
               (indignantly opening one eye)
What was that thing!

                    Petty (very solemn)
Whatever it was, his radio's gone.

                    Laverock
               (startled, repudiating it)
That boy? cracked up? He'll be back --mark my
words! Can't be cracked up! Absolutely indis-
pensable! No other Product's ever had such
publicity!
               (with a sudden inspiration)
Next time I --I'm going to send him to Mars! Mars!

                              FADE OUT:

61-61D

FADE IN:
LONG SHOT TOWERING SNOW-CAPPED MOUNTAINS

with white cumulus clouds piled up behind.
Follow with a series of slow majestic
DISSOLVES, to give the impression of a single
great PAN SHOT, from the snow-peaks, through
lovely Alpine scenery of cliff and pine
forest, and finishing in an idyllically
beautiful valley of waterfalls, much like
Yosemite National Park. The sun is shining,
and the singing of birds grows progressively
louder.

DISSOLVE FINALLY TO:

62

LONG SHOT WRECKED N74 (MINIATURE)

crashed against the steep bank of a mountain
river, which a few rods below, leaps off
into nothingness in a roaring waterfall.

DISSOLVE:

62-A

FULL SHOT

showing the current working at the wreck. As
it moves with a grating sound a few inches
out into deeper waters, BOOM AROUND the wing
into a CLOSE SHOT of the twisted-open door.
Slim lies on his back, half out of the doorway, unconscious, and with his head hanging
close above the sliding water. The plane
shifts again, settling deeper. Slim's
dangling head is dunked in the current.
After a moment he comes to, scrambles into
a sitting position. Groggily taking in his
situation, he swings out, and stands mid-thigh
in the stream. As he examines the wreck in
dismay, the whole things swings around, and
settles across the full current. Half roused
by the emergency, he wades after it.

63

MED. SHOT INCLUDING THE CABIN INTERIOR

Slims pistol and cartridge belt hanging
visible on the far side.

Slim (hoarse, anxious, reaching)
Here! - -my gun!

CONTINUED:

Two stunning pre-production landscape paintings by Leland Curtis showcase the multi-leveled beauty of the upper levels of the lost valley, as described in Scenes 61 - 61D. Images courtesy of Bob Burns.

As the plane is swept down-stream, Slim has just time to reach in, and snatch out the portable radio. Instinctively he ducks under the moving wing.

63-A   FULL SHOT (PROCESS)

Slim watches appalled as his last link with civilization is dragged spectacularly out of sight over the falls.

64   CLOSE TRUCK SHOT SLIM (REVERSE SHOT)

Standing on shore with the radio. At the foot of the steep bank, he stands stupidly, fumbling open his hot flying-jacket, and slowly moving his eyes round the circle of hills. As he mops his damp forehead, his face is serious, utterly astonished. Then he is listening - -a far shrill screaming chorus, not of human voices. The sound passes into the distance. Slim shivers, relaxes. Then suddenly behind him there is a little startling avalanche of gravel, dislodged by something among the scattered pine trees on the slope above. Slim spins round like a scared animal, and for a long time his anxious, watchful eyes peer and search for his unseen watcher. After a while he begins edging round into a new position, his eyes still probing among the trees. A single pebble comes bounding down, but still nothing appears. Slim's face sets slowly. He stands grimly waiting for the thing to show itself. Suddenly he stiffens. Behind one of the larger trees there has been a glimpse of motion.

65   MED. CLOSE SHOT BIG TREE

From behind it, there appears very slowly a white girl. She is dressed in a flimsy sleeveless gown, kilted up knee-high under her belt. She wears high sandals, and her hair is loosely bound. On her arms are heavy gold bracelets, and over her shoulder a quiver filled with formidable-looking arrows. At her belt a short, curved knife, and in her hand a big business-like bow. She stands seriously and attentively watching Slim, not directly threatening him with the bow, yet holding it easily ready for instant use, and with an arrow notched to the string.

As each waits for the other to make the
first move, Slim's first expression of blank
astonishment slowly gives way to one of
more acute anxiety.

> Slim (murmuring)
>
> Gosh! a woman!

The girl does not move. Deciding at least
to indicate friendly intentions, Slim
slowly raises both hands above his head.

67   CLOSE SHOT   GIRL (NARU)

vividly curious. Suddenly her bow-and-arrow
mood relaxes. PAN WITH HER as she comes
stepping swiftly down the steep bank.

68   MED. SHOT   SLIM AND NARU

as she pauses, watchful, a few feet off.

> Slim (smiling diffidently)
>
> Hello Miss!
>> (as she watches, alert, unanswering)
>
> Bon jour, Mademoiselle!
>> (then a final forlorn hope)
>
> Well, guten Tag then!

> Naru (unexpectedly)
>
> Skraling?

> Slim (missing the foreign word)
>
> Hm?
>> (then rather awkwardly --still his move)
>
> You see I'm a stranger here. I--
>> (gesturing limply toward the falls)
>
> --I just lost my ship.

> Naru (with a quaint inflection)
>
> Ship?

> Slim (eagerly nodding, gesturing)
>
> Yes, Mam --over the falls --my plane --avian--
>> (finally imitating with hooked thumbs)
>
> -Bzzzzzzzzzzzzzzzzzzzzzzzzzzzz!

She follows the action with startled eyes.

> Naru (at last doubtfully)
>
> Thine ern?

CONTINUED:

                    Slim (catching at the foreign word)
"Thin ern"?
          (then wearily)
Well, I guess we better start right at the begin-
ing.
          (with helpful gestures)
Me Slim Johansen - -Slim! - -Me Slim! - -You? - -You?

                    Naru (promptly)
Naru.

                    Slim (discouraged, but patient)
No, Miss - -look! Me Slim! - -me! - -Mr Slim!
- -Slim! - -You?

                    Naru (stamping in sudden temper)
Naru! Naru! Naru!

                    Slim (checking eagerly as it downs)
Naru? - -Naru?
          (then delighted, admiring as she
          nods vigorously)
Why! You got it the first time!

                    Naru (parroting the strange phrase)
Got it?

     A look of deep discouragement comes over
     Slim's face.

                    Slim (wearily)
Miss, aren't there any gentlemen around here I
could try talking to?

                    Naru (tentatively)
Gentle? man?

                    Slim (half turning away, despondent)
No, you don't understand.
          (murmuring, eyeing her sidelong)
You sure are gorgeous, though!
          (sudden anxiety)
You don't understand - -do you?
          (shaking, thrilled, as she watches him
          silently with an odd look)
No! - -you don't!
          (an overwhelming thought)
I bet I could get away with saying plenty if I
wanted to!
          (taking a deep breath, watchfully
          launching himself into romance)
I - -I bet you're the prettiest girl around here!
          (quick, horribly anxious)

                                        CONTINUED:

                    Slim (continued)
No Understand?
                    (relaxing, dazzled, almost reverent,
                    as she returns only an alert friendly
                    look)
Why, it's like I was Clark Gable!
                    (trying to imagine himself in a
                    conquering role - -but not quite
                    succeeding, due to extreme oafish
                    caution)
Boy! would I like to give you a big kiss!
                    (almost swooning with delight as
                    Naru takes this without quiver)
I dunno! I - -I must be in dreamland!

                    Naru (startled, looking around)
Greenland?!

                    Slim (weakly hysterical - -a
                    daring reference to her scanty attire)
No Miss! You'd be kind of chilly up there!
                    (a thrilled aside to the glamourous
                    universe, as Naru laughs in response)
Gosh! Would I like to know what she thinks about
me!

                    Naru (thoughtfully eyeing him)
You?
                    (then concisely after a moment)
Witless!

          She turns on her heel, walks away. At her
          shockingly apt reply, a horrible uncertainty

                              CONTINUED:

has come into Slim's mind. He stares after
her, aghast, grabs up the radio, and hurries
after her. TRUCK WITH HIM.

                    Slim (timidly overtaking her)
Please, Miss--! wait a minute!
          (tremulously, as she faces round
          sharply)
What did you say?

                    Naru
          (severe, and no mistake)
Witless, thou.

                    Slim
          (a squeak of horror)
You mean you understood what I been saying!?

                    Naru
          (primly looking away)
Not all.

                    Slim
          (wilting, relieved)
Well, that's something!

     TRUCK WITH THEM as she swishes on again.

                    Slim
          (desperate, fawning, following)
Oh, some on now, Miss Naru! you don't want to go
and get sore!
          (with passionate sincerity)
Honestly, every guy you meet's going to think
that way, even if he don't come right out and
say it.

          (then plaintively, stopping her)
Wait a minute! We're talking English. How come
you understand English --that's not right!
          (feebly, his reason reeling)
English is what we're talking, isn't it?

                    Naru
          (surprised but kindly)
Aye. --You will learn.

     As he starts on again, the full implications
     of the situation penetrate Slim's stunned
     mind.

                    Slim (wildly leaping after her)
But look! you got to be reasonable! This is
Antarctica --nobody lives down here! The biggest
                                        CONTINUED:

143

> Slim (continued)
land animal is a spider--
> (shakily, as she rounds on him in wonder)
Naru!--who are your folks?

TRUCK as they move slowly together.

> Naru (casually)
Norse-folk, we.

> Slim (blankly)
Norse?
> (then suddenly excited, getting it)
You mean Vikings?--like my old man used to keep
gassing about back in Minnesota?
> (shaking her arm)
--some lost Vikings got as far as this--?

They have come out on the crest of a low hill.

> Naru (simply, pointing down o.s.)
Aye, but not lost. Yonder we dwell.
> (smiling slowly)
Will you abide?

> Slim (incredulous)
Abide?--You mean--after all the things I said
--you're asking me to stay?

As she smiles, nods, he turns, looks o.s.

69   HIGH ANGLE LONG SHOT NORSE VILLAGE

among tremendous evergreens. At one end a
stream forms a deep clear pool. Parallel to
it runs a line of long low log houses. Many
lower rooms are open on one side like lean-
tos, with big exterior fireplaces. The visible population, consists entirely of women,
children, and a few old men.

70   MED, CLOSE TRUCK SHOT THROUGH VILLAGE

picking up group after group. Children are
spearing small fish at the lower end of the
pool. Several girls are swimming off the
rocks further up, or sitting in the sun to
dry their hair. Three older women are weaving some sort of cotton-like fabric at a
hand-loom. And old man is working at a big
strange-looking saddle which he has set upon
a rack. Another old man, with a beard, and
wearing a short cape, sits at the foot of a
great tree, with his blind face bowed over a

CONTINUED:

small harp carved in the shape of an eagle.
On his shoulder perches a big magnificent
raven. He plucks out an accompaniment to
the quiet singing of a group of girls who
are weaving big baskets. Further along a
third old man operates a forge, with a boy
assistant. Children run in and out, shouting,
and chasing each other. The atmosphere
throughout is peaceful and gay. As the
CAMERA reaches each group, the people turn
their heads, and excitedly look up o.s. The
effect produced is that the CAMERA is moving
parallel to the foot-path on the hillside
above the village, down which Naru is leading Slim. As the CAMERA passes, each group
rises, as though to start following it toward
the point where the path enters the village.
During the above--

      First (calling, pointing o.s.
Naru comes!

      Second (excitedly)
And look ye!--with a stranger!

      Third (a little boy, shouting)
A Skraling!

      Fourth (Katte)
Thora! Quick--Naru hath an outlander found!

      Fifth
An outlander comes--!

      TRUCK SHOT ends. CAMERA MOVES FORWARD INTO
      A TWO SHOT of Slim and Naru coming down the
      path just before it enters the village
      TRUCK BACK ahead of them.

      Slim (grinning, looking o.s.)
That "outlander" means me?

      Naru (nodding)
Aye--come you not from out the land?

Slim is eagerly looking ahead.

      Slim (smiling, pointing o.s.
Isn't he kind of old to be playing hobby-horse?

Two views of the Norse Village described in Scenes 69 and 70 by Duncan Gleason. Image of the painting at top is courtesy of Bob Burns. Image of the tree-house and environs sketch below is courtesy of a private collection

now perched on the saddle, testing a safety-
belt attachment as he peers at Slim.

71-73   TRUCK TWO SHOT SLIM AND NARU

          Naru (indifferently)
'Tis Halfgar, the gear-maker. To old has he
grown for the drive, and now makes gear for the
swift ones.

          Slim (puzzled)
Gear? --That thing's a saddle!
          (turning, half laughing)
How are you going to use that on a horse!

          Before Naru can answer, they are mobbed by a
          crowd of girls and children, giggling and
          pointing with the naive curiosity of primi-
          tive people. Slim is a little cvercome.

          Sixth (Thora --wide-eyed, solemn)
You are well come, outlander.

          Slim (pleased, awkward, bowing)
Thanks, that's swell.

          Naru (jealously drawing him on)
Slim, his name.

          TRUCK ON slowly, as the crowd impedes them.

          Seventh (interestedly examining
          Slim)
Strange his name and speech!

          Thora (feeling his flying jacket)
Strange his garb!

          Fourth (laughing, pointing)
Nay, but his shoon!

          First (indicating his goggles)
And these --!

          Naru (imperious, reproving)
Still, maidens! Greet you thus a guestling?!

          Slim (laughing, elevated)
No! I like it!
          (turning from one to another as he talks)
Why I was brought up on you folks! My father was
from the old country. Always telling me about the
Vikings --!
                                        CONTINUED:

                    Naru (explaining to the others)
Like the sagas he speaks.

                    Slim (exultant, laughing)
Yeah! --the long ships, and the sea fights --and
Leif the Lucky discovering America way ahead of
Christopher Columbus!

         There is a stir of excitement among the crowd.

                    Second (calling o.s.)
Of Leif Erickson he speaks!

                    Thora (wondering, moved)
Know you Vineland?

                    Slim (laughing, almost cocky)
Vineland's Minnesota now! --it's my home!

         They are stopped by the excited crowd.

                    Fifth (calling o.s.)
Bring Haakon! A norseman hath from Vineland come --!

                    Slim (eating it up)
And that ain't all!
                    (pointing up o.s.)
See that big white cloud back of the snow peaks?
                    (preparing to mow them down)
Well, believe it or not, I flew in from the dark
side of that!

         Slim's sensation falls absolutely flat.
                    Naru (casually verifying)
On a dead ern he fell. I saw him from afar.
                    Slim (comically crestfallen)
You folks sure believe things easy!
                    (then suddenly serious, remembering)
Say! I remember now--!
                    (glancing from one to the other)
Up there in the mist something crashed me!
--something big and pale--

         A quiet stir, significant glances exchanged.

                    Thora (softly)
The Storm-goer!

                    Sixth (nodding)
Aye! The White One!

                    Seventh
Last night he ranged the peaks!

                    Slim (eager, incredulous)
You know about it?

                    Second (nodding mysterious)
All know the White One!

                    Fifth (glancing up o.s.)
The wild, the unbroken --!

                    The Boy (exultantly)
None takes him!

                    Slim (incredulous)
You mean it was alive?

                    Naru (quiet, nodding)
An ern.

                    Slim (puzzled by the word)
Ern?

                    Naru (impatient, touching her arm)
An ern! an ern!

        INTERCUT with a BIG INSERT, showing a brace-
        let with a raised eagle-design.

                    Slim (slowly, stunned)
An eagle? - -big as a plane!

                    Naru (grave, watching him)
Even so have the other outlanders fallen, their
erns slain by the rage of the White One, jealous
of his realm.

                    Slim (glancing from face to face)
Others? - -outlanders? - -here?

                    Second (nodding)
Aye, now a few.

                    Slim (suddenly gasping)
Why, it must be Jerry Trailer! - -and the Argentines!
            (vehemently, glancing about again)
Where are they? - -we'll get back together- -!

                    Katte (gently)
They are not.

                    Slim (softly, sobered)
Oh - -they died when they crashed.

                    Thora (reluctant, significant)
Nay, they dwelled among us - -for a little while.

                    Slim (quiet, disturbed)
I don't get you.

                    Naru (sadly watching him)
Unskilled they were!

        He stands puzzled. All eyes are fixed on
        him in grave sympathy. As he is about to
        speak, the crowd parts. The old blind man
                                        CONTINUED:

with the harp, shuffles up very cautiously,
evidently guided to some degree by the
raven.

                    Slim (observing Naru's respect)
Who's this?

                    Naru (lowering her voice)
Haakon, the skald. Blind he is, and wise in his
singing.

                    (turning deferentially)
Haakon, greet the outlander.

          Haakon begins ceremonially chanting his im-
          provised verses --a heavily rhythmical re-
          citative to the accompaniment of his harp.

                    Haakon (facing Slim)
Greeting we give, / skoal to the guestling
That fared to the fastness / and found the folk.
Here to help him / we hold us ready,
In fighting or feasting / pledge him friendship.
So shall he live / long in the land,
Nor slow nor unskilled / die as the stranger.

          There us an impressive silence. At last - -

                    Slim (soberly bowing to Haakon)
Thanks. That was very nice.
                    (studying the solemn faces)
But it sure sounds like you folks didn't figure
me for a very good risk around here.

          Naru is troubled, unhappy, tries to say
          something, then takes him gently by the arm.

                    Naru (drawing him on)
You are weary and hurt. Katte and Thora will make
you ready food and mead- -

                    Slim (brightening)
Well if mead's what I think it is- -

          As they start out of the SHOT together- -

                                        DISSOLVE TO:

74   FULL SHOT   END OF VILLAGE

          Waited upon by Katte and Thora, Slim sits at
          a small table under a huge tree against which
          Haakon sits smiling, harp on knee. Slim has
          finished eating, but he still holds a big

                                        CONTINUED:

metal cup, and feels very good indeed. Naru
leans against the tree, disapproving of Slim's
now entirely unabashed interest in the other
girls. As Thora offers him more food--

                    Slim (sighing, waving her away)
No more, thanks, darling! --just couldn't.
          (holding out his cup)
But maybe another little shot of that mead--

                    Katte (admiringly filling the cup)
A true Viking!

     Naru sniffs, tosses her head.

                    Slim (tenderly to Katte)
Thanks, Pretty!
          (nodding toward Haakon)
Ask the Professor if he won't wet his whistle,
and tune up again.

                    Naru (sharply)
The maiden's name is Katte.

                    Slim (bowing, correcting himself)
Sorry! --Kitty!
          (then genially to Haakon)
Prof, let's hear some more about that local George
Washington of yours!
          (fuzzily)
--what's his name? Horner?

                    Naru (sniffs with impatience)
Einar, the Earl!

                    Slim (drinking again)
Good ole Einar!

     Haakon spiritedly resumes his narrative.

                    Haakon (chanting)
Into England the Earls / Einar followed,
Spoke there the Saxon, / an age stayed,
Won them wives, / and the folk waxed;
Then for freedom / fared again viking--

                    Slim (quietly cheering)
Freedom's the thing! --am I right?
          (solemnly pondering)
So your good ancestors stopped off in England!
Well, that's about the way all us square-heads
learned to talk United States back in Minnesota--
          (catching, correcting himself)
Sorry! --Vineland

                                        CONTINUED:

           Slim (continued)
        (pretending not to notice when Katte
again fills his cup)
So there was two viking Columbuses —our man,
Leif Ericksen, and your man, Earl Einar.
        (proudly)
And both of 'em heroes!

          Haakon (stirringly resuming)
Twain the worthies, / the world sharing.
Leif led the folk / westing to Vineland.
Einar the Earl / onward ever
Took the whale's way / under the sun-wrath,
Southward steered / into the ice!

          Slim (nodding, owlish)
Into the ice - -and the mountains - -and the fog.
I flew over.
        (squinting at Haakon)
My boy, if you're not a lot faster thinker than
you look your ancestors are stuck there yet!

      As Haakon strikes the harp again, all are
      smiling, as though following an Old favorite.

         Haakon
Fast and foodless / in frost held- -
        (as Thora and Katte join in unison)
Still stood the folk. /
        (as even Naru joins in, smiling)
            But skilled and strong,
Einar the Earl / tamed the wild ern!
        (exultantly in chorus)
Bridled and broken / winged ones bore them
High hills over / here to the homeland!

      All are smiling, elevated. Slim sighs
         Slim (sad to doubt them)
I get it - -your ancestors flew in here on eagles!
        (brightening, philosophic)
Well there were five-hundred thousand passengers
on the Mayflower!

      Shrugging, he empties his cup. Haakon's
      raven has been excitedly flapping, pecking
      at the eagle on the harp.

         Haakon (quiet, troubled)
Loki! Fight not the ern - -it bodes ill!

         Slim (emerging from the cup)
It was a great story!
        (very sentimental, sympathetic)
Makes a man kind of sad to think of you kids now,
with no men to take care of you except Haakon
              CONTINUED:

                    Slim (continuing)
here, and old Halfgar--
          (sighing modestly, looking into the cup)
--and now me.

                    Thora (bewildered)
What says he!

                    Katte (laughing, incredulous)
No men?!

                    Naru (indignant, with an edge)
Would you have our men stay all day like wastrels,
feasting and drinking the mead?

                    Katte (vehemently)
Mighty our men! Even now they join the drive
with the clans--!

                    Thora (joining in)
--They go to the great Rookeries where the swift
ones are mated!

                    Slim (comically long-faced)
You mean there are other towns like this among
these mountains?

                    Thora (proudly)
A score and more! Strong we go to the harvest!

                    Haakon (solemnly)
Under great Skal, the Earl.

                    Naru (proud, animated)
Aye! and first of our thorp is my brother Raud,
the Chief! Two spears can he hurl to the mark at
full course! When the mead stirs him, he can toss
his battle-axe to the tree-tops, and with a shout
catch it falling!

                    Slim (sighing, setting cup down)
Battle-axes! I knew there had to be a catch in it!

          Again the raven is flapping. With his beak
          he plucks out a single deep note on the harp.

                    Haakon (softly, raising his head)
They come! From far Loki hears them call!

                    Naru (suddenly excited)
Quick! the watch-horn!

          Katte runs to a huge long horn, chained to a
          tree, blows a single shrill blast.

One of Duncan Gleason's most spectacular and detailed production sketches depicts the arrival of the eagles in the "great Rookeries" of the ROCKY AMPHITHEATRE location in Scene 77A. Image from the author's collection.

hurrying in a single direction. Women run
out carrying cups, and big vessels of mead.
Others appear , two by two, carrying large
hampers filled with big smoked fish.

76   TWO SHOT SLIM AND NARU

hurrying after the others. Her manner is a
little cold. Noticing the big baskets of
fish being carried through the b.g. - -

                Slim (making conversation)
You sure must expect the boys to be hungry!

                Naru (grudgingly amused)
Not for the men are the baskets, but for the
steeds.

                Slim (completely bewildered)
Fish? - -for horses?

77   NEW ANGLE LONG SHOT THE CROWD
            (STRAIGHT SET)

rounding two great boulders at the end of the
village, and entering a big rocky amphitheatre.

77A   ROCKY AMPHITHEATRE

which opens over bottomless distance with
glimpses of canyons and jungles. Along both
sides of the amphitheatre stand paired posts,
carved with standing eagles, each pair
connected by a heavy chipped cross-piece,
and equipped with short dangling chains.

77B   LONG SHOT THE CROWD (MINIATURE PROJECTION)

The people crowd to the very edge of the
precipice, eagerly peering off into space.

　　　　MED. SHOT FAVORING SLIM AND NARU　　　

Slim is curiously inspecting the place.
Suddenly there comes o.s. a distant wild
shrieking, not of human voices.

Crowd (calling joyfully)
They come! They come!

Slim (incredulous, peeping over)
Up from down there!?

Naru (very impatient)
Blind in sooth is the outlander!
(pointing up and off)
There - -past the peaks!

As Slim raises his head and looks o.s.- -

79　　　　VERY LONG SHOT A DOZEN WINGED SHAPES
(ANIMATION)

soaring closer over the distant mountains.

80　　　　CLOSEUP SLIM

Slim (softly, staring)
Planes! They've got planes!

80A　　　　(MINIATURE PROJECTION) LONG SHOT

Eagles entering in far distance, making
circle, and turning in TOWARDS CAMERA.

81　　　　REVERSE ANGLE PREVIOUS LONG SHOT (PROCESS)

The shapes are approaching fast. Now they
are seen flapping their wings, and on each
one rides a human figure- -

82　　　　BIG CLOSEUP SLIM

Slim (with rising exultation)
No - -not planes! - -eagles! the erns of Einar!
- -
And men! - -men riding on them!

83   EXT. (SIDE ANGLE) LANDING FIELD AND
        DISTANT MOUNTAINS.

        LOW ANGLE FULL SHOT FAVORING SLIM AND NARU

        as the ridden eagles sweep overhead.
        Glimpses of their riders, brawny warriors
        with longish hair, and some with beards or
        big drooping mustaches. Shouting jovially,
        they brandish spears and battle-axes. They
        are dressed only in short apron-like kilts,
        wide leather belts, and heavy sandals. Each
        one wears a slotted visor which serves as
        goggles. The eagles are screaming.

          The Crowd (calling, raising its
         arms)
    Steer in the swift ones!
    Bridle them down!
    We have mead brought you!
    Take at evening thy rest!
    Well come to the home-feast!

83A   EXT. LANDING PLACE (PROCESS)

        Having circled the landing place, the birds
        now come tearing in just over the heads of
        the crowds, shrieking loud, setting up a wind.

          Naru (a warning cry to Slim)
    'Ware the claws!

        He just ducks, as a huge pair of talons
        flashes through the SHOT. As he looks again- -

84   FULL SHOT EAGLES LANDING ON PERCHES
        (MINIATURE PROJECTION)

        Before they have even folded their wings
        their riders have pushed back their visors,
        unhooked the safety belts, swung out of the
        saddles, and each one casually hitched his
        eagle with the ready chains, leaving the
        women and children to feed the flapping,
        squawking eagles with fish from the big
        baskets.

85   EXT. EAGLES PERCHES AND COOP (PROCESS AND
        STRAIGHT)

        FULL SHOT THE BIG FIERCE-LOOKING WARRIORS

              CONTINUED:

as led by Raud, they come swaggering through
the crowd toward the CAMERA. Each one is
greeted by at least one woman, holding ready
a big foaming cup of mead.

                    First (shouting as they advance)
Mead here!

                    Second
Mead ho!

                    Atok (the biggest and hairiest)
What! No mead?

                    Raud (roaring impatiently)
Where is my sister? Where is Naru - ?

          PAN HIM INTO A FULL SHOT, she is there.

                    Naru (handing him a two-quart cup)
Well come, Raud.

          Smiling, he tilts the whole two quarts down
          his throat, belches contentedly.

                    Raud (again holding his cup out)
Mead in the name of Thor! Never were the erns so
wild - -nor the hatchlings so well hid - - nor the
hens so fierce on the nests!
                    (with satisfaction, raising the full cup)
Yet we brought them in! We brought them in- -!

          About to drink, he suddenly notices Slim
          standing behind Naru. His eyes go wide.

                    Naru (quickly, a little nervous)
It is an outlander that asks the freedom of the
thorp. I - -I found him in the wood.

                    Raud (glowering, lowering his cup)
Always she finds somewhat in the wood!
                    (then more cheerful, tossing off his
                    second hooker as others gather round)
Yet, outlander, since you are come amongst us
you are well come - -as here witnesseth my naked
hand!

                    Slim (eagerly shaking)
Thanks, Chief - -
                    (then with a sudden yawp of pain as his
                    fingers are crushed in Raud's huge paw
- -ooop!

          As Raud looks mildly surprised - -

                                        CONTINUED:

                    Naru (proprietary, pleased)
Slim his name.

                    Raud (almost laying Slim low with
                    a genial wallop on the back)
If you have need of aught, Slim, take it freely
while you last living. It is our law of fellow-
ship.

          As he starts on again, Slim's eyes dart
          fascinated toward the eagles.

                    Slim (impulsively stopping Raud)
Chief, if - -if you're not just being polite, I'd
sure appreciate a practice hop on one of those
erns.

                    (Then lamely, as all turn and stare in
                    astonishment)
I'm - -I'm a flyer by profession - -

                    Raud (bellowing to the others)
This unfledged outlander would bestride a swift-
one!

          There is a roar of laughter. Slim looks
          disconcerted, Naru annoyed. Atok is strug-
          gling tremendously to control his amusement.

                    Atok (at last, indicating an eagle)
Take there my Donderwing!

85A   EXT. DONDERWING'S PERCH
                  (MINIATURE PROJECTION)

                  SHOT of big, fierce-looking bird (Donder-
                  wing). Boy is feeding the eagle with fish.

85B   BACK TO SHOT

                    Slim (dazzled)
Gee! - -Thanks!

                    Raud (laughing, protesting)
Nay, Atok! Donderwing is a war-goer, fierce and
wild!

          Naru nods vigorously. But Atok has con-
          ceived a sudden dull hostility for the
          foreigner.

                    Atok (surly, glaring at Slim)
The outlander has said he would ride! - -Ride then!

                                        CONTINUED:

                        Crowd (laughing, as Slim hesitates)
Aye! --ride, outlander!
Put Donderwing through his courses!
Ride! Ride!

85C   EXT. DONDERWING'S PERCH
                 (MINIATURE PROJECTION)

                 Slim enters a little cockily toward where the
                 eagle, a huge distinctive-looking bird, is
                 perched. Naru runs in, overtaking him.

                        Naru
Slim! --ride not!

                        Slim (winking, reassuring)
It's O.K., kid. None of these boys ever put an
experimental bomber into a power dive - -

                 His words are startlingly cut short. The
                 eagle which has apparently been taking no
                 notice of him, waits until he is within
                 reach, and then makes a lightning lunge
                 simultaneously with beak and claws. Slim
                 leaps back shaken, and minus the front of
                 his shirt.

                 Meanwhile, the crowd has followed him in.
                 and it now breaks into a great yell of
                 laughter.

                        Crowd
Ride, outlander!
Ride!
Curb the Donderwing to thy will- -!

                 Slim looks at the crowd, and starts back
                 toward the eagle, which makes another swipe
                 at him, which certainly would have killed
                 him, if Atok had not grabbed his arm and
                 jerked him out from under the beak.

                        Atok (surprised, admiring)
Nay! he hath a norse heart!

                        Naru (suddenly bursting out)
Take shame on yourselves, all! Even you, Raud!
- -To let our guest, an outlander, untried and
unskilled, be slain by a war-goer- -!

                                     CONTINUED:

                    Raud (sheepishly)
The maid is right!
                         (anxious, kindly)
Back Slim! The ern knows one master only.

                    Slim (obstinate, a little sore)
But I still want to ride one of these turkeys.

                    Naru (promptly taking his arm)
Then ride you shall! Come- -!

85D   TRUCK SHOT (FULL SIZE PROCESS)
                    EXT. EAGLE PERCHES AND COOP

                    Naru (drawing Slim along)
I will take you up with me on my Rainflower.
She is a small hen, and gentle - -a mount for a
child- -

        Followed by the amused crowd, they reach a
        big covered coop. Naru draws aside a
        matting, and reveals inside a huge, fierce-
        looking hen eagle, sitting on its nest.

                    Naru (practically in baby talk)
Come, darling! - -spread thy pretty wings!
                         (as the brute waddles slowly off the
                         nest)
Are thy young still unhatched?

        In the nest are three enormous eggs. As
        Slim cranes his neck to see, the eagle
        pecks at him with a sudden daunting squawk.

                    Slim (ducking, covering up)
Say!

85E   EXT. EAGLE COOP (STRAIGHT SHOT)
                    FULL SHOT

        crowd laughing. SHOT featuring Atok
        in foreground.

85F   EXT. EAGLE COOP (FULL SIZE PROCESS)

                    Naru (laughing lightly)
'Tis naught, Slim - -she but plays, sweet sparrow!

                                        CONTINUED:

She reaches in and fastens rope to a ring
which is in eagle's beak, and commences to
lead the bird off the nest, out of scene.

85G   EXT. MOUNTING BLOCK (MINIATURE PROJECTION)
          FULL SHOT

          Naru mounts eagle from block, fastening
          safety belt.

                    Naru (to Slim)
          Now up behind me!
                    (when Slim has clumsily obeyed)
          Hold hard by my belt --here!

85H   MED. SHOT CROWD, FEATURING ATOK
          (STRAIGHT SHOT)

          The crowd has watched in rather patronizing
          amusement. But Atok is horrified.

                    Atok (groaning, covering his face)
          A man! --to ride a hen! --behind a maiden!

86   (EXT. THE LANDING PLACE (SIDE VIEW)
          (MINIATURE PROJECTION) LONG SHOT

          as the eagle, with Slim and Naru on its
          back, makes a long waddling run, and
          finally takes off.

                    Crowd (mockingly cheering)
          Hail to Slim Henrider!

86A   EXT. NARU'S EAGLE (MINIATURE PROJECTION
          AND ANIMATION)

          Slim and Naru, flying

EXT. NARU'S EAGLE (PROCESS) CLOSE SHOT
SLIM AND NARU ON EAGLE

The landscape (PROCESS) tilts and sweeps past
below them, The heads of both are bowed
into the wind, and their hair is streaming.

                Slim (exultantly yelling)
Say! This is great!

His words are blown away.

                Naru (leaning back toward him.
Shout! - - the wind —!

Slim withdraws nervously.

88-88B   EXT. NARU'S EAGLE (PROCESS)
                BIG DOUBLE CLOSEUP SLIM AND NARU

                Slim (shouting but shy)
All you need on this thing is a radio and a clock!

She gives him an amused back-glance, and with
a twitch of the rein puts the eagle into a
sharp spin. Slim saves himself by wild grab
with both arms round her waist. But when
she flirtatiously lets her head fall back on
his shoulder, he stiffens in panic, lets go.

                Naru (impatient with the boob)
Nay! You must hold me hard!

                Slim (just the tips of his fingers
                hooking the back of her belt)
I - -I'm all right thanks.

She gives him a back-glance of angry con-
tempt, puts the eagle into another spin.

                Slim (scrambling, yelling)
Hey! - -left rudder! - -Left rudder! - -LEFT RUDDER!

88C   EXT. NARU'S EAGLE (MINIATURE)

She puts the eagle into a steeper spin.
Slim's legs fly off both on one side, and he
is left clinging only by the safety belt,
while Naru grasps him, not too gently, by
the hair.

89   EXT. LANDING PLACE LONG SHOT THE UPROARIOUS   46-B
            GROUP ON GROUND

            As Naru and the eagle bring Slim in dangling.

89A   EXT. LANDING PLACE (MINIATURE) LONG SHOT

            as the eagle comes to a full stop in front of
            the crowd.

90   EXT. COOP (MINIATURE) FULL SHOT

            Eagle stops.

90A   EXT. COOP (PROCESS) CLOSEUP NARU

            on eagle's back. She lets go of Slim's hair,
            and he drops out of SHOT.

90B   EXT. COOP (STRAIGHT SET) FULL SHOT

            Slim drops into picture and lands on ground.
            (As seen from Naru's angle)

90C   EXT. COOP PROCESS FULL SHOT

            Naru on eagle. She looks down at Slim,
            glaring at him. She dismounts.

90D   EXT. COOP (MINIATURE PROJECTION) NARU,
            SLIM, CROWD AND BIRD

            Naru hits the ground. She looks down at
            Slim, glaring.

                        Naru (mockingly to crowd)
            Our new flyer has yet to learn how to cling!

            The eagle exits from scene.

91   EXT. COOP (STRAIGHT SHOT)
            CLOSE PAN SHOT SERIES OF LAUGHING FACES

            ending on Raud, watchful, very grave.

as laughter continues at Slim's expense.

                    Slim (scrambling up, following Naru)
Gosh , Naru! I just haven't got the hang of it yet.

She turns coldly from him. Then suddenly - -

                    Naru (brightly, looking o.s.)
Rainflower! thy hatchlings break the shell!

PAN HER as she runs for entrance to nest.

92A   INT. COOP (MINIATURE PROJECTION)

The little, hideous, featherless eaglets
are beginning to hatch. Naru enters, runs
up to nest. She plays with the little
eaglets. Then puts her arm around the
eagle's neck, as the mother eagle puts her
head into SHOT.

                    Naru (arm around eagle's neck)
Another! - -and so fierce and sturdy! Great war-
goers will they be! Are you not proud, my
darling?

93-93   EXT. EAGLE COOP (STRAIGHT SHOT)
               CLOSE SHOT SLIM WATCHING

A hand enters the SHOT, falls heavily on
Slim's shoulder. TRUCK BACK to include
Raud, very grave. Slim faces round.

                    Raud (a sober warning)
The maid, Naru, my sister, is of the blood of
chiefs. - -At the last harvest, even in the
welter and slaying of the mighty ones, great
Skal himself looked softly on her.

When Slim gets the idea, he is outraged by
the injustice of it all.

                    Slim (indignant, sputtering)
Who! - - me?- -up there? - -just now? - -why don't
you bawl her out! Are you crazy?

                    Raud (firm, checking him)
I speak in friendship. Naru's love can be given
to none less than a warrior and a breaker of
erns- -

                        CONTINUED:

                    Raud (continued)
                (Very serious, significant)
- -one fit for the great harvest.

                    Slim (furious)
I get it! You're to hand her over to some big
shot with a white beard!
                (with extreme bitterness)
Well, I'm sorry for the guy!

            As Raud looks mildly astonished, there is a
            great noise of excitement o.s., shouts, etc.

                    Voice (o.s.)
The storm-goer!

            Raud looks up, and Slim follows his gaze.

95   EXT. SKY AND WHITE EAGLE
            LOW ANGLE EXTREME LONG SHOT INTO SKY
            (MINIATURE)

            The white eagle sails majestically over. The
            late sun shines on his breast and underwings.

96   EXT. EAGLE PERCHES AND COOP (STRAIGHT SET)
            MED. SHOT GROUP AROUND RAUD

                    Raud (as all look upward)
The White One!

                    Slim (excitedly)
Why, that's the man that crashed the N74!

                    Raud (to Slim)
Mark how our erns cower beneath his wings!

                    Slim (eager, admiring)
But who owns him?

                    Raud (turning startled)
None rides the White One! Old he is, and wild
beyond all the erns- -

                    A Boy (estatically looking up)
None takes him!

                    Fifth (explaining to Slim)
Too crafty is he to come near.

                    Sixth
Too fierce to take.

                    Raud
In times past our fathers and our fathers' fathers
went out against him, and in each age hath the
White One slain his man.

              Atok (regretfully looking up)
We trouble him no more.

              Boy (again)
None takes him!

              Haakon (listening sadly)
In my youth I, Haakon, the skald, dared dream of
taking him - -that now walk in darkness all my days.

         As they continue staring up, awed and moved, a
         startled look slowly comes into Slim's face.
         He begins glancing from one to another. Pre-
         sently he smiles, shoots a long glance across
         at Naru, and then again raises his head like
         the others.

97   EXTREME LONG SHOT WHITE EAGLE (MINIATURE)

         sailing off out of sight.

98   FULL SHOT GROUP AROUND SLIM

         as all come back to earth with a sigh.

              Slim (softly)
So the big fellow don't belong to anybody!
         (looking eagerly from one to another)
Nobody here has any sort of claim on him?

              Raud (shaking his head)
None.
              Slim (with extreme diffidence)
Then none of you gents would care if - -if I was
to ketch him for me?

         Every head flashes round, startled. Then all
         at once, the yelling chorus of laughter.
         They howl, and practically blow their belts.

              Raud (when he can speak finally)
Come, Slim - -the feast waits!
         (slapping Slim's back, hooking his arm)
We will keep thee with us always for the mirth - -!

         As they move off, Slim is still smiling.

99   BIG CLOSEUP NARU

         looking after him, startled and serious
                       DISSOLVE TO:

100   EXT. CAMOUFLAGE (PROCESS AND STRAIGHT)
         lying on a ledge of rock which overlooks
         a tremendous gorge.

101   MED. CLOSE SHOT SLIM (PROCESS AND STRAIGHT)
         He has arranged a camouflage of stones and
         small branches through which he motionlessly
         watches. His clothes are now worn and tattered.

his face lean and deeply tanned, and his whole
manner more grim and serious than before. Pre-
sently Naru softly enters the SHOT, looks down
at him for several moments before he realizes
she is there.

                    Slim (starting, glancing up)
Oh! - - it's you - -
               (gruffly returning to his watch)
Keep low.

          She stretches out beside him, watching him
          sidelong. He obstinately averts his face.

                    Naru (troubled, hesitant)
Slim - - why lie you out all day alone on the ledges?

                    Slim (steadily watching o.s.)
It's narrowing down, Naru! Yesterday I spotted
him just after sunrise, and again just before
sunset - -
               (indicating the surrounding hills)
- - coming in here!

                    Naru (anxious, incredulous)
You think indeed to take the White One?

                    Slim (softly, still looking off)
Or else.

                    Naru (watching him sidelong)
If it is for me you make this foolish hunt, it
- - it is bootless!

                    Slim (bitterly, still watching o.s.)
I know that. You can't even manage to say something friendly when I come home to get the big
laugh in the evening!

                    Naru (indignant, half rising)
Why should I speak! Why should I look, or think,
or anything!
               (faltering)
Am I a fool, to give my heart to a man already dead?

          He glances hopefully at her. Then slowly
          his face sets again.

                    Slim (turning away obstinate)
Don't ask me to give up White Eagle, Naru!

                    Naru (sad bitter)
Nay! I pray that you may be hurt by the White One.
               (soft, impressive)
So shall you be spared going down unskilled into
the dale of the great harvest.

                Slim (turning back in sudden temper)
What is all this about the great harvest? I asked
the blacksmith, and he says you only go for fish
and fruit to carry you through the rest of the year
up here- -

                Naru (her eyes very grave)
Igor is kind. To an outlander - - doomed - - he
would not speak of the Mighty Ones.

        Slim studies her face seriously. At last - -

                Slim (quietly)
Maybe you better tell me about the Mighty Ones,
Naru.

                Naru (turning away, distressed)
Ask me not, Slim!
              (wide eyed, visualizing)
Awful they are beyond our very dreams of dread!
              (softly, shivering)
Else might we all die in sleep.
              (turning her eyes back to him)
And the time comes - -!

        Slim has suddenly seen something far o.s.
        He stiffens, watches in tense excitement.

                Slim *whispering, watching)
Down! - - Don't move!
              (hardly breathing himself)
Don't breathe - -!

102   REVERSE ANGLE - LONG SHOT - THE CLIFFS
            (PROCESS☐ STRAIGHT☐ AND ANIMATION)

            on the opposite side of the canyon. White
            Eagle sweeps in, carrying a large fish,
            circles, and settles down on a steep pinnacle,
            part way up the cliffs, and overhung inacces-
            sibly by them.

103   EXT. WHITE EAGLE'S PINNACLE - FULL SHOT
            WHITE EAGLE - (ANIMATION)

            tearing and eating his fish. When he has
            finished, he sits ruffling his feathers.
            At last, he spreads his wings, drops off,
            banks, and sails away down the canyon.

104   MED. SHOT - SLIM AND NARU - (PROCESS & STRAIGHT)

            watching breathlessly. At last they relax.

                Slim (sighing, ecstatic)
Wasn't he Something, Naru!
              Rising, pointing across the canyon)
And there! - - that pinnacle half way down the red
cliff! - - that's his place!

                    Naru (awed)
But, Slim! - - how?

        Slim smiles slyly, winks.
                    Slim (thinking about it)
Toots, I got a scheme - -!
                                        LAP DISSOLVE

105   EXT. VILLAGE STREET - CLOSE SHOT - FORGE

        On an anvil, a hammer is shaping a red-hot
        grapnel, with three hooks and a looped
        shank. TRUCK BACK to include SLIM and
        IGOR. Igor plunges the hissing grapnel
        into a tub of water, takes it out, and
        bends on a stout, light line.

                    Slim
                    (offering his goggles)
Look - - all I got is these - -
                    (hopefully)
- -but a lot of the folks seem to think they're
pretty snazzy- -

                    Igor
                    (laughing, waving goggles aside,
                    handing Slim the grapnel)
Nay! - - a gift! - - a gift from the smith!

                    Slim
                    (touched, protesting)
But listen - -!

        Igor waves him off, turns away, laughing.

                    Igor
                    (entering his smithy)
A gift! - - a gift- -!

        Slim stares after him, moved. Then suddenly
        he comes to himself, coils up the line,
        fastens the grapnel at his belt, picks up
        another longer and heavier coil of rope,
        slings it over his shoulder. BOOM WITH HIM
        as he moves abstractedly out of the village,
        half smiling, eyes fixed on the hills.

EXT. CAMOUFLAGE (PROCESS)

Slim goes through SHOT, exits toward
White Eagle's peak.

DISSOLVE:

107   EXT. BASE OF PEAK (PROCESS)

Slim throws his grapnel hook up. It catches.
He pulls the line taut, and begins to climb
on rope.

DISSOLVE:

108   EXT. SIDE OF PEAK (PROCESS)

Slim climbing up rope against side of
peak.

DISSOLVE:

109   EXT. SUMMIT OF PEAK (PROCESS)

Slim coming out, sweaty and breathless,
against the skyline.

110   EXT. CAMOUFLAGE (PROCESS)

Naru in foreground, sees the small figure
of Slim in far distance, on top summit of
peak.

111   EXT. SUMMIT OF PEAK (PROCESS)

Slim crosses the bar rock, and looks down
the sheer far side. He fastens his rope
around a projection of rock, and lets himself down over the brink. He lowers himself hand over hand. Due to the overhang
the farther he descends, the farther he
is from the cliff face.

EXT. CAMOUFLAGE (PROCESS)

Naru watches Slim descending on rope, hanging far out from side of cliff.

112-A   EXT. WHITE EAGLE'S PINNACLE (PROCESS)
                  CLOSE SHOT

                  Slim, hanging on rope, throws a half-hitch around his foot, and begins to swing his body back and forth on the end of the rope, like a pendulum. (White Eagle's pinnacle is just below him, and the cleft is right in front of him.)

112-B   EXT. CAMOUFLAGE (PROCESS)

                  Naru, watching Slim swing back and forth.

113   BIG CLOSEUP - NARU

                  watching anxiously through the line of camouflage established in the previous scene.

113-A   EXT. WHITE EAGLE'S PINNACLE (PROCESS)

                  Slim swings himself into cleft.

113-B   INT. CLEFT

                  CLOSEUP Slim. He looks into distance, and shrinks back to hide himself in the cleft.

113-C   EXT. WHITE EAGLE IN DISTANT PEAKS (ANIMATION)

                  LONG SHOT, White Eagle sailing in.

113-D   EXT. CAMOUFLAGE (PROCESS)

                  Naru sees White Eagle sail in and land on pinnacle.

EXT. CAMOUFLAGE (STRAIGHT SET)

CLOSEUP Naru, reacting.

114   EXT. WHITE EAGLE'S PINNACLE (MINIATURE
PROJECTION)

MED. SHOT, SHOWING the big rope leading down
like a vine along the face of the cliff, and
running into the cleft behind White Eagle's
eating a fish. Slim is in cleft in background, watching.

115   INT. CLEFT (STRAIGHT SET)

CLOSE SHOT SLIM, tensely waiting for the
right moment.

116   EXT. WHITE EAGLE'S PINNACLE (MINIATURE
PROJECTION)

MED. SHOT White Eagle is suspicious and alert
in intervals of eating. Slim is watching in
background.

117   EXT. WHITE EAGLE'S PINNACLE (MINIATURE
PROJECTION)

CLOSER SHOT, White Eagle turns his head, and
Slim hides just in time. White Eagle, suspicious, turns away, spreads wings, is just
about to fly.

118   INT. CLEFT (STRAIGHT SHOT)

CLOSE UP Slim. Gets ready to jump.

119   EXT. WHITE EAGLE'S PINNACLE (MINIATURE
PROJECTION)

FULL SHOT as Slims crabs himself into position
and just as White Eagle is about to take off,
he swings down in a big arc, and lands on
the broad, feathered back. At the shock they
drop together off into space.-

Slim leaps from the cliffs to begin his taming of White Eagle as Naru looks on in Scene 119A. By Duncan Gleason. Image from the author's collection.

119-A   EXT. CAMOUFLAGE (PROCESS)   53A-53B

As White Eagle takes off, raising a terrific
battle, Naru jumps to her feet, watching
White Eagle and Slim fly out of scene.

120   CLOSE UP - NARU WATCHING

in terror.

121   EXT. CAPTURE OF WHITE EAGLE (MINIATURE)

LONG SHOT, White Eagle and Slim, fighting.

121-A   EXT. CAPTURE OF WHITE EAGLE (PROCESS)

CLOSE UP Slim on White Eagle's back. As
White Eagle beats through space, Slim desper-
ately holds on to line which he has already
noosed around White Eagle's neck. He slips
and falls entirely out of picture. Rope is
taut and swinging.

121-B   EXT. CAMOUFLAGE (PROCESS)

CLOSE UP Naru. She screams.

122   EXT. CAPTURE WHITE EAGLE (ANIMATION)

FINAL LONG SHOT. Slim being carried off out
of sight, disappearing into clouds, clinging
to the line.

122-X1 -
122-X2 -   EXIT. CAPTURE OF WHITE EAGLE

fighting and breaking him.

                                  DISSOLVE TO:

123   EXT. GLEN (STRAIGHT SHOT)

FAST DOLLY SHOT, ahead of Naru, running
wildly down the hillside, toward the
village. She catches up with and
passes CAMERA.

                    Naru (calling frantically)
Raud! —Raud!
                    (pausing, desperate, looking around)
Where is Raud? - -Where are the men?

124   EXT. ENTRANCE TO LANDING FIELD (VILLAGE SIDE)
             MED☐ SHOT - RAUD AND OTHER MEN APPEARING

                    Raud (calling as he appears)
Naru! - -Sister! - -here!

                    Naru (running in, clinging to him)
Oh, Raud, he is gone! - -gone!

                    Raud (anxious, shaking her)
Who? - - who?

                    Naru (sobbing)
The outlander! - -borne off by the White One!

                    Atok (astounded)
Rode he the Storm-goer?

          TRUCK THEM toward the landing -place.

                    Naru (sobbing, hauling Raud)
He clung by his cord! The White One struck at
him! Quick! - - mount the erns!

                    Raud (gently, restraining her)
Little sister, it cannot be that Slim yet lives.

                    Naru (weeping, stopping)
Oh, no!

                    Atok (suddenly leading on)
By Thor! The body of him that strove with the
Storm-goer shall have Viking burial!

125   FULL SHOT - GROUP ENTERING LANDING PLACE
             EXT. EAGLES PERCHES & COOP - (PROCESS & STRAIGHT)

          The tethered eagles are on their perches.

                    Raud (shouting)
Mount erns, all - -!

          The raven on Haakon's shoulder is flapping
          and cawing wildly.

                    Haakon (stopping Raud)
Hold! Loki skreaks of a great fight afar!
          As all pause, tense, listening
                                        CONTINUED:

           Atok (suddenly pointing up o.s.)
Raud! - - past the peaks!

126   EXT. LANDING FIELD AND DISTANT MOUNTAINS
           (PROCESS EXTREME LONG SHOT, White Eagle

           flying toward the CAMERA.

127   EXT. EAGLE PERCHES & COOP (GROUP IN FORE-
           GROUND) FULL SHOT GROUP LOOKING UP

           Raud (sadly nodding)
Aye! The White One in his pride! - - having cast
his rider down - -!

           Naru (suddenly shrill, pointing)
Nay! - - there! - - see! - - on his back!

128   EXT. LANDING FIELD & DISTANT MOUNTAINS (MIN.
           PROJECTION) SIDE ANGLE - LONG SHOT WHITE EAGLE

           approaching in wild erratic flight. On his
back a figure is visible.

129   EXT. LANDING FIELD (PROCESS)
           FULL SHOT GROUP TREMENDOUSLY EXCITED)

           First (gasping, incredulous)
The Storm-goer! - - ridden!

           Naru (shrieking, exultant)
Slim! - - Slim! - - Slim!

           Raud (admiringly)
How the ern droops!

           Atok (wonderingly)
Aye! ridden near to death!

           Naru (excitedly)
He brings him in! - - here to the very landing-
place!

           Raud (suddenly anxious)
On the ground comes the death-fight!
           (starting forward, shouting orders)

               (CONTINUED)

Slim guides White Eagle in for his first landing in Scene 130. The painting is unsigned, but is very likely the work of production illustrator Stanley Johnson. It is the only painted image of White Eagle that has been recovered. Image courtesy of Mark Berry.

Quick - - the shackles! - - the poles! - - Atok! the
hood from thy Donderwing.

As the men run to obey, we hear all the
eagles on their perches screaming and flapping.

130   EXT. LANDING FIELD AND DISTANT MOUNTAINS
(MIN. PROJ. SIDE VIEW MED. SHOT

as Slim rides White Eagle steeply toward the
ground.

130-A   EXT. EAGLE PERCHES (FULL SIZE PROJECTION)
MED. SHOT RAUD (PERCH #1)

snatching hood from eagle perch. Eagles
screaming and flapping.

130-B   EXT. EXT. EAGLES PERCHES & COOP (FULL SIZE
PROJECTION) MED. SHOT (PERCH #2)

Two men run in and snatch poles with hooks on
them.

130-C   EXT. EAGLE PERCHES & COOP (FULL SIZE PROJEC-
TION) MED. SHOT (PERCH #3)

Three men run in and grab sticks and shackles.

130-D   EXT. REVERSE SIDE OF LANDING FIELD (MIN PROJ.)

White Eagle lands on ground. It struggles and
flaps exhaustedly, but Slim now has it bridled
with a half hitch of grapnel line.

130-E   EXT. REVERSE SIDE OF LANDING FIELD (MIN PROJ.)
MED. SHOT WHITE EAGLE AND SLIM

In the b.g. Raud and the others advance cautiously, carrying their poles, shackles, etc.

                    Raud (calling, cautious)
Now - - from all sides - -!

131   EXT. REVERSE SIDE OF LANDING FIELD (MIN.
PROJ.) CLOSER SHOT SLIM

sliding limply from White Eagle's back. As
his feet hit the ground, he hangs on, or he
would fall with exhaustion. His clothes are

                              CONTINUED:

in ribbons, there are deep gashes on his face
and arms. His eyes are hollow, his face
drawn, but when he sees the group advancing - -

      Slim (horse, panting)
Never mind that!
  (weakly, snarling, as they still advance)
Lay off of him, I tell you!

      Naru (calling a timid warning)
He is yet wild! - - he will kill!

    Slim does not reply. Staggering a little,
    he walks round to White Eagle's head, as it
    stands with drooping wings, evidently as
    exhausted as Slim.

      Slim (heedless of the audience)
Sorry I had to rough you around, old man - - it was
you or me.
  (ruefully stroking the neck feathers)
You see I didn't know what you were really like
or I'd have left you alone.

131-A   CLOSE UP SLIM AND HEAD OF WHITE EAGLE (MIN.
       PROJ.)

      Slim (quickly unfastening the
grapnel cord, as the men (o.s.) cry
out in warning)
So long - -

131-B   BACK TO PREVIOUS SHOT (131)

      Slim (stepping back, tears in his
      eyes)

Now Go back to where you belong, you big, white - -

131-C   EXT. REVERSE SIDE OF LANDING FIELD (MIN.PROJ)
       MED. SHOT

    His last words are lost, as White Eagle, feel-
    ing himself free, screams and flaps his tre-
    mendous wings. Slim has turned away blindly.
    He walks away from CAMERA, stumbling through
    the crowd, towards the turn in the rock.

EXT. REVERSE SIDE OF LANDING FIELD (AROUND
TURN IN ROCK) (MIN.PROJ.) MED☐ SHOT

Slim has just turned around corner of rock, and
is stumbling through crowd. The eyes of all
the watchers are big and incredulous. Suddenly
they turn, not looking at Slim. Around the corner of the rock comes White Eagle, slowly
waddling after Slim, head low like a tired
horse. Slim turns, and a look almost of dismay
comes into his face as he sees White Eagle.
White Eagle comes to him and hangs his head
close to Slim's own.

132   MED. SHOT SLIM (MIN. PROJ.)

as White Eagle walks into the SHOT, and stands
hanging his head close to Slim's own.

                    Slim (his face working)
No! Go on!
          (hoarsely as the Eagle does not move)
Don't you understand? You're free! - - Think I'd
make a chained parrot out of something like you?
          (then wildly, his voice breaking)
Beat it! do you hear me?

Still the Eagle does not move. Slim glances
helplessly right and left. Raud comes up.

                    Raud (gently, almost sadly)
Nay Slim - - the war-ern that has found his rider
stays now whether you will or no.

                    Slim (weakly)
Yeah?
          (stupidly turning back to White Eagle)
Gee!

Suddenly his face contorts and he pats the
big neck.

                    Slim (muffled, brokenly)
No kiddin', I'm awful sorry.
          (finally straightening, trying to grin)
Well, I guess I'd better fix him up a hangar - -

As though he understood, White Eagle
slowly turns toward the CAMERA. He sees
something, and cocks his head on one side.
We hear the screech of an eagle o.s.

132-A   EXT. DONDERWING'S PERCH (REVERSE SHOT)
(MIN.PROJ.)

Boy by perch, staring goggle-eyed. Donderwing
screeches at White Eagle.

EXT. DONDERWING'S PERCH (PROCESS)

(B.G. MINIATURE WITH ANIMATION AND REAR PROJ.)

White Eagle lowers his head, and starts pigeon-
towing over, ominously trailing his wings.

       Slim (anxiously plucking at his
         tail feathers)
Here! wait a minute! You can't start picking
trouble already -- !

       Raud (restraining him)
It is his right -- the erns know.

All watch as White Eagle continues his daunting
advance. Donderwing on the perch also lowers
his head, snaps his beak defiantly, half
spreads his wings. But at the last moment, he
thinks better of it, hops down on the far side
and waddles away. White Eagle steps up into
the vacated perch, and postures magnificently.
The crowd laughs and cheers.

       Second (shouting as all advance)
He hath overthrown Donderwing!

       Fifth
Now the Storm-goer cocks it over the roost!

133   EXT. DONDERWING'S EX-PERCH (MIN. PROJ.)
       FULL SHOT WHITE EAGLE

as Slim and others walk into SHOT

       Slim (grinning, proud)
Well, big boy, I guess you kind of showed 'em who's
head man around here.

Curses and the scream of an eagle are heard
o.s. O.S. laughter from the crowd.

133-A   EXT. EAGLE PERCHES (MIN. PROJ.)

MED SHOT Donderwing is on the first perch.
Atok stands in front of him, with a heavy
massive-looking chain in his hand. He slaps
Donderwing.

       Atok (in disgust)
Broody crow!

The crowd roars with laughter. Atok leans down
and starts to secure eagle with chain.

133-B   CLOSE UP (FULL SIZE FOOT AND PERCH   57B

        Atok fastens huge chain around Donderwing's
        foot, securing it to the log.

133-C   EXT. DONDERWING'S EX-PERCH (MIN. PROJ.

        Slim sees Atok tethering Donderwing, smiles,
        tears a long tatter off his shirt.

                        Slim (fastening White Eagle's claw)
        There! Now remember - -you're tied!

133-D   EXT. EAGLE PERCHES AND COOP
                    MED. SHOT

        The crowd has been watching in wonder.
        (Raud is in f.g.) Suddenly Raud's emotion
        boils over. He comes forward past CAMERA.

-133-   EXT. DONDERWING'S EX-PERCH (STRAIGHT)
                    CLOSER SHOT RAUD AND SLIM

                        Raud (fiercely to Slim)
        I am a Chief and an ern-breaker, and I say that
        since the days of Einar never was it better done!
                        (grabbing Slim's hand)
        And I say, Slim, that from henceforth - - at board
        or in battle - - in flight or in death - - we are
        one, bone and blood!

        As Slim heartily returns the handshake - -

134   BIG CLOSEUP NARU WATCHING

        startled, almost scared.

                                LAP DISSOLVE:

135   EXT. VILLAGE CLOSE SHOT NIGHT SLIM'S
                    PORTABLE RADIO

        TRUCK BACK to include Slim and Igor with his
        blacksmith's tools. Igor is tinkering.

                        Slim (amused, as Igor finishes)
        Think your work's going to hold up, Igor?

        As Igor doubtfully scratches his head, PAN
        INTO AN INT. FULL SHOT one of the log buildings
        which is open on one side like a lean-to.
        Facing it is a big out-door fireplace, brightly

                                CONTINUED:

burning, and casting up light on the tree
trunks. Slim has set the radio on a wooden
bench between the fire and his large audience
inside the room. All are watching seriously
and expectantly. The men have paused with
poised mead cups. The women - -particularly
Naru and several other girls at work around a
hand loom - -keep glancing over. During the
following scene, in spite of his assumed
"public-speaking" manner, Slim keeps glancing
over seriously at Naru, who takes pains not
to meet his eyes.

     Slim (cheerfully to the group)
Well, ladies and gentlemen, I was sort of hoping
I'd be able to forget about this crowning triumph
of civilization, but if you've all decided it's
a "magic box" who am I to argue!
     (pausing, hand on the dial)
Incidentally, has anyone here by any chance ever
heard tell of Bi-Car-Brome?

136   CLOSE SHOT NARU, GLANCING OVER STARTLED

     Naru (involuntarily anxious)
Is - -is it a maiden?

137   FULL SHOT GROUP

     Slim (piously)
On the contrary!
     (then spinning the dial)
Well, suppose we start with dear old Station BCAX - -!

     Radio (instantly coming through a
     burst of static)
- -brrrrrrrpp sour stomach! - -And, friends, let's
all remember one thing: Good digestion is good
business! So-o - -
     (that objectionable optimism)
- -Bi-Car-Brome!

Over the end of the speech- -

138   CLOSE SHOT ATOK

winding up to buzz his battle-axe.

     Atok (hoarse, horrified)
An evil voice!

Slim cleverly slides the radio a couple of
feet down the bench just as the battle-axe
sings in, and embeds itself in the wood.

Slim (in mild reproof)
Be yourself, Atok. You're a big boy now.

Radio (heartily resuming)
Good evening, friends! This is King Rideout. Now
before we get on with our progrum, I'm sure there's
one question that all you good people are anxiously
waiting to have answered: Is there as yet any word
from our young Bi-Car-Brome Knight Errant-of-the
Air, Lt. Slim Johansen, lost now these many weeks
in the frozen wastes of Anar--
          (stumbling over it)
--Antic --the south polar regions?

Naru (voicing the astonishment of all)
Slim! speaks the evil voice of you?

Slim (winking conspiratorially)
Couple of other boys.

Radio (after a solemn pause)
Well, folks, Bi-Car-Brome is sorry to have to in-
form you that the answer is still no. But I'm
absolutely certain --absolutely certain! --that
one day the Lieutenant will bob up in civilization
with a story that will absolutely wow the radio-
audiences of America and the entire world!

Slim (devoutly aside)
In a pig's eye!

Radio (that Moral Rearmament voice)
Let's try to hold that thought --what do you say!
          (then shaking off the somber mood)
And now, folks, Bi-Car-Brome takes pleasure in
turning you over to Hex Faversham and his Jolly
Jivers. Take it away, Hex--!

There is a burst of orchestration, and a
crooner begins lugubriously singing an ultra-
modern torch song, which cues the following
dialogue. Up to this point the audience has
sat in shocked astonishment, but now it begins
to betray signs of actual distress.

Raud (at last, uneasily)
Hath he some great grief?

Slim (rather embarrassed)
It seems some other guy walked off with his girl.
Naru (in blank astonishment)
But why slays he not the man?   CONTINUED:

         Slim (in wry amusement)
Back home I could give you a dozen answers, Naru.
But here, I can't figure it out myself.

      There is a murmur of bewilderment. Suddenly
      Atok voices the enormous contempt of all pre-
      sent by spitting loudly on the floor. Slim
      double-takes this violently. Then slowly his
      face lights up.

         Slim (snapping radio off)
Second the motion!

      He stands smiling thoughtfully, eyes on Naru.

         Raud (beckoning Slim over)
Haakon, strike the harp!
         (handing Slim a cup of mead)
Drink, friend! Haakon's song will make thy
heart forget the evil voice of the Outland.

      As Haakon strikes his harp, Slim tosses off
      the cup of mead, glad to sink into the sur-
      rounding friendliness. Across the loom Naru
      is watching him shyly.

         Haakon (singing exultant)
Hail to the harvest / and the moon hanging.
White in the welkin, / and Death with her.
So to each sweetness / a sorrow is given.

      Under the influence of the harp-song, Slim is
      more and more powerless not to look across at
      Naru in the firelight. And although she does
      not once look up, her fingers begin fumbling
      at the work, and the other girls exchange
      smiling glances.

         Haakon (continuing to sing)
Doomed all my days / to walk in darkness,
I sail not sunward / on my swift one.
Neither know I / the norse war-joy.

      Raud is watching Slim very seriously.

         Raud (clearing his throat)
You think deeply, Slim.

         Slim (startled)
Yes, I - -i - -
         (lamely, as his eyes go back to Naru)
- -yes!

         Raud (grimly watching)
I, also.
         (leaning forward a little)
Soon come the messengers of Skal   CONTINUED

                        Slim (murmuring, absent)
Messengers of Skal?

                        Raud (trying for his attention)
Daily we look for them in this season, bearing to
all the clans Skal's call to the great harvest.

                        Slim (murmuring, looking o.s.)
Oh- -

                 Haakon (continuing to sing)
Yet cry the youths to me, / endless yearning:
"Happy is Haakon / that has not seen her,
In face and fairness / the maid like a glower- -

That has not known / the sheen of her tresses,
The soft smile, / nor the eyes shining.
Else were he also / lost in love's longing."

        The following speeches are played partly in
        the interludes of Haakon's song, and partly
        over the song itself, with INTERCUT CLOSEUPS
        bringing out Slim's and Naru's preoccupation
        with each other —noticed by everyone.

                        Raud (grave, trying again)
Great now will be the grief of the folk if Slim
lives not through the year.
                (glancing meaningly at Naru)
It is well that - -that as yet there be none whose
grief will be more than mine.

                        Slim (careless, absent)
I have White Eagle now. I'll be O.K.

                        Haakon (continuing to sing)
Blind though I be / my youth was better!
I can recall / the loosed ern's night cry,
The stars far-flashing / over my love-flight!

Bold in battle / and fear you blushes?
What more woeful / than youth wasted- -
Eld, not death / is the darkest dread.

        Raud is determined to be heard.

                        Raud (grasping Slim's wrist)
Other outlanders have learned to ride the erns.
Yet even the best and bravest came not back from
the dale of the Might Ones.

        At his insistence, Slim turns reluctantly.

                        Slim (quiet, smiling)
Are you afraid I won't be able to take whatever's
going, Raud?
                                        CONTINUED:

                       Raud (with soft vehemence)
Not I, by Odin!
             (continuing anxious and preoccupied, as
             CAMERA TRUCKS into a CLOSEUP, excluding
             Slim)
Yet the skill must be learned in boyhood! Even
to look upon the wyverns and grendels, the heart
must be strengthened like the wrist upon the
bridle, and the mind toughened like the hand upon
the bow.
             (his eyes darkening as he visualizes)
In that time when the Mighty Ones rear up in
their dread, I have seen even skilled men stand,
and die outward through their eyes- -

        As he speaks, he has glanced back at Slim.
        Slowly his words trail off. A look of
        helplessness comes into his face. TRUCK BACK
        to INCLUDE SLIM, whose whole spirit goes out
        through his eyes toward Naru across the room.
        As Haakon sings on, TRUCK BACK FURTHER to
        INCLUDE SEVERAL OTHER MEN glancing gravely
        from Slim to Raud. As the song nears its end- -

140   MED. SHOT NARU

        fumbling fitfully over her embroidery.

             Haakon (continuing to sing o.s.)
Her then hale / away from the hearth-side!
Weary she waits / the arm of her warrior,
Steering his swift one / down the star-ways.

141   CLOSEUP HAAKON

        There is a smile on his blind face, as though
        he senses that his song had taken effect.

             Haakon (softly finishing song)
Hail to the harvest / and the moon hanging
White in the welkin, / and Death with her
So to each sweetness / a sorrow is given.

142   REVERSE ANGLE MED. LONG SHOT

        SHOWING Naru's chair empty, and all the girls
        gravely looking o.s. after her. PAN SWIFTLY
        to Slim's empty chair. All eyes are upon
        Raud, who stares indecisively into his cup.

                    WIPE TO:

MED. LONG SHOT WHITE EAGLE NIGHT   63
     (GLASS SHOTS AND ANIMATION)

> flying upward in silhouette against the moon,
> with Slim on his back, holding Naru before
> him.

                              DISSOLVE TO:

144   EXT. MOONLIT PINNACLE NIGHT (GLASS SHOTS,
     MIN. PROJ. AND ANIMATION) FULL SHOT
     WHITE EAGLE PERCHED ON PINNACLE OF ROCK

> with the moon behind him. Slim and Naru have
> just dismounted.

144A   EXT MOONLIT PINNACLE (FULL SIZE SET)
     (PROCESS) (B.G. SHOT ON PAINTED GLASS
     MED. SHOT

> Naru runs down ahead of Slim to a little shelf
> with grass growing on it, and a few young
> trees. She turns and waits for Slim, who
> comes down more slowly, his eyes fixed on her
> face. When she meets his look, her expression
> changes. Slim takes her hands.

                    Slim (huskily)
> I guess you're in my blood, Naru. From the way it
> feels, you've been there for about a thousand years.

> She looks frightened for a moment, but cannot
> quite make herself tear her hands and eyes
> from his hands and eyes.

                    Naru (her voice breaking)
> I have no more strength to strive with such a
> power! Let the doom take me - -!

> As he draws her into his arms,

                              SLOW DISSOLVE:

144-B   EXT. MOONLIT PINNACLE NIGHT (GLASS SHOTS
     AND ANIMATION) FULL SHOT

> A beautiful shot of White Eagle, motionless
> staring off fiercely at the moon.

                              DISSOLVE:

EXT. MOUNTAINS PEAKS NIGHT (GLASSES)   63A

Another beautiful shot of clouds drifting in
the moonlight, across the mountain peaks.

                                    DISSOLVE:

144-D   EXT. MOONLIT PINNACLE AND WHITE EAGLE
         (GLASS SHOTS, MIN. PROJ. AND ANIMATION

         FULL SHOT Slim sitting at base of tree near
         precipice. Naru leans back in his arms.
         White Eagle on top of pinnacle.

144-E   EXT. LEDGE (PROCESS) CLOSE SHOT

         Slim and Naru, seated at base of tree. Her
         head is against his shoulder. They are look-
         ing out into the beautiful moonlit night.
         Suddenly, from the distance o.s. comes shrill
         wild cries. Naru's face becomes frozen with
         fear and horror. The long cries come louder
         and closer. At last--

                    Naru (shuddering, whispering)
         The messengers of Skal!

145   EXT. LEDGE (PROCESS)

         LONG SHOT, Slim and Naru in F.G. as two
         eagles sweep past the pinnacle. On their
         backs are wild riders, carrying streaming
         torches, and uttering their shrill cries.
         As they sweep on o.s.--

145-A   CLOSE SHOT (PROCESS)

         Slim and Naru. She is clinging desperately
         about his neck.

                    Naru
                 (sobbing bitterly)
         The messengers of Skal --!

         As the voices of the messengers pass into the
         distance, there comes faintly from the village
         an answering blast on the watch-horn.

                                    FADE OUT.

FADE IN:

146   EXT. VILLAGE - DAY
LONG SHOT

It is in a turmoil of preparation, with
the men, fully armed, carrying equipment
toward the landing place, and each one
accompanied by one or more women, and
perhaps a child or two, to see him off.

DISSOLVE TO:

147   EXT. EAGLE PERCHES AND COOP (PROCESS)

CLOSE SHOT - RAUD

standing leaning on his sword. In the
b.g. some of the women are quietly
weeping.

> Raud
> (shouting)
Haste all! - -great Skal waits us! - - No more
leave-taking! - -Look to the lading of the erns!
There can be no halting for the slipped load!

148   EXT. VILLAGE - THE FORGE
CLOSE SHOT

Igor is proudly showing Naru the big
straight-bladed sword which he has just
completed.

> Igor
> (brandishing it)
Weighty, yet nimble! - -seven times forged!
- -the sword crowns my smith-craft!

> Naru
> (anxiously glancing around.
Nay! - -Belike we yet shall have no call for it.

As he puzzledly puts the sword out of
sight - -

149   EXT. EAGLE PERCHES (MIN.PROJ. AND ANIMATION)
MED. SHOT

as Raud arrives at the perch of his own
eagle, which greats him excitedly. As
CONTINUED:

he soothes it, he glances over at Atok
who is gloomily loading his own now
very bedraggled eagle.

> Raud
> (in sly amusement)
> I fear thy Donderwing comes early into the moult.

> Atok
> (bitterly)
> His comb is clipped by the White One, once for
> all.
> (angrily jerking on a strap)

Naru enters the shot. Draws Raud away.

149-A   INT. EAGLE PERCHES (STRAIGHT SET)

MED. SHOT NARU AND RAUD. (The following
scene is played quietly against a noisy
b.g. (o.s.) of preparations.

> Naru
> (quiet, tense)
> Raud!--Slim must not go!

> Raud
> (laughing after a moment of
> astonishment)
> Is he then like to stay with the old women
> and the babes?

> Naru
> (steadily, glancing o.s.)
> Aye, if you bid him--with some smooth tale
> of need at home.

> Raud
> (starting to scowl)
> With a lie shall I dress my friend in the
> feathers of his own ern?

Naru cleverly changes her tactics.

> Naru
> (gently, pleading)
> Raud--when I was little, never would you
> withold aught from me.
> (putting her hand on his)
> Give me now this last kindness to end my
> girlhood.

CONTINUED:

Slowly Raud's resistance gives way.

                    Raud
              (troubled and puzzled)
My sister, think you Skal would have a chief's
daughter wed with a laggard and a home-stayer?

                    Naru
              (passionately)
By the death of Baldur, I care not what comes
to me if Slim lives!

Both look o.s., doubtful, grave

149-B   EXT. DONDERWING'S EX-PERCH (MIN. PROJ.
                         AND ANIMATION)
                         CLOSE SHOT SLIM AND WHITE EAGLE

Slim has fastened his radio onto the
broad back. Of all the men, only he
is unarmed.

                    Slim
              (as he finishes)
There, big boy! --now we're class.
              (pondering, still dissatisfied)
One of these days I got to figure out some
kind of dash-clock --

150   EXT. DONDERWING'S EX-PERCH
                        (FULL SIZE SET)

Slim turns as Raud walks in, looking
anxious.

                    Raud
              (overdoing astonishment)
What, Slim! --readying to ride

                                        CONTINUED:

          Slim (cheerfully kidding)
No, I'm stayin' here with Haakon and the kids.

          Raud (heavily regretful)
Against my heart I must leave you here.

          Slim (astonished, dismayed)
What's the idea?

          Raud (much too hearty and easy)
Ever one stout warrior stays to look to the thorp.

    After a pause- -

          Slim (detecting something fishy)
What are my duties supposed to be?

          Raud (off guard, improvising)
Well if - -if need were, a- -
          (brilliantly)
- -a messenger!

          Slim (coldly)
Messages about what?

          Raud (fluffing, starting to sweat)
About? - -About things - -and - -and things!

          Slim (face hardening, nodding o.s.)
Is she goin'?

          Raud (very smooth)
As a Chief's sister and a maid yet childless - -aye.

    Slim looks him in the eye until Raud is
    forced to look down. Then slowly Slim grins.

          Slim (gently, touched)
Thanks for trying, Raud, but I- -
          (patting White Eagle's neck)
- -I just wouldn't know how to explain it to White
Eagle here.

    Raud tries to keep his attitude for a moment.

          Raud (at last, sheepish, relieved)
In truth I am but a sorry liar!
          (warmly)
- -and in truth I am glad!
          (turning away, bawling to the crowd)
Mount erns, all!

    As he hurries toward his own eagle- -

152   EXT. DONDERWING'S EX-PERCH (MIN.PROJ, AND
             ANIMATION) CLOSE SHOT SLIM BESIDE WHITE
             EAGLE

             As he prepares to mount, Naru walks in, carry-
             ing the sword, and a sort of Sam Browne attach-
             ment. As she hands it to him, she is smiling,
             but her lips tremble, and she does not attempt
             to speak. Slim delightedly accepts the sword,
             is about to thank her, when he is checked by
             her expression. He gravely fastens the belt
             around his body so that the sword hangs against
             his left thigh. Then he bends down and kisses
             her. She stares at him a moment frightenedly,
             then turns, and runs off toward her own eagle.

153   EXT. LANDING FIELD AND DISTANT MOUNTAINS
             (MIN. PROJ.) (ANIMATED B.G. OF BIRDS FLYING
             TO HARVEST) MED. LONG SHOT

             Raud stands beside eagle. Other eagles and
             people in the b.g.

153-A   CLOSEUP RAUD

                         Raud
             Haste! Skal is already a-wing.

153-B   EXT. LANDING FIELD AND DISTANT MOUNTAINS
             (MIN. PROJ. & ANIMATION) FULL SHOT

             Raud takes off, followed by several birds.

154   EXT. LANDING FIELD & DISTANT MOUNTAINS
             (ANIMATION) EXTREME LONG SHOT

             of Raud's clan, Slim and warrior girls flying
             off into distance.

                                          DISSOLVE TO:

155   EXT. GEORGE (ANIMATION) EXTREME LONG SHOT

             of a huge gorge like the Grand Canyon, running
             down into mist and darkness. From wall to wall
             it moves solid with eagle wings.

                                          DISSOLVE TO:

155-A   EXT. EXTRANCE TO VALLEY (ANIMATION)
EXTREME LONG SHOT

of Valley. Eagle tribes entering valley.

155-B   EXT. VALLEY (ANIMATION)

Eagles landing, showing geography of valley.
DISSOLVE TO:

156   EXT. ROCK PLATEAU (A HUGE BLOCK OF ROCK)
(MIN. PROJ.) LONG SHOT

flat-topped, about sixty feet high, and with
room for football field on top, set among
scattered trees, with a dense jungle on one
side. Far off in the jungle rise a group of
thin volcanic smokes. Very small above the
rock, a single eagle with its rider flies in,
and begins circling for landing.

157   EXT. ROCK PLATEAU (PROCESS) FULL SHOT
SKAL'S EAGLE CIRCLING

The eagle lands on the plateau in left b.g.
Skal dismounts. He is a huge bearded middle-
aged man, armed with sword and battle-axe,
and carrying a long spear. He takes a few
impressive strides, and stops face to face
with Raud. Raud salutes by bending from the
waist, and touching the ground at Skal's feet.

         Raud (with formal respect)
Hail Skal!

         Skal (dignified, shaking hands)
Raud!

The following scenes reveal the top of the
rock as the encampment of Raud's group.
At present only a few of the temporary
perches are occupied by eagles, in charge of
a couple of boys. Nearby, rough drying-racks
have been built, with unlighted fires laid
under them. Big open bins wait empty. At
one end of a group of warriors, armed with spears,
lounge among the saddled eagles, like a
troop of cavalry in reserve. The camp is
reached from below by long tree trunks into
which footholds have been chopped. Most of
the clan is unaccounted for - as Raud and
Skal greet each other.

"Hail Skal!" Raud's eagle from Scene 157, by Duncan Gleason. Image from the author's collection.

EXT ROCK PLATEAU (FULL SIZE SET) ＼   69
                         CLOSER SHOT SKAL AND RAUD

                              Skal (serious, military)
                    You have set out watches?

                              Raud (nodding, pointing o.s.)
                    Aye, and ever two by two - -a lad for sharp eyes,
                    and a gray-beard for cool wits.

157-B   EXT. SENTRY ROCK POST (PROCESS AND ANIMATION)

                         Two-man sentry team posted on pinnacle of
                         rock, gazing off unwaveringly toward the
                         jungle.

157-C   EXT. SENTRY TREE POST (PROCESS AND ANIMATION)

                         Two-man sentry team posted in tree, gazing off
                         unwaveringly toward jungle.

157-D   EXT. ROCK PLATEAU (FULL SIZE SET)
                         CLOSE SHOT SKAL AND RAUD

                              Skal (checking, nodding)
                    It is well done.
                              (then gravely)
                    Move "They" yet in the wood?

                              Raud (quick, constrained)
                    Not yet. - -Have They struck elsewhere?

                              Skal (seriously shaking his head)
                    It is here I look for the first danger.
                              (as both glance absently toward
                              volcanoes)
                    Our fathers thought their lair to be among the
                    earth-smokes.
                              (abruptly shaking off the mood)
                    Well - -get the fruits in.

                              Raud (pointing down o.s.)
                    The gatherers have been at work since dawn.

158   EXT. ROCK PLATEAU (PROCESS)
                         HIGH ANGLE LONG SHOT RAUD'S PEOPLE
                         (RAUD AND SKAL IN FOREGROUND OF SHOT

                         scattered below between trees and jungle, are
                         the harvesters. FOLLOW WITH A ROUTINE of
                         anxious haste, showing some (mostly women and

                                             CONTNUED

The harvesters in the Valley of the Ancients. Scene 158, by Duncan Gleason. Image from the author's collection.

boys) gathering big melon-like pods from the
trees. Elderly men collect the pods into
baskets fastened on their backs. Swaggering
among the others, but doing no work at the
moment,is a band of heavily armed warriors commanded
by Atok. As they move, they keep
glancing alertly toward the jungle.

159   EXT. HARVEST FIELD (PROCESS & STRAIGHT)
             FULL SHOT SLIM AND ATOK

             Atok gives Slim a boost with his loaded
             basket, starts him toward the rock. PAN ATOK
             among the pickers.

                     Atok (glancing toward jungle)
             Haste, friends! Haste!
                     (with grim, quiet humor)
             Think you to live forever?

             As the others glance anxiously o.s.- -

160   EXT. ROCK PLATEAU (PROCESS)
             MED. SHOT SKAL AND RAUD, WATCHING

                     Skal (turning, dissatisfied)
             Leads that lack-wit thy sword crew?

                     Raud
                     (laughing)
             Nay! Sword in hand, Atok is the wisest of our
             clan!
                     (as Slim climbs up sweating from
                     below)
             Ah! the first-fruits!

             Raud picks one of the pods out of Slim's
             basket, winking as Slim continues o.s.
             with a respectful glance at Skal. Then
             splitting the pod with his battle-axe,
             Raud munches one of the kernals inside.

                     Faud
                     (offering the pod to Skal)
             They are sweet this year.

             Skal accepts, looking after Slim.

Naru signals Raud from aloft in Scene 165. By Duncan Gleason. Image from the author's collection.

Slim dumps his basket in on of the bins.

> Skal
> (munching, nodding toward Slim)
What strange man is that?

> Raud (with an uneasy glance)
He is our outlander.

> Skal (quickly remembering)
Oh, but I had heard!
> (Then looking toward Slim, laughing,
> munching)
A sorry sight!--like some plucked fledgling!
> (shrugging, throwing the pod away)
Well, he may fall in the place of some needed
warrior--

Out of scene an eagle screams. As Skal
turns--

161   OUT

162   EXT. ROCK PLATEAU (PROCESS AND ANIMATION)

Skal, glancing toward the jungle.

One comes from the wood!

The eagle can be seen flying in distance.

163   EXT. PLATEAU (PROCESS AND ANIMATION)
                 LONG SHOT AN EAGLE FLYING TOWARD CAMERA

164   EXT. PLATEAU (FULL SIZE SET) FULL SHOT
                 RAUD AND SKAL

> Raud (hasty, anxious)
A maiden that I sent out to spy the Mighty Ones,
if she could, from aloft.

165   EXT. NARU'S EAGLE (PROCESS)
                 CLOSEUP NARU AND EAGLE

She leans over, makes a sign signals to Raud.

Skal is looking up, his eyes following the
flight of the eagle.

               Raud (interpreting Naru's signals)
They begin to move abroad - - come not yet this way.

               Skal (elaborately casual)
Was not the scout thy sister, Naru?

               Raud (with another anxious glance)
Aye, Skal.
               (then ostentatiously shouting o.s.)
Ho Warders! keep sharp watch!

               Skal (benevolently persistent)
A seemly maiden always, and a fair.
               (glancing over after a soggy pause)
Belike, Raud, when the harvest is in I shall have
words for thee- -

               Raud (sweating, business-like)
The fishers have I also told off as spearmen,
should the watch cry the warning- -

               Skal (annoyed, astonished)
Raud! It is of the maiden Naru, thy sister, that I
would speak.

His voice dies. He is staring open-mouthed
o.s.

166-A   EXT. NARU'S EAGLE (PROCESS) CLOSEUP NARU

               throwing kisses and smiling.

167   EXT. ROCK PLATEAU (FULL SIZE SET) (SKAL &
               RAUD IN B.G.) MED. LONG SHOT

               Slim, leisurely preparing to climb down with
               his basket. Naru has circled back on her
               eagle, and they are smiling, waving, kissing
               hands. Slim smiles, waves, kissing his hand.

168   EXT. ROCK PLATEAU (FULL SIZE SET)
               TWO SHOT RAUD AND SKAL

               Skal, on the verge of apoplexy, turns, glares.

                    Raud (sulky, avoiding his eyes
               You have seen, Skal.

                              CONTINUED:

                    Skal (finally exploding)
Her love is given?
          (furiously, as Raud nods silently)
--to an unhatched outlander? -- Naru, a chief's
sister!
          (glaring, bull-like)
By Thor and Odin, this may not be!

          CAMERA TRUCKS with them as they start walking.

                    Raud (stiffening, meeting his look)
Until Skal shall put me down from my chiefship in
full mote, it is mine to say what shall come to my
sister and my clan.

                    Skal (bleakly, as Raud stands firm)
And in the harvest-time the Mote meets here--
nightly!

          Raud scowls, says nothing. Skal turns away
          heaving with wrath. Then comes another shock.

                    Skal (gasping, looking o.s.)
The White One!

169   EXT. PERCHES ON PLATEAU (MIN. PROJ.)
                  FULL SHOT WHITE EAGLE ON HIS PERCH

                  Skal's eagle is in scene, held by a couple
                  of boys. Skal and Raud walk into the SHOT

                    Skal (quiet, incredulous)
Tamed!!
          (then turning with an admiring bellow)
Wht worthy has done this!?

                    Raud (casual, malicious)
For our outlander it was a morning's sport.

169-A   CLOSE TWO SHOT

                    Skal (his eyes starting)
The outlander?
          (choking, pulling his beard)
--but but but but but but but but how?

                    Raud (warmly, plugging Slim)
By craft and daring -- and alone, as in the old
time did Einar.

But Skal is lost in admiration of White Eagle.

                    Skal (soft, his eyes shinging)
In truth it is a steed meet for an earl only!   CONTINUED:

"Tamed!!" Raud and Skal encounter White Eagle in Scene 169. By Duncan Gleason. Image from the author's collection.

                                    Skal (Cont'd)
                              (then very sly and oily)
                    --and --and should it happen that in the mischances
                    of the harvest the rider have ill luck--
                              (breaking off as he meets Raud's glare)
                    --Well, I must look to the other clans.

                    Skal mounts and takes off.

169-B   CLOSEUP

                    Raud, looking up after him, for a moment.
                    Then, serious and commanding, he turns
                    towards eagles.

169-C   FULL SHOT

                    The eagles begin to flap and squawk nervously.

                              Raud (glancing toward the jungle)
                    The erns are troubled.
                              (very gravely to the boys)
                    See they are double-shackled.

                    The boys start to obey, looking back wide-
                    eyed toward the jungle.

170   CLOSER SHOT - WHITE EAGLE AND RAUD

                    The big bird is fretting. Raud hesitates.

                              Raud (starting to shackle one claw)
                    You also, White One.

170-A   CLOSE UP FULL SIZE CLAW

                    Raud fastens shackles.

                              Raud (thoughtfully)
                    It will be best.

170-B   MED. SHOT

                    Raud looks toward jungle, and exits. White
                    Eagles pecks at its shackles irritably.

                                        LAP DISSOLVE TO:

The harvesters at work from the montage Scenes 171- 175. By Duncan Gleason. Image from the author's collection.

171-175   MONTAGE - LONG AND CLOSE SHOTS - THE HARVEST

        Picking - hauling - filling bins - fish
        being smoked on the racks.

176   EXT. HARVEST FIELD (PROCESS AND STRAIGHT)

        TRUCK RAUD, as he moves through the harvesters.
        The harvesters are working and carrying their
        produce to the rock. Raud stops to speak to
        Slim, who is re-loading his basket. A low
        whistle from overhead is heard o.s. Raud looks
        up.

177   EXT. SENTRY ROCK POST (PROCESS)

        An out-post sentry team. The elder sentry
        looks down, makes a warning gesture.

          Elder Sentry (calling down quietly)
     Raud! They move!

          Raud's voice (o.s.)
     Hitherward?
          Elder Sentry (hollow-voiced,
         looking toward jungle)
     Not yet. We have still the wind of them.

178   EXT. HARVEST FIELD (PROCESS AND STRAIGHT)
       FULL SHOT

        Raud quietly turns to Atok.

          Raud
     Atok! Begin now to draw the folk in.

        The nearby people have stopped working, their
        eyes fixed on the jungle, listening.

        CLOSE PAN SHOT, Atok moving among the people,
        getting them started toward the rock.

          Atok (cheerful, drawling)
     To the rock, all! - - take only what ye have.

179   OUT

180   OUT

181   OUT

"To the rock — to the rock!" The harvesters flee the approaching allosaur in Scene 182. By Duncan Gleason. Image from the author's collection.

> First Guard
> ("Break it up!")
To the rock - - to the rock!

183   EXT. HARVEST FIELD (PROCESS & STRAIGHT)
                        LONG SHOT TOWARD ROCK

as all start slowly, looking back wild-eyed.

> Second Guard
> (in f.g.)
Nay - - no more gathering!

Atok stands steadfast, as people pass him.

> Atok
> (cheerful, ironical)
Softly! - - softly! Now we shall rest us for a
little above - -

183-X1   EXT. CHARGE OF ALLOSAURUS (MINIATURE
                        PROJECTION)

FULL SHOT people passing by guards, scurrying
along softly, looking back over their
shoulders.

183-X2   EXT. BASE OF PLATEAU (FULL SIZE SET)

LONG SHOT people entering and beginning to
crowd around poles, scrambling up, milling
around. The women are going up first.
Everyone glancing back over shoulders, scared.

183-X3   EXT. HARVEST FIELD (PROCESS & STRAIGHT)

LONG SHOT SHOOTING TOWARD ROCK Slim moving
along with people, CAMERA PANNING WITH HIM.
He is a little bewildered, breathless, find-
it it hard to smile. He reaches Raud.

> Slim
> (touching Raud's arm)
Raud - - what - -

As Raud turns to reply, suddenly o.s. - -

                                        CONTINUED:

>   Sentries
>   (loud, unguarded o.s.)
They come!
'Ware all! 'Ware! - - 'Ware! - - Ware!

183A   EXT. SENTRY ROCK POST (PROCESS) -
                        CLOSE SHOT

>   Sentry
They come!
'Ware all!

183B   EXT. SENTRY TREE POST (PROCESS) -
                        CLOSE SHOT

>   Sentry
They come!
'Ware all!
'Ware - - 'Ware! - -Ware!

183C   (SAME AS 183)

>   raud
>   (suddenly shouting, urgent)
Bring the folk in! - - bring them in!

>   CONTINUED:

As the last stragglers run through - -

FLASH ROUTINE

184-188   ATOK'S GUARDS

                    4th Guard (roughly pushing)
Haste- -!

                    1st
The rock - - !

                    3rd
Run!
                    Atok (over a dropped basket)
Let it go - -
                    (grinning grimly toward the jungle)
- - thy fruit will be safer now than thy head - -!

189   EXT. HARVEST FIELD REVERSE ANGLE (PROCESS
                       AND STRAIGHT) LONG SHOT

                       Out from behind the distant trees stalks an
                       allosaurus, his little forelegs tucked up,
                       glancing fiercely right and left. (Slim,
                       Atok, Raud and warriors in f.g.)

190   BIG CLOSEUP - SLIM

                       Staring almost insanely o.s.

191   MED. SHOT - SLIM AND RAUD

                       Slim stares frozen. Raud enters, sees him.

                              Raud (touching his arm)
                       Friend!
                              (gentle, pointing, as Slims atarts,
                              comes to)
                       Yonder lies the rock - -

                       As Slim, still staring o.s., tries to reply - -

191A   EXT. SENTRY ROCK POST (PROCESS)

                              Sentry
                       More come!
                       More!

The allosaur appears, from Scene 189. By Duncan Gleason. Image from the author's collection.

EXT. SENTRY TREE POST (PROCESS)

                    Sentry
More!
'Ware westward!

191C   EXT. HARVEST FIELD REVERSE ANGLE (PROCESS
                        AND STRAIGHT) LONG SHOT

                        Raud (shouting up to the congested mob)
Up! - - to the rock! - - up! - - up!

192   EXT HARVEST FIELD (PROCESS AND STRAIGHT
                        REVERSE ANGLE LONG SHOT

                        Two more allosauri join the first from the
                        jungle. Suddenly the first snaps his head
                        round, looks directly toward CAMERA.

193   FULL SHOT
                                Atok (cheerfully drawing his sword)
- -out swords!

                        As his men obey like a well-trained team,
                        Raud also draws his sword. Slim shivers.

                                Slim (pawing Raud's arm)
What - - what do I do?

                                Raud (impatient, shaking him off)
Nay, the rock! - -you are unskilled.

                        ZOOM INTO A CLOSEUP OF SLIM. He is haggard,
                        his teeth are chattering, but he manages to
                        grin. Slowly he slips his basket, takes a
                        deep breath.

                                Slim (drawing his sword)
Well, I got to learn some time - -

194   EXT. PERCHES ON PLATEAU (ANIMATION)
                        FULL SCREEN CLOSEUP WHITE EAGLE SCREAMING

                        flapping, straining against his shackle.

The warriors make a stand in scene 194A. By Duncan Gleason. Image courtesy of Ronald V. Borst.

194A   EXT. HARVEST FIELD (PROCESS AND STRAIGHT)
REVERSE ANGLE - LONG SHOT

Allosaurus charges towards group. Men throw
spears, shoot arrows, etc.

194B   EXT. CHARGE OF THE ALLOSAURUS
(AMIMATION AND MIN. PROJ.)

Warriors holding back allosaurus, while
people rush toward rock. (Rock is not seen
in picture)

195   EXT. BASE OF PLATEAU (STRAIGHT SHOT)

LOW ANGLE - FULL SHOT

The mob is swarming up the poles, others on
the ground milling and struggling for their
turn.

196   EXT. CHARGE OF ALLOSAURUS (ANIMATION AND
MIN. PROJ.)

Man throws spear.

197   EXT. HARVEST FIELD (FULL SIZE PROCESS AND
MIN. PROJ. AND ANIMATION)

Guards retreat from allosaurus. People
swarming up poles.

198   EXT. BASE OF PLATEAU (MIM. PROJ. AND
ANIMATION)

Allosaurus grabs man off pole. Warriors
throw spears into allosaurus. Women scrambling
up poles.

199   CLOSEUP - FULL SIZE HEAD OF ALLOSAURUS

Allosaurus swallows man, feet first. Man
screams.

The retreat up the poles from Scene 195. By Duncan Gleason. Image from the author's collection.

199X1   MED. SHOT (MIN. PROJ)

Men throwing spears into allosaurus. Slim in
position near tail.

199X2   CLOSE SHOT (MIN. PROJ.)

Women scrambling up pole. Allosaurus just
about to grab her.

199X3   CLOSE SHOT (MIN. PROJ.)

Slim slashes off tail with his sword.
Allosaurus starts to turn and Slim backs
away. Atok and his band back towards
rock.

199X4   FULL SHOT (FULL SIZE PROCESS, B.G. MIN.
         PROJ. AND ANIMATION)

Allosaurus turns with a bellow, and Slim backs
away from it. Atok and his men back towards
rock. Slim retreats farther, as allosaurus
comes toward him.

199X5   EXT. HARVEST FIELD (FULL SIZE PROCESS, MIN.
         PROJ. AND ANIMATION)

Slim in miniature is standing on CAMERA
side of allosaurus. He is hit by tail and
comes rolling toward CAMERA.

199X6   REVERSE SHOT (STRAIGHT SET)

Slim lands at edge of jungle, unconscious.

199X7   EXT. HARVEST FIELD (FULL SIZE PROCESS,
         MIN. PROJ. AND ANIMATION.

Slim lying in f.g. Fighting allosaurus
by rock.

199X8   EXT. BASE OF PLATEAU (MIN. PROJ.)

CLOSE SHOT - Atok slashes hind leg of
allosaurus.

199X9   EXT. HARVEST FIELD (FULL SIZE PROCESS,   78
                 MIN. PROJ. AND ANIMATION

                 LONGER SHOT - Allosaurus turns away from Slim,
                 who lies unconscious on ground. (He is
                 clearly recognizable in scene)

199X10   EXT. SENTRY ROCK POST (MIN. PROJ.)

                 Allosauri swarm by sentry post. Birds
                 scream and flap wings wildly.

                                Sentries
                              (shout)
                 Quick - quick - the herd!

                 They jump on their eagles and fly off,
                 toward CAMERA

199X11   EXT. CHARGE OF ALLOSAUI HERD (ANIMATION)

                 LONG SHOT - Allosauri charging out of jungle.

199X12   EXT. BASE OF PLATEAU (FULL SIZE SET)

                 CLOSE SHOT - Atok and last of guards start
                 scrambling up poles.

199X13   EXT, HARVEST FIELD (NEW ANGLE)
(FULL SIZE PROCESS & ANIMATION)

Slim in f.g. just beginning to come too,
dazed. Only two men are left on poles.
Allosauri tear down poles, eat up last two
men. They paw and jump at face of rock.

119X14   EXT. CHARGE OF ALLOSAURI HERD (ANIMATION)

Eagles attack allosauri from air.

199X15   ZOOM SHOT (FULL SIZE PROJ.)

Warrior on eagle dives at allosaurus, throwing spears.

199X16   EXT. CHARGE OF ALLOSAURI HERD (ANIMATION)

Eagle dives down, warrior throws spear
into allosaurus.

199X17   OUT

199X18   OUT

199X19   OUT

199X20   OUT

199X21   OUT

199X22   OUT

199X23   EXT. NARU'S EAGLE (ANIMATION)

Naru's eagle circling over fight.

199X24   CLOSEUP - NARU (FULL SIZE PORTION EAGLE)
(DULL SIZE PROCESS)

peering down, anxiously.

199X25   EXT HARVEST FIELD (FULL SIZE PROCESS,   79A
MIN.PROJ. & ANIMATION

LONG SHOT - fighting in progress. Slim in
foreground, sitting up, holding his head,
still dazed. One allosaurus, slightly
detached from herd, turns toward him.

199X26   CLOSEUP - NARU (FULL SIZE PROCESS)

Reacting in fear.

199X27   EXT. NARU'S EAGLE (ANIMATION)

Naru puts her eagle into steep dive.

200-202   EXT. HARVEST FIELD (FULL SIZE PROCESS,
MIN. PROJ. & ANIMATION)

LONG SHOT - fight in b.g. Slim in f.g. is
just becoming conscious of fight, and of
the danger of the approaching allosaurus,
which has not sighted him yet. Naru's
eagle flashes in past allosaurus, lands
in clear space close to slim and Naru slides
to the ground.
PAN HER as she runs up to Slim. catches
his arm, and shakes him. He staggers
to his feet, and they turn back toward
direction from which Naru came.

PAN Naru and Slim run toward eagle.
Allosaurus grabs eagle, shakes it and
kills it. Naru and Slim turn and run
to try to get back towards plateau.
One of the allosauri, which has been at
base of plateau, sees them and starts after
them. They turn and run off screen towards
CAMERA. Allosaurus runs past CAMERA in
pursuit.

203   EXT. JUNGLE CHASE #1 (FULL SIZE SET)   79B

             DOLLY SHOT - Slim and Naru running desperately
             through jungle.

204   OUT

205   EXT. JUNGLE CHASE #1 (MIN. PROJ., MINIATURE
             AND GLASS

             Slim and Naru running desperately through
             jungle, pursued by allosaurus.

205X1   EXT. JUNGLE CHASE #1 (FULL SIZE SET)

             DOLLY SHOT - Slim and Naru running desper-
             ately through jungle.

205X2   EXT. JUNGLE CHASE #1 (MIN. PROJ.

             Slim and Naru running through jungle, pursued
             by allosaurus.

205X3   EXT. JUNGLE CHASE #1 (FULL SIZE SET)

             DOLLY SHOT - Slim and Naru running desper-
             ately through jungle.

205X4   EXT. JUNGLE CHASE #1 (FULL SIZE SET)

             CLOSE SHOT - Slim and Naru running past
             CAMERA, stumble over log and fall. They
             look back in terror.

205X5   BIG TWO HEAD CLOSEUP

             Slim and Naru, staring back in terror.
             They get up and run from CAMERA, CAMERA
             TILTING UP AFTER THEM.

205X6   EXT. JUNGLE CHASE #2   (MINIATURE AND
             ANIMATION) CLOSE SHOT -

             The allosaurus, as it comes straight towards
             and directly over CAMERA. LOW CAMERA ANGLE.

208   EXT. JUNGLE CHASE #3 (MIN. PROJ.)

                   LONG SHOT - Slim and Naru run in, look back
                   and commence to climb tree.

208X1   EXT. JUNGLE TREE #1 (FULL SIZE PROCESS)
                   B.G. OF ANIMATION

                   Slim and Naru climb up tree, out of scene.
                   Allosaurus enters and runs toward tree.

208X2   EXT. JUNGLE CHASE #3 (MIN. PROJ.)

                   LONG SHOT - Allosaurus charges in to base
                   of tree, as Naru and Slim climb up out of
                   his reach. Allosaurus jumps at them.

208X3   EXT. JUNGLE TREE #2 (FULL SIZE PROJ.

                   MED. CLOSE SHOT (REVERSE) Allosaurus
                   jumping for branch on which Naru stands.

208X4   EXT. JUNGLE CHASE #3 (MIN.PROJ.)

                   MED. CLOSE SHOT - Allosaurus catches
                   branch on which Naru is standing, just
                   as Slim reaches down to help her up higher.
                   Allosaurus pulls down branch, and Naru is
                   about to fall to the ground with branch.
                   She grasps tree trunk and hangs on.

208X5   EXT. JUNGLE TREE @2 (PROCESS)

                   Slim grabs Naru's wrist and swings her up
                   out of danger, as Allosaurus' jaws snap
                   just missing her feet. Naru and Slim
                   climb up out of SHOT.

208X6   EXT. JUNGLE TREE #3 (PROCESS)

                   Slim and Naru climb into picture. Allosaurus
                   jumps, trying to reach them.

208X7   EXT. JUNGLE CHASE #3 (MIN. PROJ.)   79D

LONG SHOT - Allosaurus grabs big branch with
mouth and begins to shake tree.

209-211   EXT. JUNGLE TREE #3 (PROCESS)

CLOSE SHOT - Slim and Naru, with tree
shaking. Slim starts to descend.

          Slim
A few more of those and the tree goes over - -!

          Naru
          (restraining him)
Wait!

She points. Through the jungle comes a
big triceratops, plodding peaceably.
Naru whips an arrow from her quiver,
puts it to her bow. Slim grabs her
arm.

          Slim
Want him after us too!

                              CONTINUED

                    Naru (excited)
          Ever these twain are foes!
                    (shakes his arm off)

211X1   EXT. JUNGLE TREE #3 (PROCESS)

               CLOSE SHOT, Naru shoots arrow.

211X2   EXT. JUNGLE CHASE #3 (MIN PROJ.)

               Naru rattles three arrows off the armor
               of the stupid monster. It turns, thrashing
               its horns, looking for trouble. The allo-
               saurous now sees its enemy, bellows, and rushes
               instantly to the attack. There follows a
               terrific battle between the two animals.

211X3   EXT. JUNGLE TREE #3 (PROCESS)

               Slim and Naru looking down at the fight
               going on below.

                         Naru
                    (grasps Slim's arm)
          Come. They will not see us.

               They descend out of picture.

211X4   EXT. JUNGLE TREE #3 (MIN. PROJ.)

               Slim and Naru descend into picture. In
               the f.g. the terrific battle continues.

211X5   EXT. JUNGLE CHASE #3 (MIN. PROJ.)

               Slim and Naru are almost down. The tricera-
               tops makes a fierce charge, and pins the
               allosaurus against the tree. The tree starts
               to fall.

211X6   EXT. JUNGLE TREE #2 (PROCESS)

               Naru and Slim on falling tree, (WITH MOVING
               B.G.

211X7   EXT. FALLING TREE (PROCESS)

CLOSEUP Tree falls to ground. Naru's leg is pinned under tree. Slim is thrown clear, and tries to pull Naru loose. (Fight continues in b.g.)

211X8   EXT. FALLEN TREE (MIN. PROJ.)

Naru is still pinned under tree, and Slim is trying to free her. (Fight still continues in b.g.)

211X9   EXT. FALLEN TREE (FULL SIZE SET)

CLOSE SHOT Slim and Naru stare at fight, frightened. Still trying to get Naru loose.

211X10   EXT. FALLEN TREE (PROCESS)

Allosaurus kills triceratops. Triceratops falls across log, lifting it enough to free Naru's leg.

211X11   EXT. FALLEN TREE (MIN. PROJ,)

Allosaurus staggers out of picture, in opposite direction from which he entered.

211X12   EXT. FALLEN TREE (PROCESS)

Slim frees Naru from log. They get to their feet, watchfully.

212   EXT. FALLEN TREE (FULL SIZE SET) -
MED. SHOT - SLIM AND NARU

              Slim
           (standing up, grim)
Well -- let's get started back.

              Naru
           (holding him)
Nay! They swarm between us and the rock!

                    Slim (obstinately leading on)
I don't trust these trees.

                    Naru (suddenly pointing o.s.)
They come! --many! Slim, let us run--!

213   EXT. FALLEN TREE (MIN. PROJ.)

                  REVERSE ANGLE - LONG SHOT - ALLOSAURUS HERD

                  As they come bellowing through the jungle.

214   EXT. FALLEN TREE (FULL SIZE SET)
                  TWO SHOT - SLIM AND NARU

                    Slim (drawing her back into cover)
Lie low! -- get in there!

215   EXT. FALLEN TREE (MIN. PROJ.)

                  FULL SHOT as the allosauri troop through.

216   EXT. FALLEN TREE (FULL SIZE SET)

                  MED. SHOT - SLIM AND NARU

                  emerging. Slim looks o.s. after the herd.

                    Naru (sick, shaken)
Come! -- the way is now clear!

                    Slim (anxious, detaining her)
What makes you so sure?

                    Naru (distracted, eager to go)
Ever at this hour they go to their earth against
the chill of night.

                    Slim (tense, turning on her)
Where?

                    Naru (blank, impatient)
None knows. Even our fathers knew not.

                  Slim is thinking eagerly, eyes, o.s.
                  Suddenly --

                                      CONTINUED:

                    Slim
               (pushing her back into cover)
     Wait here!

                    Naru (horrified, struggling)
     Slim!--no!--They go to the place of death!

                    Slim (rough, preoccupied)
     You shut up and do what you're told!

               Before she can speak, he runs o.s.
               after the herd. On Naru, haggardly
               looking after him--

                                        DISSOLVE TO:

217   EXT. JUNGLE CHASE #4 (MIN. PROJ.)

               LONG SHOT SLIM TRAILING THE HERD

               as it moves away beyond the trees toward
               rocky chasm.

                                        DISSOLVE TO:

218   EXT. VOLCANO REGION (MIN. PROJ.)
               LONG SHOT ALLOSAURUS HERD

               reaching a stony region. Like a line of
               monsterous ducks they turn down a steep
               gully which passes below a fuming volcanic
               crater. As the last tail wriggles out of
               sight, Slim cautiously appears above
               among the trees.

218-X1   EXT. VOLCANIC REGION #2 (MIN. PROJ.)

               The allosaui disappear down gully, which
               leads to the black mouth of a cave (Cave
               not seen in this set). Slim climbs rock
               to get view of where they are going.

219   EXT. VOLCANIC REGION (PROCESS)

               Slim on rock, sees the last of the allosauri
               disappear into the black mouth of a cave
               of hell. He looks at this, then looks off
               at the volcano, then back at the cave.

EXT. VOLCANIC REGION (FULL SIZE SET)   81
                 REVERSE CLOSE SHOT SLIM

          thinking vehemently. He looks eagerly from
          the crater, down the gully, and to the cavern
          from which rumblings still come. Suddenly,
          he hears a soft whistle below him. He turns
          and looks o.s.

219-X2   EXT. VOLCANIC REGION #2 (MIN. PROJ.)

          Naru has crept into scene, and stands
          below Slim.

                    Naru (frightened, urgent)
          Come! - -here it smells of death.

          Slim beckons her to come up beside him.
          She starts to climb up rock.

219-X3   EXT. VOLCANIC REGION (PROCESS)
                 CLOSE SHOT SLIM AND NARU

                    Slim (tense, eyes still o.s.)
          You're sure they stay holed-up in there all
          night?

                    Naru (nodding)
          Until they feel the warmth of the morrow's sun.
                    (then anxious as he grins,
                    bangs his fist)
          Slim! - -come! What ails thee?

219-X4   EXT. VOLCANIC REGION (FULL SIZE SET)
                 REVERSE

                    Slim (still grinning)
          I'm not sure, Toots - -
                    (slowly turning his eyes
                    toward the crater)
          - -but I'm afraid I got another scheme.
                    (then coming to earth, seeming to
                    see Naru for the first time - -
                    mock severe)
          Wait a minute! Haven't you ever heard of the
          word obey?
                    (then smiling, kissing her)
          Well, you're going to!

          She returns his kiss uncomprehending - -

As Naru breaks from his kiss. She turns
and starts to climb back down the rock.
CAMERA PANS, and above them at the head
of the steep-walled gully, appears a
single belated allosaurus, wounded and
raging, cutting off their retreat. As
it starts toward them with a bellow - -

219-X6   EXT. VOLCANIC REGION (FULL SIZE SET)

FLASH CLOSE UP Naru, horror-stricken,
reacting.

219-X7   FLASH CLOSE UP SLIM

reacting.

219-X8   EXT. ALLOSAURUS HEAD (FULL SIZE)   82A

                      FLASH CLOSEUP, full size head of allosaurus,
                      wounded and raging. It starts forward.

219-X9   EXT. VOLCANIC REGION - PROCESS #2

                      Slim reaches down to try to snatch Naru
                      from danger. She starts to scramble up.
                      Allosaurus charges in to picture, intent
                      after Naru.

219-X10   EXT. VOLCANIC REGION #2 (MIN. PROJ.)

                      Slim leaps on to head of allosaurus, just
                      as animal is about to grab girl.

219-X11   EXT. VOLCANIC REGION (FULL SIZE SET)

                      Slim, astride allosaurus' head, attacks
                      monster with sort-handled knife, which
                      he unsheaths from his belt. There is a
                      terrific struggle. Naru crouches against
                      rock.

219-X12   EXT. VOLCANIC REGION #2 (MIN. PROJ.)

                      The struggle between Slim and the allosaurus
                      continues, as allosaurus tries to claw Slim
                      from his head. Naru climbs up rock in
                      b.g., farther from danger.

219-X13   EXT. VOLCANIC REGION (FULL SIZE SET)
                      CLOSE SHOT - NARU

                      She hears shrill cry above, and looks up and
                      o.s.

219-X14   EXT. WHITE EAGLE AND TREE TOPS (ANIMATION)

                      LONG SHOT - White Eagle streaking over
                      tree tops.

219X-15   EXT. VOLCANIC REGION #2 (MIN. PROJ.)   82B

                           SLIM is thrown from allosaurus' head, and
                           falls to the ground. Allosaurus starts
                           after him. Naru snatches up rock and slams
                           it at the beast's head. Allosaurus gives her quick
                           glance, then turns back toward Slim. It
                           starts in for the kill.

219-X16   EXT. VOLCANIC REGION (PROCESS #3)

                           Slim on ground. Allosaurus head shoots
                           into picture, ready to grab boy. There
                           seems no escape.

219-X17   EXT. VOLCANIC REGION #2 (MIN. PROJ)

                           Off Stage comes a loud whistling of wings
                           and a shrill cry. White Eagle flashes
                           in, strikes allosaurus' head like a white
                           thunderbolt, throwing animal on its back
                           among the boulders. White Eagle wheels and
                           lands beside Slim.

220-   EXT. VOLCANIC REGION #2 (MIN. PROJ.)

                           (White Eagle's legs in b.g.) Slim is just
                           scrambling to his feet, as Naru jumps down
                           into picture.

                                    Slim (looking at white Eagle)
                           Big fellow!
                                    (sees eagle's bloody ankle and
                                    dangling chain)
                           He'd have torn loose from his claw if he had to.

229-X1   EXT. VOLCANIC REGION #2 (MIN. PROJ.)

                                    Naru (with an anxious shriek)
                           Quick - - mount!

                           The allosaurus has regained its feet, and
                           as Slim and Naru scramble up on White
                           Eagle, it rushes at them. As White Eagle
                           rises.

                                         232

220-X2   LONGER SHOT   82C
                The allosaurus springs into the air, but falls
                back, clutching only a few white feathers.
                As White Eagle sails o.s., the allosaurus
                stands hissing and glaring upward.

220-X3   EXT. WHITE EAGLE AND TREE TOPS (ANIMATION)
                White Eagle, with Slim and Naru on his back,
                sails away over the tree tops.

                                        DISSOLVE TO:

220-X4   EXT. ROCK PLATEAU (MIN.) NIGHT
                A beautiful scene of a campfire burning on
                top of the plateau.

                                        DISSOLVE TO:

221   EXT. ROCK PLATEAU (FULL SIZE SET)
                NIGHT - FIRELIGHT - FULL TRUCK SHOT

                The smoking-racks - the bins full of fruit - -
                into a FULL SHOT of a dance group about the
                central campfire on the rock. Men of all
                clans centered about Skal, who sits on a stone,
                flanked on either hand by a stooge. On one
                side, Raud's group - - Slim, Atok, Naru, etc.

                        Skal (ceremonially raising his axe)
                The Mote is met.
                        (glancing balefully toward Slim)
                Who speaks?

                As Slim raises jauntily, Raud is anxious.

                        Slim (beginning, very friendly)
                Well, ladies and gentlemen - -

                        1st Stooge (angrily interrupting)
                By what right speaks an outlander in our Mote?

                Slim stops, looks very crestfallen.

                        Skal (quiet, scowling at Slim)
                It is well asked.

                No one dares speak. Slim is about to sit down
                when Naru jumps up behind Raud.

                        Naru (advancing, vehement)
                Once was even Einar such an outlander!
                        (appealing to the crowd)
                You know him all for a breaker of erns - none bet-
                ter! You have seen him face the Mighty Ones - -
                none more stoutly! And me a norsewoman, and a
                chief's daughter - a clansfellow of many here - he
                has this day brought back living from the Place of
                Death.
                A murmur of excitement through the crowd. CONTINUED:

>   Voices (much impressed)
> The place of death!
> They have seen the place of death! etc. etc.

>   Atok (calling out)
> The maid has well spoken!

Suddenly, tipped by a glare from Skal--

>   2nd Stooge (jumping up)
> By what right speaks any maid in the Mote?

At once the sensation Naru has made is lost.

>   Voices (objecting and laughing)
> Aye, by what right!
> Bid her hold her tongue!
> Back to thy weaving, Naru!

As the uproar grows, and Skal brightens --

>   Raud (suddenly rising, loud)
> Mark me, norsemen!
>   (scowling round as silence falls)
> You will now hear this man because he speaks for
> me! His is my friend and my brother --
>   (challengingly slapping his sword)
> --and with my head I vouch for him!

>   Atok (rising, grinning round)
> Such as it is, my head lies with Raud's head!

There is a growl of hesitant anger. Raud
and Atok wait. Skal hesitates.

>   Skal (at last: "Any objections?")
> Cries out any still against this thing?
>   (grumpily, after a long silence)
> Speak outlander!

Slim now advances very diffidently.

>   Slim (shyly scratching his head)
> Well, fellers, there's nothing much to it--

                                     LAP DISSOLVE:
222   EXT. VOLCANIC REGION (PROCESS #3)
        EARLY MORNING FULL SHOT HUGE TREE TRUNK
        slung beneath two scissors made of smaller
        trees. Ropes are attached, upon which Skal's
        men are beginning to take hold. Raud and Slim
        (Slim is on top of battering ram) are in charge,
        while Skal stands in f.g. sourly watching. TRUCK
        BACK TO SHOW the tree set as a battering ram
        against the rather fragile side of the volcanic
        crater above the cavern.   CONTINUED:

CONTINUED (2)   84
O.s. a continued muffled roaring of allosauri,
and shouts of men.

                    Slim (calling as the men hang back)
        Catch hold of those ropes! --line them up, Raud!

222-X1   EXT. BATTERING RAM (PROCESS) (B.G. MIN. PROJ.)

        SLIM standing on top of battering-ram.

                    Slim (calling anxiously)
        Atok! how long can you hold them?

222-X2   EXT. ENTRANCE TO CAVE (PROCESS)
                (MIN. PROJ. B.G.)

        Under the direction of Atok another group has
        built a big smoky fire at the entrance of the
        cave. Through the smoke and sparks the head of
        an allosaurus appears now and then, blinking
        bellowing, and withdrawing. Others are crowd-
        ing behind. Arrows fly steadily. Another group,
        on top of the cave, are rolling huge boulders
        down.

                        Atok
                    (cheerfully yelling back to Slim)
        Nay, I know not.

222-X3   EXT. BATTERING-RAM (PROCESS) (B.G. MIN PROJ.

                        Slim (to Atok)
        .....Feed 'em more smoke!

222-X4   EXT. ENTRANCE TO CAVE (PROCESS) (MIN. PROJ. B.G.)

                        Atok (bawling to his crew)
        Brush here! More brush!
                    (then flinging his battle-axe as an
                    allosaurus charges the fire-makers)
        Back wyvern!

223   OUT

224   EXT. BASE OF BATTERING RAM (FULL SIZE SET)

        FULL SHOT Raud now has four men on each rope.

224-X1   EXT. BATTERING-RAM (PROCESS) (B.G. MIN.PROJ.)

                 Slim (anxious, impatient to Raud)
All set?

224-X2   EXT. BASE OF BATTERING-RAM (FULL SIZE SET)

                 Raud (also anxious)
Aye! Ready!

224-X3   EXT. BATTERING-RAM (PROCESS) (B.G. MIN. PROJ.)

                 Slim (yelling to the men)
Now - -everybody! - -all together!
        (pounding the cadence with his sword)
Heave! - -Heave! - -Heave!

224-X4   EXT. VOLCANIC REGION (PROCESS #3)

Straining, the men get the ponderous ram
swinging, very slow at first, but then with
a longer and longer stroke. INTERCUT with
Atok having greater and greater difficulties
keeping the allosaui penned up.

224-X5   EXT. BASE OF BATTERING-RAM (PROCESS)
                (B.G. SHOT IN GILLESPIE MIN. FROM UNDERNEATH
RAM TOWARDS ROCK)

Finally the ram just taps the crater wall,
then again and again with heavier and heavier
blows. Suddenly a blazing crack appears,
smoke rises.

225   EXT. VOLCANIC REGION (FULL SIZE SET)

                 Skal
         (staring, shaken)
It cracks!

226   EXT. BASE OF BATTERING RAM (FULL SIZE SET)   86
               FLASH CLOSE UP

                    1st Man (dropping rope)
It cracks!

227   FLASH CLOSE UP

                    2nd Man
The earth-fire!

228   FLASH CLOSE UP

                    3rd Man
Run!

229   FLASH CLOSE UP

                    4th Man
Run!

230   EXT. BATTERING-RAM (PROCESS)

         CLOSE SHOT SLIM

         as the ram stops striking, slows down.

                  Slim (yelling after the men)
Come back here - - it's not through!
             (desperately to Raud)
Get those men- -!

231   EXT. BASE OF BATTERING RAM (FULL SIZE SET)

         CLOSE SHOT RAUD IN THE MOB

         striking with the flat of his sword.

                  Raud (hoarse, raging)
Back to the ropes! Back - - fools! - - women!

         The men push past him heedless, headlong.

232   EXT. ENTRANCE TO CAVE (PROCESS) (MIN.
         PROJ. B.G.
         FULL SHOT ATOK AMID SMOKE

         Allosauri trample the sinking fire.

                  Atok (shouting o.s.)
Slim! The Mighty Ones burst forth!

EXT. BATTERING RAM (PROCESS)
                    CLOSE SHOT SLIM

                              Slim (pleading, struggling)
                    Gang! It's our last chance! Come back- -!

234   EXT. ENTRANCE TO CAVE (MIN. PROJ.)
                    FULL SHOT - AN ALLOSAURUS

                    plowing through the dying fire. All run but
                    Atok and two other men. They catch up fire
                    poles and thrust them into the mouth of the
                    allosaurus.

235   OUT

236   EXT. VOLCANIC REGION (PROCESS #3)
                    CLOSE SWIFT PAN SHOT SKAL

                    suddenly alive, charging into the mob, driving
                    them back out of sight toward the ram.

                              Skal (tremendously bellowing)
                    What! Fear you fire? - -Back! - - to the ropes!
                              (drawing his sword as the men waver)
                    Back cravens!

237   EXT. ENTRANCE TO CAVE (MIN. PROJ.)
                    LONG SHOT

                    Two more allosauri begin to force themselves
                    out. The last two men run, leaving Atok
                    alone.

237-X-1   EXT. BATTERING RAM (PROCESS)
                    CLOSE SHOT SLIM

                              Slim (glancing o.s., crying out)
                    Atok!

                              (then slowly relaxing)

238   EXT. BASE OF BATTERING RAM (FULL SIZE SET)
                    FULL SHOT, FAVORING SKAL

                    Most of the men are taking hold of the ropes.

                              Skal (bawling to Slim)
                    We are ready, Outlander!

EXT. BATTERING RAM (PROCESS #2)   87-A
CLOSE SHOT SLIM

exultantly running along top log towards
crater. He starts to beat time.

                    Slim (wildly yelling)
Now heave! - - All together!
              (as the ram starts swinging again)
Bust your gizzards!
              (as the ram starts swinging again)
She's caving in! - -One more! - -Heave! - -Come on!

240   EXT. BASE OF BATTERING RAM (PROCESS) (B.G. IN
           GILLESPIE MIN. FROM UNDERNEATH RAM TOWARDS ROCK)

           FULL SHOT THE RAM CRASHING THROUGH

           A gush of molten lava. Then as the men turn
           and run for safety, a whole section gives way,
           and a flaming flood pours down into the gully.
           Men scramble for safety.

240-X1   EXT. VOLCANIC REGION (PROCESS #3)

           Men running from lava. The frame work of the
           battering-ram begins to collapse under pres-
           sure of lava.

240-X2   EXT. BATTERING RAM (PROCESS)

           The frame of the battering ram begins to fall
           with Slim, carrying him straight down towards
           lava. People in gully scrambling to safety.
           Lava flowing down towards allosauri.

240-X3   EXT. WREAKED BATTERING RAM AND LAVA FLOW
           (PROCESS) FULL SIZE PORTION OF WRECKAGE

           with Slim hanging on, lands in scene.
           B.G., by Gillespie, of rocky region and flow-
           ing lava

241   OUT

242   EXT. WRECKED BATTERING RAM AND LAVA FLOW   87B
               (PROCESS #2) (CONTINUATION OF 240X3)
               (F.G. FULL SIZE LAVA AND LOG)

               Slim scrambles to his feet, balances him-
               self precariously on log. Log begins to ride
               the lava flow towards precipice, below which
               are the allosauri. Log begins to smoke.
               Slim rides it like a lumberjack. He whistles
               shrill for White Eagle.

242-X1   EXT. SLIM RIDING LOG (PROCESS)
               (B.G. BY GILLESPIE) CLOSE UP SLIM'S FACE

               As he tries to keep his balance. He whistles
               again for White Eagle.

242-X2   EXT. WREAKED BATTERING RAM AND LAVA FLOW
               (ANGLE SHOOTING TOWARD BRINK) (GILLESPIE
               MIN. MAN AND WRECKAGE IN LAVA FLOW

               LONG SHOT of Slim riding log in lava flow.
               In b.g. can be seen allousauri charging out
               of cave, with men running to safety.

243   EXT. VOLCANIC REGION (FULL SIZE SET)
               CLOSE SHOT NARU

                         Naru (screaming)
            Slim!

            She runs out of scene.

               THE FOLLOWING SHOTS OF NARU'S
               RESCUE OF SLIM ARE TO BE INTER-
               CUT WITH SLIM RIDING LOG.

243-X1   EXT. VOLCANIC REGION #2 (MIN. PROJ.)

               Naru rushes in and mounts White Eagle, and
               flies off.

243-X2   EXT. NARU ON WHITE EAGLE (PROCESS)
               CLOSE SHOT

               Naru in air, takes lariat from saddle and
               throws it.

243-X3   EXT. BATTERING RAM (PROCESS)   87C
                              LONG SHOT

                              Naru throws lariat. People watching in f,g,

243-X4   EXT. WRECKED BATTERING RAM IN LAVA FLOW
                              (FULL SIZE)

                              Slim grabs lariat, just as he is about to
                              go over falls.

243-X5   EXT. VOLCANIC REGION #2 (MIN. PROJ.)

                              White Eagle and Naru, with Slim hanging
                              from rope. White Eagle gently deposits Slim
                              on ground.

244   EXT. ENTRANCE TO CAVE (MIN. AND ANIMATION)
                              FULL SHOT

                              as the lava starts pouring over the allosauri,
                              and into the cavern.

245   EXT. ENTRANCE TO CAVE AND LAVA (MIN.)

                              Cave completely fills with lava. The fright-
                              ful bellowing of the allosauri is drowned
                              out in the roaring lava.

246   EXT. VOLCANIC REGION (FULL SIZE SET)
                              CLOSEUP SKAL WATCHING

                        Skal (breathless, big-eyed)
He has broken open the earth! It is Einar that
has come back!

PAN HIM, swift and imposing, through the
crowd. Way is made until he comes to Slim
and Naru in each other's arms. He stops,
waits. Raud comes up quickly as though to
interpose. At last Naru sees him, jumps back
from Slim, who prepares for the worst. But
Skal slowly bends forward, and with great
dignity touches the ground at Slim's foot in
an impressive gesture of respect and homage.

                              LAP DISSOLVE:

wearing a long cloak of feathers, and a conical
iron helmet ornamented with a pair of raven
wings. The lines of the wings are enormously
and impressively extended by the carved stone
spread-eagle directly behind. O.s. Haakon's
voice recites to his harp. TRUCK BACK to show
Skal standing at his throne - a big stone block,
set before a huge monolith which bears the
eagle carving. One step below is Haakon.
Continue TRUCKING BACK to reveal Slim and Naru
facing them at the foot of three steps. Slim
is at last completely in Viking costume. Naru
wears white. On her head is a wreath of
flowers, below which her hair hangs unbound.

                    Haakon (as the TRUCK SHOT begins)
Death has he driven / out of the dales
And filled forever / our homes with fruits!

                    Skal (loudly as Haakon ends)
To his face I say it: This is Einar that has come
back to his folk!

                    Haakon (ecstatic, snapping the
                       strings of his harp)
I have sung!

     Continue TRUCKING steadily back to open up a
     magnificent LONG SHOT of the out-door temple-
     like meeting-place of Skal's people. A rough
     circle of fifty evenly spaced monoliths, very
     big, though less than Skal's. Before each one
     sits the Chief of a clan, his own people crowd
     ed around him, warriors seated, and women and
     children standing behind. At the center, con-
     tained by a wide circular curb, blazes a big
     flickering fire, the only light. Outside the
     circle on one side is a straight double row
     of perches, occupied by the eagles of the
     whole tribe. Just beyond, a sheer cliff drops
     away into darkness and distance, above which
     are stars. Women move quietly amoung the crowd
     with jars of mead and baskets of cakes. The
     whole atmosphere is one of solemn festivity.

                    Skal (as the TRUCK SHOT continues)
Vinelander, in quittance of what we owe, have we
a small gift to give - - yet that which our hearts
hold ever the highest: Henceforth to be called
Norseman, speaking by thine own right in the Mote
                    (after an impressive pause)
Beyond this, you shall be known as Earthbreaker,
to rule over all the clans as earl - -
                    (glowering as the crowd murmurs gladly)
- -in that day when I shall be no more!   CONTINUED:

The TRUCK SHOT ends with Skal very small in
perspective. At once there is a roar of
cheering. Mead cups are raised and emptied.

                    Voices (rising above the roar)
Skoal to Slim Earthbreaker! Skoal! Skoal! Skoal!

248   TWO SHOT SLIM AND NARU

She is smiling up at him proudly.

                    Slim (wretched, sheepish, grinning)
Hello, kid.

249   MED. SHOT FAVORING SKAL

                    Skal (watching their preoccupation)
In love, even as in battle, the worthy heeds not
much-speaking.
                    (smiling ruefully in his beard)
Then seethes his heart with the earth-fire.
                    (abruptly turning to Haakon)
Haakon, speak the words that wed.

Skal sits down, arranging his robes. A
stooge hands him a golden cup, holding more
than a quart of mead. A hush falls.

                    Haakon (to Slim as silence falls)
Take now the maiden's hand.
                    (quiet, solemn, as Slim obeys)
From this day out shall ye be no more twain, but
one thing. And in all things one - -as to the hand,
the sword - -and to the wind, the ern - -and to the
heart, the blood. Ye shall have one life, and one
will, and one longing- -
                    (softly)
- -as may the Gods grant you at last also one death!
                    (Then in a loud voice, raising his arms)
Viking! take they bride!

                    On another great roar of friendly cheering- -

250   CLOSE TWO SHOT SLIM AND NARU

He is panicky, but she firmly puts both arms
round his neck, and kisses him. O.s. the
cheering is shaken with laughter.

251   MED. PAN SHOT SLIM AND NARU

running hand in hand toward the eagle perches.
The crowd surges after them, the men laughing
and shouting, the women pelting them with
flowers

Skal is whispering earnestly to the stooge.

253   EXT. WHITE EAGLE AT PRECIPICE OF TEMPLE
(MIN. PROJ.)
MED. SHOT - WHITE EAGLE

perched at the edge of the precipice against
a b.g. of stars. He is saddled for a journey,
and round his shoulders hangs a huge garland
of flowers. Slim and Naru reach him, nearly
mobbed by good-natured well-wishers.

253A   EXT. PRECIPICED OF TEMPLE (FULL SIZE SET)

Raud (pumping Slim's hand)
Now we are in truth one blood!

Atok, a little drunk, and finding the whole
thing enormously comic, gaily pounds Slim's
back, nearly flooring him with each blow.

Atok (in time to his terrible swats)
Earthbreaker! Earthbreaker!

Slim (ready to help Naru up)
Hop up there, kid - -before this gorilla makes a
widow out of you!
(then plaintively to Atok)
Hey! go easy!
Stooge (entering, buttonholing him)
Earthbreaker! - -ere you go - -great Skal is sore
grieved he has not yet heard thy magic box!
(blandly nodding o.s. as Slim's eyes pop)
If you will- -
Slim (a slow burn)
A time like this, and the guy wants a concert!

Naru (grave, hand on his shoulder)
My husband - -you must!

Slim (wildly to Raud)
Hear that? - -my husband!
(with extreme bitterness to Stooge)
O.K., pal!

253B   EXT. WHITE EAGLE AT PRECIPICE OF TEMPLE
(MIN. PROJ.
Snorting with sulkiness, Slim unstraps the
radio from White Eagle, and followed by the
others, starts back. PAN WITH THE GROUP

254   EXT. TEMPLE OF THE GODS (FULL SIZE SET)
FULL SHOT FAVORING SKAL
as Slim enters and sets the radio down.

Skal (eager, but a bit nervous)
So this is the magic box?

244

                    Slim (viciously twisting the dial)
This is the magic Box!

                    Radio (instantly loud, vital)
- -before wireless contact faded out on the whole
region, the enemy air fleet was reported concen-
trating off the Azores- -

                    Slim (dialing a new station)
Sorry! - -guess that don't affect us.

                    Radio (same voice, new station)
All house-holders of the Greater New York area
whose cellars have been officially designated as
"bomb-proof" will conspicuously display the bill-
posters furnished by the mail-carrier- -

                    Slim (frowning, puzzled, dialing)
Must be a practice blackout even at home- -!

                    Radio (same voice, new station)
- -otherwise conform exactly to the safety measures
adopted by the local authorities.

                    Slim (suddenly very startled)
Every station!

                    Radio (continuing)
That's all for the present. - -We now rebroadcast
by transcription yesterday's address.

        The soft noise of a needle on a phonograph
        record. At the first words of the following
        speech Slim grows rigid, bends forward hag-
        gardly, with his face almost against the grill.
        INTERCUT the following with SHOTS of norsemen
        listening, watching Slim as they realize some-
        thing is the matter, exchanging looks, whispers.

                    Radio Voice (rich and familiar)
And in conclusion, The Generalissimo of That Nation
boasts that his bombers will be supplemented by a
ray capable of preventing a single American inter-
ceptor squadron from rising along the Atlantic
Seaboard.
                    (a pause - -then loud and solemn)
This is the answer of the United States to that
ultimatum: By the authority constitutionally
vested in me as Commander-in-Chief of the armed
forces, I hereby proclaim a State of National
Emergency. All branches of the Service will cooperate in repelling any invasion.
                    (another pause - -a crackling of manu
script - -then gentle and intimate)
And to you, the people, let me, my friends, now add
that even though at the beginning of this war we   CONTINUED:

                        Radio Voice (con'd)
may have inflicted upon us actual disasters - -yet
you and I know that in the end we shall find ways
and means - -not to retaliate in kind - -but broadly
to do our full part in defeating once and forever
this brutal, wanton, and unprovoked assault upon
the free peoples of the earth.

            A band breaks into stirring patriotic airs,
            so that when they speak at last, Slim and
            the others have to raise their voices. Slim
            has straightened slowly, his face harsh, his
            eyes far away. Suddenly- -

                        Slim (starting toward White Eagle)
Got to go!

                        Naru (incredulous, stopping him)
Slim! - -my husband!

                        Slim (brushing past)
The Fourth Pursuit Squadron's up the creek!

                        Raud (shocked, spinning him round)
Would you leave your bride?

                        Slim (brought back to earth)
You don't understand - -it's war! My people- -!

            A stir of excitement among those nearest.

                        Voices (calling to the others)
Vineland goes to war!
The evil box hath said it!

            Slim again tries to pass.

                        Raud (indignant, blocking him)
No longer outlander! - -we are now your people!

                        Slim (wryly, doggedly, facing Raud)
That's what I thought- -
            (nodding toward the blaring radio)
- -until something in me heard that!

                        Raud (bitter, scowling)
And the blood oath you and I have sworn- -is that
nothing in thee?

                        Radio (as music breaks off)
All National Guard units of Greater New York will
report immediately at their several- -

            In a spasm of bitterness Raud draws his sword,
            and with three blows silences the radio.
                                        CONTINUED:

                Slim (in the tense silence)
Raud! Raud!--my friends are being attacked!
           (desperately appealing to all)
The bombers are on their way --now! --the Skralings!
And not for a clean fight with our men!--but to
rain down death and fire and disease on a whole
vast defenseless city full of women and children!

A general gasp of astonishment and horror.

255   CLOSE SHOT HAAKON

                Haakon (softly, sternly)
Oh shame!

256   FULL SHOT GROUP ABOUT SLIM

The murmur continues, but no one speaks.

                Slim (turning in desperate appeal)
Naru!
    After a long moment of hesitation--

                Naru (quietly, eyes on Slim's face)
I bid my husband go!

                Raud (as Slim grabs her hands)
And I --I fly with my friend!

                Atok (with a shout)
I am Raud's man by Thor's hammer!--I follow!

One after another Raud's warriors spring up.

                1st (with a yell)
And I!

                2nd
I also!

                3rd
Slim's and Raud's men all!

257   NEW ANGLE LONG SHOT
    as another chief jumps up on his stone chair.

                Chief (bawling)
Who of my clan flies with Raud and the Earthbreaker?

                5th (Chief's man, jumping up)
I!

                                    CONTINUED:

6th

I!

Another Chief (jumping up)
All follow!

The excitement grows to an uproar. Slim
stands bewildered, moved, looking from face
to face.

Voices (rising over the roar)
All follow!   All!   All!

258   NEW ANGLE TO INCLUDE SKAL ON HIS THRONE

Skal (furious, threatening)
I, Skal, speak! - -Yet am I earl, and I say that
you go not! - -no, not one!

The roar grows less assured, starts to sub-
side. As Raud's band faces Skal defiantly- -

Skal (glaring at them)
Would ye break Einar's great oath, sworn of old
time for us and our children?

Haakon (solemnly quoting)
Never to go back to the outland! - -Never to
steer beyond the peaks!

Raud (grim dogged)
Blood is a stronger oath!

Atok (pushing past him)
Haste! the war may be ended!

Raud (defiantly leading on)
Men of my clan - -to the erns!

Slim has stood speechless with surprise and
gratitude, tears in his eyes. But now he
intercepts them with arms outstretched.

Slim (anxious, shrill voiced)
No! - -gang! - -wait! Listen to Skal! - -he's
absolutely right!
          (then quiet, smiling, as they pause)
Do you guys really think I'd lead you into that
kind of fighting! You don't know the odds you'd
be in for - -swords against pom-poms and machine
guns- -!

CONTINUED:

                    Raud (impatient, grabbing his arm)
Thy death is mine!

                    Atok (hooking the other arm)
Enough speaking!

                    The Others (pushing them forward)
Onward!
To the erns- -!
                    Slim (breaking free, desperately)
I tell you it's sure death! Dead erns - - a sky
full - -ridden by devils - -diving, and spitting
fire five miles above the earth- -!

259   MED. CLOSE SHOT SKAL ON HIS THRONE

          Mead cup in hand, he has listened during the
          previous scene, with his eyes growing bigger,
          and bigger. For Slim's last speech he is
          leaning forward, his beard quivering with
          excitement. Suddenly - -

                    Skal (dashing down his cup)
Where is this war?
                    (jumping up roaring, drawing his sword)
By Thor and Odin, we also are a free folk!

          As Slim turns, open-mouthed, astonished - -

260   FULL SHOT THE CROWD

          all now on their feet. Swords are drawn
          and waved, mead cups emptied and thrown away.

                    Atok (in f.g. laughing, shouting)
Great is Slim Earthbreaker!
                    (tossing his battle-axe high in air)
- -he hath taken away our war-play with the Mighty
Ones- -
                    (catching it as it comes down)
- -and now gives us back to fight with devils.

          Suddenly over the tumult - -

                    Naru's Voice (shrill, triumphant)
Look, ye folk!

261   EXT. AURORA AUSTRALIS
          NEW ANGLE LONG SHOT NARU

          perched above the cheering, milling mob on a
          high stone outside the circle. Behind her the
          night sky is filled with the long shaken beams
          of the Aurora Australis. (This must be a shot of
          extreme dramatic beauty and realism.   CONTINUED:

                    Naru (continuing, pointing)
A sign in the sky!

          As the crowd turns with a shout--

262   EXT. TEMPLE OF THE GODS (FULL SIZE SET)
             CLOSEUP HAAKON

             the light flickering on his blind face.

                    Haakon (softly, awed)
The swords!--the swords of Einar!

263   FULL PAN SHOT OVER THE CROWD

             looking off, pointing, brandishing weapons.

                    Voices (above the others)
A sign!
A sign!
The gods call to battle!

          PAN SHOT ends as it picks up Skal on throne.

                    Skal (taking command with a shout)
War-goers only!--Bring weapons and water-flasks!
                    (striding toward the eagles)
Lead on, Slim! We are thy men!

          As the principal group starts almost running
          toward the eagles, and as the rest of the
          mob sweeps after them, BOOM AWAY and UP FROM
          THEM, BACK into an increasingly LONGER SHOT,
          the whole tribe flooding through the flickering
          firelight shadows in the stone circle, and
          rushing for the eagles. Swords are brandished
          battle-axes tossed up.

                    Voices (fainter and fainter)
Skoal to the sword-work!
Skoal to Vineland!
Skoal to the death-goers!
Einar and Eriksen!
Skoal to the Norse way!
Mightly will be the slaying!
Glad are we!

          As the SHOT grows darker, and the noise and
          the scale of the figures swiftly diminish--

                              SLOW FADE OUT:

FADE IN:

264   OUT

265   INT. H.Q. MITCHELL FIELD (PROCESS & STRAIGHT)
             BIG CLOSEUP GOLD EAGLE ON WOODEN COLOR-STAFF

             TRUCK BACK to include the American flag on
             which it perches. PAN INTO FULL SHOT,
             GROUP H.Q. MITCHELL FIELD. Outside the win-
             dows, the field, with planes ready to take
             off. Outside the door an orderly is on duty.
             In the radio room inside, Group Comm. Haslip
             is tensely listening in. The Operator-
             Sergeant hovers respectfully. Presently the
             Group Adjutant enters hastily, face strained,
             eyes sunk, forgetting even to return the
             orderly's salute.

                    Haslip (seeing him, rising)
             Oh - - Adjutant!
                    (handing head-phones to Sergeant)
             Take over - - I'll be here.
                    (controlled, tense, crossing to Adjutant)
             Scouter Flight's swept the whole off-shore area.
             Still no enemy contact- -

                    Adjutant (with an odd bitterness)
             At least that's an hour gained for those mobs
             trying to leave the city.

                    Haslip (eyeing him sharply)
             You have any trouble getting out?

                    Adjutant (reticent, ironical)
             None whatever, sir - - I "comandeered" the Mayor's
             autogyro off the roof of the Municipal Building.

             After a shocked start - -

                    Haslip (quietly, watching him)
             City's a bit - - congested, eh?

                    Adjutant (sickly turning away)
             Just now, sir, New York doesn't bear thinking about.

                    Haslip (disturbed)
             But I understood the Governor's Committee was doing
             wonders!

                    Adjutant (still sneering, bitter)
             Considering our simple democratic faith in never
             being ready, they've done miracles!
                    (with growing restrained excitement)
             - -fifteen per cent of the civilian population
             poured over into Jersey in two days!
                    (as Haslip listens gravely)
             Guns are in battery, and those heart-breaking Fifth

                    Adjutant (continued)
Avenue picnic-busses of school-kids are rolling
through the Holland Tunnel.
                    (his voice cracking)
But for blocks around every General Transport
depot, it's - - it's like Armistice Night!

                    Haslip (with a rueful nod)
I remember.

                    Adjutant (continuing, wry, mocking)
And when you look at the bridges, they seem to
drip!
                    (illustrating with his two hands)
You keep waiting for them to bend in the middle!
                    (then suddenly almost shockingly serious)
Those bombs can't be allowed to fall!

        Halip checks him with a gesture. The Ser-
        geant stands in the doorway, white, dazed.

                    Haslip (turning, brisk)
Well, Sergeant?

                    Sergeant(quiet, breathless)
I - -I've lost contact with the flight, sir.

                    Haslip (starting to explode)
You've- - !
                    (then quiet, studying the man's face)
What do you mean?

                    Sergeant (voice jumping an octave)
Their signal was coming through regular, sir. When
they checked us, I could even hear their motors.
                    (weakly, swallowing)
Then - -everything just went dead!
                    (then impulsively stepping forward)
Colonel! Is the whole First Flight down at sea?

                    Haslip (barking, sending him back)
Get back on it! - - stay with it!

        TRUCK INTO TWO SHOT. HASLIP AND THE ADJUTANT
        looking haggardly into each other's eyes.

                                    DISSOLVE TO:

266   EXT. WASHINGTON BRIDGE (STOCK)

           MONTAGE of all kinds of traffic on a holiday,
           people trying to get out of New York.

                                    DISSOLVE:

266-X1   EXT. WASHINGTON BRIDGE (STOCK) - LONG SHOT

                                    DISSOLVE:

267   FULL SHOT EXT. SECTION OF BRIDGE (NEWCOMBE
                SHOT)

                All lanes jammed, bumper to bumper, with
                stalled Jersey-bound traffic. A steady
                blare of horns. Squeezing from car to
                car, New York cops and helmeted National
                Guardsmen are trying to bring order to
                the chaos of pathetic and fantastic
                refugee salvage.

268   EXT. WASHINGTON BRIDGE (FULL SIZE SET)
                CLOSE PAN SHOT A COP

                sweeping down on a big limousine, whose
                chauffeur is steadily giving it the horn.

                        Cop
                (knocking the man's hand aside)
                Whaddya think this is - -Halloween?
                        (then as the car ahead advance
                        a yard)
                Come on! - -git it along!

269   CLOSE PAN SHOT NATIONAL GUARDSMAN

                stopping beside a rather shabby sedan.

                        Guardsman
                        (swinging his arm)
                Close it up here! - -close it up!

270   CLOSE SHOT A LITTLE GIRL

                her leg in a brace, lying in a broken-
                down station wagon, holding a parrot
                cage.

                        Little Girl (thrilled, whispering)
                Maybe when we get to the country I'll let you out
                for a little while.

                        Parrot (genially)
                Swing it, babe!

                                    WIPE TO:

INT. LAVEROCK'S OFFICE
CLOSE SHOT LAVEROCK AT OFFICE WINDOW

> Laverock (indignantly looking out)
> Right in the middle of the week! Right in the
> middle of the week! --Planes! Bombs! Guns!
> --Fantastic! --How am I going to do any business
> with a war on my hands!

PAN TO INCLUDE PETTY ducking in at the outer
door, and trying to duck out again unseen.

> Laverock (turning, catching him)
> Petty! order the office staff up to the roof --I
> want The Sign stored in the cellar--!
> (then heroically changing his mind)
> No! --not that! --never! --Second thought, get a
> hundred thousand sand-bags --pack 'em all around
> the whole contraption--!

As bitter tears spring into Petty's eyes--

WIPE TO:

271-X1   EXT. N.Y. STREET TRAFFIC (THREE SHOTS)
               (BLARE OF HORNS)

271-X2   EXT. WASHINGTON BRIDGE

               CLOSE SHOT of people on bridge. (Blare of
               horns)

272   EXT. WASHINGTON BRIDGE (NEWCOMBE SHOT)

               FULL SHOT TRAFFIC JAM ON BRIDGE

               the horns are still a solid blare. Suddenly
               the sound stops dead. A moment of absolute
               silence.

272-X1   CLOSER SHOT

               smaller group of traffic. Heads begin to
               pop out, look upward, straining doubtfully
               to listen. There comes o.s. very faint,
               continuous, sinister, a modulated electric
               whine.

of startled people reacting to stopping
of motors and horns.

272-X3   CLOSE SHOT

Small group of traffic on bridge. As
isolated voices begin to call out, ZOOM
in to a CLOSE SHOT of a big open truck
crowded with standing occupants. The driver
climbs down, grinning grimly.

                 Driver (fumbling for a cigarette)
Brothers and sisters - -this is IT!

273   CLOSE PAN SHOT ANOTHER COP

                 Cop (bawling in the grip of habit)
Git it along! - -git it along! - -git it along!

As he realizes his own futility, and stops- -

                 Driver (leaning out, confidential)
Motor's dead.

                 Voices (o.s., shouting)
Juice's off!
Lights! - -everything!

274-278   OUT

278-X1   EXT, N Y. STREETS

SHOTS of panic on streets. People getting
out of cars and running in a mad scramble,
looking up at sky, which is heavily clouded.
Above the panic is heard shouts:

                 Voices (shouting)
It's come!
They've come!
Our planes won't be able to get up!
Let's get out of here!
Hurry!
Hurry!

2780X4   EXT, WASHINGTON STREET BRIDGE
278-X5

SHOTS of panic. People getting out of cars
and running in a mad scramble, looking up
at sky, which is heavily clouded. Above
the panic, shouts:

                               CONTINUED:

                         Voices (shouting)
Let's get out of here!
They're here!
They've got it!
Hurry!

279   INT. H.Q. MITCHELL FIELD
                         CLOSEUP RADIO IN GROUP H.Q.

                         Sergeant (hoarse, turning)
                         to CAMERA, fussing with dials)
Everything's dead! Can't receive! Can't send!

                    TRUCK SWIFTLY BACK INTO A FULL SHOT AT
                    GROUP H.Q. HASLIP frowning in the doorway--

                         Haslip (turning to Adjutant)
Send out the Second Flight!--I must have information!

                    The Adjutant jumps down the steps, runs to
                    the waiting side-car.

                         Sergeant
                         (desperately attempting to start it)
The magneto doesn't work!

                    The Adjutant doesn't answer, but runs
                    past CAMERA.

                         Adjutant (shouting)
Second Flight!--off-shore patrol!

                    FAST DOLLY TO CLOSE UP Haslip at the window.

                         Haslip
Come on, Second Flight! Come on, Second Flight

281   OUT

282   EXT. MITCHELL FIELD
                         FULL SHOT THE LEAD-PLANE SECOND FLIGHT

                    Adjutant runs in, desperately yelling.

                         Adjutant
Take off with your flight, Captain Lang.--Off
shore patrol!

                                          CONTINUED:

Captain Lang jumps out of his plane.

                    Lang
My ship's dead!
          (calling to the ground crew)
Boys! wheel me out of the way!

Major Aving enters Shot.

                    Aving (grim, grabbing him)
Keep your ship in formation! - - stay in it!
          (quiet, grim)
You're not the only one, Lang. Every motor on
this field is dead.

Far above the clouds is heard a whine and
an ominous crackling. They all look up.

283   MED. SHOT TWO PLANES IN FORMATION

                    1st Pilot (head out, listening)
So they really got what it's going to take!

                    2nd Pilot
          (bitterly pressing starter)
And were we getting good!

As both look slowly up into the sky - -

284   EXT. DIRIGIBLE IN CLOUDS

A monster dirigible moves through the clouds
preceded by flashes as though of lightning.
The whine increases. On the belly of the
ship the source of the whine becomes visible
- -a sparkling, pulsing point of radiation.

285   EXT. ANTI-AIRCRAFT BATTERY MED. SHOT

Guns and crew look formidable and efficient.

                    1st Soldier (quietly to Commander)
Range-finder's out, sir.

                    2nd (calling from the truck)
No juice at all!

                    3rd (spitting on the ground)
Can't even move the guns!
          As the Battery Commander takes it, turns - -

286-X1   EXT. DIRIGIBLE IN CLOUDS (MIN.)

                    The Dirigible noses its way up through the
                    roof of clouds.

                                        DISSOLVE:

287   INT. DIRIGIBLE ABOVE CLOUDS (MIN.)

                    Its design is new, impressive, and enormous.
                    It's motors are idling.

288   INT. DIRIGIBLE CONTROL CABINET - MED. SHOT

                    The Commandant is grizzled, short-bearded,
                    tough, while his first and second officers
                    are younger and starchier. Non-commissioned
                    officers woodenly stand at various control
                    instruments. The uniforms are of a
                    peculiar design which suggest no known
                    nationality.

                              Commandant (into speaking-tube)
                    There! - - now hold her to the wind.
                              (placidly taking out his watch)
                    In twenty-seven minutes our bombers arrive.

                              1st Officer (looking down outside)
                    Undisciplined fools!

                              2nd Officer (young, self-conscious)
                    But what a romantic panorama!

289   INT. DIRIGIBLE CONTROL CABIN - (PROCESS)

                    In the b.g., seen through a hole in the
                    clouds, is the N.Y. harbor. (SHOOTING
                    over man's shoulder.)

290   INT. DIRIGIBLE CONTROL CABIN - MED. SHOT

                    The three officers are looking down,
                    brooding.

                              Commandant (nodding, with a sigh)
                    It is a great pity.

                              1st Officer (bristling, suspicious)
                    Sir. You pity a people which does not obey our
                    Generalissimo?!
                                        CONTINUED:

                         Commandant (weary, shrugging)
I'm only thinking what a city for plunder.

                         2nd Officer
                         (grinning oafishly)
That will come later - -after our Generalissimo
accepts their submission!

        Suddenly one of the non-coms at the window
        gives a muffled exclamation.

                         Non-Com
                         (turning, pointing o.s.)
Sir!

        As they turn, raise their glasses in unison - -

290-X1   INT. CONTROL CABIN (PROCESS & STRAIGHT)

        SHOOTING OVER backs of officers. Tiny specks
        can be seen in the distant sky.

                         1st Officer
                         (dismayed, incredulous)
Pursuit ships! - - still in the air!

                         Commandant
                         (into speaking-tube)
Ray nacelle! - - more emission!

291   INT. DIRIGIBLE RAY CABIN - FLASH FULL SHOT

        packed with weird machinery. The electric
        whine which continued even in the sound-
        proof control cabin, is here loud and
        intolerable. As a quiet crew, wearing
        helmets, and ray-proof armor, make adjust-
        ments, the sound becomes shattering, the
        shot is diffused with milky light.

292   INT. DIRIGIBLE CONTROL CABIN (PROCESS &
        STRAIGHT) MED. SHOT

                         2nd Officer
                         (shakily staring o.s.)
No effect! - - Do these people think to come against
us with gliders?

                         CONTINUED:

                    1st Officer (stiff, contemptuous)
Gliders!? - - See! The wings flap - - like birds!
              (oddly stirred, poetical)
- - like great eagles!

                    Commandant (quietly into tube)
Landing deck! - - send out interceptors.

293   INT. DIRIGIBLE CONTROL ROOM (B.G. ANIMATION)

               Skal's eagles, advancing in a huge, loose
               formation, White Eagle a gleaming speck at
               their head.

294   EXT. WHITE EAGLE (PROCESS)
               (PROJ. B.G.)

               FULL SHOT Slim, Skal, Raud and Atok, mounted.
               Suddenly Slim leans forward and points o.s.

295   EXT. THE DIRIGIBLE ABOVE CLOUDS
               (O'BRIEN MIN. AND ANIMATION)

               HIGH ANGLE - EXTREME LONG SHOT

295-A   EXT. DIRIGIBLE ABOVE CLOUDS
               (O'BRIEN MIN. AND ANIMATION) HIGH ANGLE

               CLOSER SHOT. The whole upper surface is a
               landing deck, which at the forward end runs
               into a hanger set into the hull. As inter-
               ceptor planes are run out, take off, and
               quickly come into formation between the
               dirigible and CAMERA.

296   EXT. WHITE EAGLE (PROCESS)

               CLOSE SHOT over Slim's shoulder, shooting
               toward dirigible and approaching planes.
               Slim peels off and starts diving.

296-A   EXT. WHITE EAGLE - (PROCESS)

               Portion of full size eagle. ZOOM SHOT behind
               Slim, using dirigible and plane as b.g.

296-B   INT. COCKPIT (PROCESS)

SHOT over pilot's shoulder. White Eagle
diving on him.

297   EXT. DIRIGIBLE ABOVE CLOUDS (O'BRIEN MIN)
MED. LONG SHOT

Slim and White Eagle in power dive. White
Eagle strikes plane, rips off tail surfaces.
Plane falls out of shot.

297-A   INT. CONTROL CABIN (PROCESS)

Dog fight between eagles and planes outside
dirigible.

297-B   EXT. DIRIGIBLE ABOVE CLOUDS (O'BRIEN MIN)
MED. LONG SHOT

SHOT eagles and planes fight by dirigible.

297-C   INT. DIRIGIBLE CONTROL CABIN (PROCESS)

Eagles and planes streak by windows of
dirigible. Dog fight between planes and
eagles.

297-C-1   INT. MACHINE GUN NEST (PROCESS)

SHOT of machine gun nest on dirigible.
Gunners shooting at eagles. One or two
eagles are hit, and fall.

297-C-2   INT. MACHINE GUN NEST ON DIRIGIBLE

REVERSE SHOT into faces of machine gunners.

297-D   EXT. DIRIGIBLE ABOVE CLOUDS
(O'BRIEN MIN. & ANIMATION)

General dog fight between birds and planes.
Eagles being shot down. Planes being
disabled and going down.

| 297-E | EXT. DOG FIGHT IN CLOUDS (MIN.) | 107 |

| 297-E-1 | INT. COCKPIT OF PLANE (PROCESS) |

CLOSE SHOT on pilot's face, with eagle
and rider on tail of plane.

| 297-E-2 | EXT. DOG FIGHT BREAKING THROUGH CLOUDS
(ANIMATION) |

SHOOTING from behind, eagle pursuing plane
down through clouds in steep dive.

| 297-F | EXT. WASHINGTON ST. BRIDGE (PROCESS) |

People looking up at clouds. Planes and
eagles dive out of clouds in dog fight.

| 298 | EXT. ATOK'S EAGLE (PROCESS)
(PORTION OF FULL SIZE EAGLE) |

CLOSE SHOT on Atok's face, as he dives after
plane.

| 298-A | EXT. DOG FIGHT BREAKING THROUGH CLOUDS
(ANIMATION) |

SHOOTING from behind, eagle pursuing plane
as they break through clouds.

| 298-B | EXT. DOG FIGHT OVER N.Y. (O'BRIEN MIN.) |

TRAVEL SHOT over New York.
Atok jumps from eagle to top of plane
smashes cowling.

| 299 | INT. COCKPIT OF PLANE (PROCESS) |

CLOSE UP Atok jumps into cockpit, grabs
pilot, overpowers him, and throws him
overboard.

| 300 | LONG SHOT - CAMERA SHOOTING STRAIGHT
DOWN OVER NEW YORK CITY |

Pilot falling away from CAMERA

INT. COCKPIT OF PLANE (PROCESS)

> Eagle's feet and wings, with trailing rope,
> come into picture. Atok grabs rope, and
> is lifted out of plane.

302   EXT. DOG FIGHT OVER NEW YORK (O'BRIEN MIN.)

> TRAVEL SHOT. Atok hanging on rope, is
> carried out of picture. Plane spins down
> out of SHOT.

303   EXT. DOG FIGHT OVER NEW YORK (O'BRIEN MIN.
> #2)

> White Eagle pursuing plane out of picture,
> towards CAMERA.

304   INT. LAVEROCK'S OFFICE (PROCESS)

> MED. SHOT - Laverock at window, with
> binoculars. In b.g. Petty impatiently
> waits his turn.

>   Laverock (whooping, exultant)
> See him up there? - - see him? That's my boy!
> Got him under contract! Got him under contract!

305   EXT. DOG FIGHT OVER NEW YORK (O'BRIEN MIN #3)

> White Eagle strikes wing of plane and rips
> it off. Plane falls.

306   EXT. DOG FIGHT OVER NEW YORK (O'BRIEN MIN.#2)

> A wounded eagle flutters helplessly. As the
> plane wheels and dives on him, the eagle
> falls and disappears between buildings.

307   EXT. NEW YORK STREET (MIN. PROJ.)

> Wounded eagle with dead Vikings lands in
> crowded street.

The only existing Duncan Gleason artwork depicting a scene from the climactic aerial battle in War Eagles.
Image courtesy of the Duncan Gleason Archives.

307-A   EXT. DOG FIGHT OVER NEW YORK
307-B   (PROCESS & ANIMATION & MIN. PROJ.)
307-C

General dog fighting over New York.

307-D   EXT. MITCHELL FIELD (PROCESS) FULL SHOT

crowded with planes. Pilots staring up,
desperate, furious, a few exhausted
mechanics futilely spinning propellers.

            Pilot's Voices (irritably o.s.)
Contact! Contact!   Contact!

Mechanics desperate, sweating, indicate
"no soap", either in dialogue or otherwise.

308   EXT. DIRIGIBLE ABOVE CLOUDS (O'BRIEN MIN. #3)

Slim and three other eagles are in a dog fight
with plane. They finish off plane, and Slim
gestures with his arm, and flies up. The
three other riders follow him. They all rise
out of scene.

309   EXT. DIRIGIBLE ABOVE CLOUDS (O'BRIEN #2)
            DIRIGIBLE in b.g.

Slim and his group appear above clouds. A
dog fight is till going on. Slim, unaware
of his danger, suddenly has a plane on his
tail. As birds and plane recede from CAMERA,
Naru's eagle appears, banks in front of
CAMERA, and follows plane. Naru is fitting
an arrow to her bow.

310   EXT. NARU'S EAGLE (FULL SIZE EAGLE) (PROCESS,
            ANIMATED B.G.)

CLOSE UP - Naru, fitting arrow to her bow
B.g. action, birds   circling.

311   INT. COCKPIT PLANE (PROCESS)

Pilot brings his sights to bear on White
Eagle from above and behind.

EXT. COCKPIT OF PLANE (PROCESS)

CAMERA SHOOTING INTO PILOT'S FACE, as he
aims machine gun. Naru on her eagle is
in b.g. She shoots arrows. Pilot is
hit and slumps forward over the stick.
Plane starts to fall.

313   EXT. DIRIGIBLE ABOVE CLOUDS (O'BRIEN MIN.#2)

Plane falls, as Slim and his group go on
toward DIRIGIBLE. Naru wheels her eagle up
out of scene.

314   EXT. WHITE EAGLE (PROCESS)

ClOSE SHOT Slim, waving eagles on to
attack. (Other eagles in b.g.)

315   EXT. SKAL'S EAGLE (PROCESS) (FULL SIZE EAGLE)

Skal, fixing spear for charge.
(Eagles in b.g.)

316   EXT. RAUD'S EAGLE (PROCESS) (FULL SIZE EAGLE)

Raud, fixing spear for charge.

317   EXT. ATOK'S EAGLE (PROCESS) (FULL SIZE EAGLE)

Atok, fixing spear for charge.

318   EXT. ATOK'S EAGLE (PROCESS)

Atok on eagle in f.g. Ahead of him, Slim,
Raud and Skal, White Eagle in lead dives
at DIRIGIBLE. White Eagles strikes and
tears of cover of machine gun nest with
claws, and zooms off. Other three eagles
dive down, hurl spears, zoom up after White
Eagle.

319   INT. MACHINE GUN NEST (PROCESS)

Birds in b.g. making a turn. Machine gunner
is killed by spear. Another gunner lies dead
                              CONTINUED:

with spear though him. A machine gunner
aims at eagles in b.g. Eagle and rider
are hit. Rider falls off and falls out
of picture.

320   EXT. DIRIGIBLE ABOVE CLOUDS (O'BRIEN MIN. #2)

Eagles banking sharply above DIRIGIBLE.
They start diving. Two of the men have
dropped from their eagles and are hanging
on ropes.

321   EXT. WHITE EAGLE (PROCESS)

CLOSE SHOT - Slim, securing rope and swinging off eagle.

322   EXT. ATOK'S EAGLE (PROCESS)

Three riders in front dive at DIRIGIBLE.
Slim is swinging on rope from White Eagle
Machine gunners firing.

323   INT. MACHINE GUN NEST (PROCESS)

Slim swings in on rope. Lands on back of
machine gunner, and goes to work with his
sword, in a desperate fight. He is out-
numbered, and is about to be overpowered,
when Atok drops in from rope.

324   EXT. DIRIGIBLE ABOVE CLOUDS (O'BRIEN MIN.#2)

Men dropping off ropes into machine gun nest.

325   INT. MACHINE GUN NEST (PROCESS)

Atok finishes off gunner, throws him
over side.

326   EXT. MACHINE GUN NEST AND SIDE OF DIRIGIBLE
             (FULL SIZE SET)

Man thrown over side of nest, rolls down toward CAMERA

327   LONG SHOT - SHOOTING STRAIGHT DOWN,   112

                       as machine gunner falls away from CAMERA.

328   INT. MACHINE GUN NEST (PROCESS)

                       Another gunner thrown over side.

329   EXT. MACHINE GUN NEST AND SIDE OF DIRIGIBLE
                       (FULL SIZE SET)

                       Man thrown out of nest, rolls down toward
                       CAMERA.

330   LONG SHOT - SHOOTING STRAIGHT DOWN,

                       as machine gunner falls away from CAMERA.

331   INT. MACHINE GUN NEST (PROCESS)

                       Another man being thrown over side.

332   EXT. MACHINE GUN NEST AND SIDE OF DIRIGIBLE
                       (FULL SIZE SET)

                       Man thrown out of nest, rolls down toward
                       CAMERA

333   LONG SHOT - SHOOTING STRAIGHT DOWN,

                       as machine gunner falls away from CAMERA.

334   INT. MACHINE GUN NEST (PROCESS)

                       Slim struggles with gun.

                                    Slim
                       Can't be dismounted - -!

                       Sees trap door. Jerks it open. He jumps
                       down, followed by Vikings

Slim, followed by Vikings, comes down
spiral stairway (or ladder). As they
reach the floor, from a rear door of
hangar, three of the enemy appear with
a Tommy gun. They open fire. One of
Slim's men drops. The Vikings pull
back into cover. Skal comes bounding
down stairway, and is hit by machine gun
bullet. Slim and Atok rescue him.

> Skal
> (grunting in pain)
> Skilled are the Skralings!
> (then gravely looking at Slim)
> Slim - - you will be earl - -

> Slim
> (anxious, holding Skal)
> You're O.K. Skal - - lie low.
> (glancing toward enemy)
> We'll pick you up on our way back.

> Skal
> (incredulous, sitting up)
> Back!?

> Slim (quietly)
> It's got to be done.

With sudden sly strength, Skal grabs his
own axe and Atok's.

> Skal (jumping up)
> Watch over the folk - - !

336   REVERSE ANGLE - LONG SHOT FROM BEHIND
               MAN WITH GUN

Holding the broad axe-blades over his body
Skal lumberingly charges. He is hit repeatedly, but the ringing axe-blades delay
his being shot to pieces. As he reaches
them, he is practically shot to pieces,
but grabs the two gunners and falls in
death hold.

337   FULL SHOT - SLIM'S GROUP

The enemy with Tommy guns has just reached
his knees, and is getting ready to aim
gun, when Atok grabs him and slings him out
through porthole, gun and all. Slim dives
after the three soldiers.

Through the ship's vitals. In the b.g.
glimpses of cat-walks among globular balloon-
ettes, two or three crew-members taking to
their heels. Slim, Atok, Raud and the others
pound down after the fleeing soldiers.

                    Soldier
               (yelling wildly as he runs)
Captain! - Captain - - the enemy has taken the ship!

At the bottom, he darts down the short
passage to the control cabin.

                    1st Officer (in doorway)
In here, you fool!
               (as the man ducks inside)
They can do nothing now!!!

As the doors slams in Slim's face, Raud's
spear flashes over his shoulder. It rings
against the door, and rebounds harmless.

                    Slim (disconcerted)
Duralumin doors!

                    Raud
               (calling his men)
Axes here!

The whine of the ray is now loud behind
them.

                    Slim (checking Raud)
It's the ray we're after.
               (posting men at the control cabin door)
Anybody sticks his head out, you four do your
stuff.

He turns, leads Raud and Atok down the
passage. At the other end is a second door,
slightly ajar. The blinding light of the
ray comes through. The door is closing slowly.

                    Slim
               (wildly starting forward)
Come on!
               (checking, bitter, as the door clangs to)
Clever people these Skralings

339   INT. RAY CABIN - FULL SET

Out of the small loudspeaker in the ceiling:

                              CONTINUED:

                    Commandant's Voice
Ray nacelle! - - Disregard enemy boarders and maintain emission at all costs.

340   FULL SHOT - THE PASSAGE

             Slim, listening at the metal speaking-tube
             which connects control and ray cabin.

                    Commandant's Voice
Our bombers are now nearing the Atlantic coast.
                    (suddenly louder, as Slim hacks through
                    the speaking-tube with his sword)
Stay tuned with their motor frequencies for 20
minutes longer, and the battle of New York has
been won!

                    Slim
                    (fiercely anxious)
Axes! - - Get through that door.

             Raud and Atok rain ringing blows which
             hardly dent the metal surface. As they
             give up, look anxiously at each other, a
             small peep-hole opens, and a grenade drops
             through.

                    Slim (dully as it fumes)
Gas! - - we're cooked!
                    (as all begin coughing, strangling)
Come on - - ! Get out of here!
                    (coming to life, calling his sentries)
Up those stairs everybody! - -maybe we'll have
time to slash up some of the baloonettes - - !

             As the others start up the stair, he is
             taken with a paroxysm of coughing, braces
             himself on a third door handle. It opens
             inward. He peers in with streaming eyes.

341   INT. SHIPS BOMB ROOM

             Rack after rack of big demolition bombs.
             Slim struggles to lift one. It is beyond
             his strength. Coughing, Raud joins him,
             but cramped together, the can only rock
             it. Slim looks from Raud to Atok.

                    Slim (strangling, but smiling)
Well - - glad to have metten you both.
                    (drawing his sword)
Batter up!
                                   CONTINUED:

As Slim is about to strike the detonator
with the hilt, Atok casually taps his
shoulder.

>   Atok
>   (gagging, indicating bomb)
> You want this?

>   Slim
>   (staggering aside)
> Plenty!

With a gigantic effort Atok lifts the huge
capsule onto his shoulder.

342   THE PASSAGE - BOOM AFTER THEM

as they stumble and stagger into the passage,
up the awkward stair, Raud and Slim anxiously
boosting from below. Half way up the stair,
they leave the gas behind.

>   Atok
>   (gasping, pausing)
> Rest Now!

>   Slim
>   (squawking, as Atok prepares to
>   set the bomb down, detonator first)
> Don't set it on its nose!

The whole party boosting from behind, Atok
completes the ascent in a staggering rush.

343   FULL SHOT INT. DIRIGIBLE RAMP (PROCESS)

Slim and group walking away from CAMERA
with bomb. Eagles in b.g. Naru's eagle
lands. She jumps off, Group continues
toward eagles. Naru runs up to Slim from
side of set.

>   Naru
> Slim! -- More come! -- Many of them!

>   Slim
> It's their bombers!

344   EXT. DIRIGIBLE RAMP (MIN. PROJ.)

Slim runs quickly around and mounts
White Eagle.   CONTINUED:

Slim
(quickly to Atok)
Now, muscles - - let's have that baby!

345   INT. DIRIGIBLE RAMP (REVERSE SHOT)
             (PORTION OF FULL SIZE EAGLE)

             Slim and eagle in immediate f.g. As Atok
             heaves the bomb across Slim's thighs, White
             Eagle sags, visibly braces himself.

                         Slim
                    (cursing, balancing the bomb)
             O.K. all of you - - get clear! Fast!
                    (then gently, affectionately to White
                    Eagle)
             Take off, big feller! If you ever flew - -!

             White Eagle starts to turn toward CAMERA.

346   EXT. DIRIGIBLE RAMP (PROCESS) FULL PAN SHOT

             White Eagle running heavily down the deck
             under his tremendous load, the group watch-
             ing anxiously. At the take-off he still
             lacks flying speed, at once starts to lose
             altitude.

347   EXT. WHITE EAGLE (PROCESS)

             CLOSE SHOT - Slim on White Eagle, the
             DIRIGIBLE visible above and behind. The
             other eagles taking off from ramp.

                         Slim
                    (desperate, urging)
             Up! UP! - - come on!

348   EXT. DIRIGIBLE ABOVE CLOUDS (O'BRIEN MIN #2)

             White Eagle circling desperately, just
             holding his own.

348-A   EXT. WHITE EAGLE (PROCESS) CLOSE SHOT

                         Slim
                    (pleading, urging)
             Up! - - Big Feller, you got to get up!

EXT. DIRIGIBLE ABOVE CLOUDS (O'BRIEN MIN. #2)   118

FULL SHOT - White Eagle beating painfully
above the dirigible.

350   EXT. WHITE EAGLE (PROCESS)

CLOSE SHOT - Slim on White Eagle, slowly
tumbling the bomb off. Bomb drops from
SHOT.

351   EXT. DIRIGIBLE (MIN.)

The bomb falls down from CAMERA toward
DIRIGIBLE. It strikes the deck. Almost
instantly there is a tremendous explosion
and the DIRIGIBLE bursts into flame.

352   EXT. BOMBERS (STOCK SHOTS)

EXTREME LONG SHOT - THE APPROACHING BOMBERS

SWIFT LAP DISSOLVE:

353   INT. BOMBER CABIN (PROCESS)

MED. SHOT - the horrified pilots watch the
long flaming fall of the DIRIGIBLE FAR
ahead.

                    Chief Pilot (at last, firmly)
They are too late! We still bomb them!

354   EXT. BEDLOW ISLAND (MIN. PROJ.)

LONG SHOT - the DIRIGIBLE still falling.
As it strikes the ocean, there is an explosion like a super bolt of lightning.

355   EXT. MITCHELL FIELD (STOCK SHOT)

FULL SHOT - a single overpowering roar of
motors. Pilots visible cheering as they
take off.

LAP DISSOLVE:

356   INT. BOMBER CABIN (PROCESS)

MED. SHOT - in leading bomber, showing
                                   CONTINUED:

attacking bombers in b.g. Again the pilots
tensely point forward.

357   NEW YORK SKY LINE (MIN.)

LONG SHOT - Bombers in f.g. B.g. full of
American pursuit planes, coming toward
CAMERA. The bombers bank in f.g. and turn
off in retreat, as the American ships sweep
forward in overpowering numbers.

358   EXT. STATUE OF LIBERTY (MIN. PROJ)

FULL SHOT - Perched on its shoulder is
White Eagle, Slim and Naru beside him.
Above, the circling, screaming eagles, and
behind a magnificent sky of broken clouds.
o.s. a huge roar of motors. The American
pursuit ships flash through, squadron after
squadron, headed out to sea. Suddenly the
last flight has swept past. As the thunder
of motors diminishes, and the steady victory
roar of New York City, punctuated by steamer
sirens, becomes audible below, BOOM INTO
A CLOSER SHOT.

Slim stands beside White Eagle, one arm
around Naru, the other raised after the
planes. BOOM into a big magnificent
CLOSEUP WHITE EAGLE, as he screams in
triumph, and wildly beats his great
shining wings.

                                        FADE OUT:

                     THE END

Post-script: Crash and Recovery

"Oh, I had a very big project called War Eagles, which I would have produced if I hadn't gone back to war. But it was a kind of King Kong type of picture and I thought I had a brilliant, BRILLIANT idea and script and I did a test reel on it which was just great. But self-evidently I couldn't go to war and make this picture because this was a picture that would take me at least two years to make..."

—Merian C. Cooper, From an audio interview with Rudy Behlmer, circa 1965.

The monument to the September Veterans of 1939, near Krakow, Poland. Merian C. Cooper's beloved White Eagle presides. Image courtesy of Mark A. Wilson.

The quote above is the only public statement ever given by Merian Cooper about the fate of *War Eagles* and it can hardly be disputed. Although sporadic work on the script continued into the next year, and a final reader's report was issued on July 24, 1940, the German invasion of Poland on September 9, 1939 is the traditionally accepted date of the project's demise. Cooper did not reenlist in the Army Air Corps immediately, but he had been expecting full war to break out in Europe since 1937 and had begun divesting himself of business ties to aircraft manufacture ever since. He did not want to be perceived as a war profiteer, especially when he knew for certain that when the fighting started, he would definitely be involved. His nature would never have allowed otherwise.

It must have been the fulfillment of a personal prophetic nightmare for Coop, since the two invading forces—first Germany, and then, a week later, Soviet Russia—overran his beloved Poland simultaneously. He had fought both countries before, and had been shot down and imprisoned by both as well. When the Nazi's unleashed *blitzkrieg* on Poland, nearly 200, 000 fell attempting to defend their country. The villains, thinly masked in the *War Eagles* screenplay, and beginning the rout of Europe in real life, turned out to be the same.

Cooper became a bombing logistics planner, served as Claire Chenault's Chief of Staff, and saw action throughout the war, eventually retiring from service as a brigadier general. He returned to his twin loves of aviation and motion pictures, and worked with his *Kong* collaborators and their young associate Ray Harryhausen one last time on *Mighty Joe Young*, released in 1949. Throughout the 1950's Cooper produced a string of hits with director John Ford, including *The Quiet Man* and *The Searchers*. Ever the cinematic innovator, he became one of the major investors and promoters of Cinerama, the super-widescreen process that was briefly embraced by the movie industry in its war with television. Naturally, Coop took to it because it was bigger than anything anyone had ever seen. He died on April 21, 1973.

Willis O'Brien was past service age when war broke out and remained in Hollywood. He returned to RKO, partnered with Marcel Delgado, Jack Shaw and scripter Harold Lamb to create *Gwangi*, an ambitious tale of a Wild West Show that attempts to capture an allosaurus found living in a lost valley with other prehistoric denizens. Over $50, 000 was spent developing it, but it suffered the same fate as *War Eagles*, as budget restraints and shaky support from the studio took their eventual toll. Without Cooper in place as the 'bulldozer" it had no chance. Obie worked sporadically afterwards, always waiting for the producers to come calling, but found his elaborate, meticulous methods rarely called for and rapidly becoming obsolete. Whenever Ray Harryhausen could collaborate with him, they did, as on the prehistoric sequences of 1956's *Animal World*. Obie passed away on November 8, 1962, while working on stop-motion sequences for *It's a Mad, Mad, Mad Mad World*.

Ray Harryhausen spent the war years serving in the Army Signal Corps, working on Frank Capra's *Why We Fight* series and producing stop-motion animated instructional films for the service. One of his frequent collaborators was Theodor Geisel, better know now as Dr. Suess. Ater the war, he became Obie's assistant on *Mighty Joe Young* and

276

eventually enjoyed the long, successful career that had eluded his childhood hero. Among the many legendary pictures in his canon is 1969's *The Valley of Gwangi*, in which Ray not only resurrected one of the lost dreams of Willis O'Brien, but finally managed to get an image from *War Eagles* onto the screen as well.

At long last, an allosaurus is confined a very familiar-looking wooden cart in the 1969 production The Valley of Gwangi. *From the author's collection*

Harryhausen eventually went on to be the undisputed Dean of special effects artists and continued to work with stop-motion animation as his specialty through his last feature film, MGM's *Clash of the Titans*, in 1981. He celebrated his 90th birthday on June 29, 2010.

Echoes of *War Eagles* found their way into various productions over the years, most directly in Universal's 1957 adventure *The Land Unknown*. A naval Antarctic expedition's helicopter is forced down into a lost, volcanic valley by a huge pterodactyl, where they discover a thriving prehistoric world and a survivor of a previous expedition. No Vikings or giant eagles appear in the script, but it all seems *very* familiar, and the film's producer William Alland made a revealing statement about the production to interviewer Tom Weaver in his book *Monsters, Mutants and Heavenly Creatures*:

"He (production department head Jim Pratt) got hold of this script which was originally written by an old timer who had been involved with the making of King Kong. *It was an old-fashioned, tired script. I should have refused to do it, but I didn't; I never refused to do anything. So I then took it on."*

Titles as diverse as Disney's *The Island at the Top of the World"* to *Sky Captain and the World of Tomorrow* (whose creators have shown recent interest in reviving the *War Eagles* concept) all exhibit similar themes and visuals, though not so obviously cribbed as those found in *The Land Unknown*. Even James Cameron's hugely successful *Avatar* is a cousin of sorts, though the action has been transferred to a distant time and planet.

A good story never dies.

And bodies sometimes don't stay buried.

Eagle model armatures began to reappear, beginning with the unearthing of a trunk in the 1970's. Pete Peterson had been one of Obie's primary animators and a small group of young effects pros—ILM's Dennis Muren and Dave Allen among them—tracked down some of the late Peterson's belongings that were on the verge of being thrown away. There, among the remains of many of Obie's creations, was a complete war eagle. It later found its way into the collection of Jim Danforth, and now resides with movie memorabilia expert Ronald V. Borst. I had the opportunity to examine it in 2006, and it is a beautifully-crafted piece of engineering, and also quite a bit smaller than often reported, standing slightly less than 12 inches high when extended.

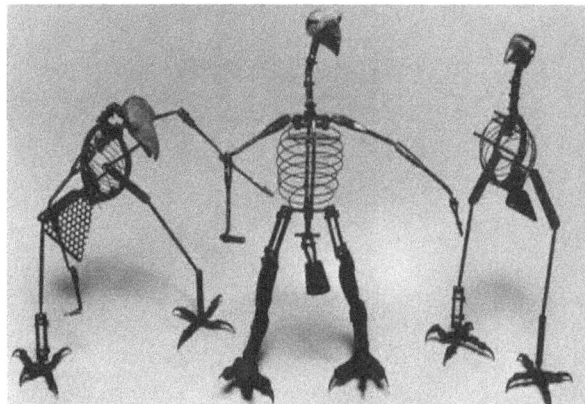

The four surviving eagle animation armatures. The wingless model in the group shot above is the one now owned by Lord of the Rings director Peter Jackson. Below: The armature recovered from Pete Peterson and now in the collection of Ronald V. Borst. Images courtesy of Jack Polito and the author.

Three more armatures appeared in a Camden House auction lot of MGM props on November 5, 1989. They were mistakenly labeled as "Three dinosaur armature models used in *One Million B.C.*, 1937 (MGM)" and were purchased by an anonymous collector for $1870.00.

Fourteen years later, one of the same armatures was auctioned by Profiles in History for considerably more. Director Peter Jackson paid $16, 000.00 to obtain it.

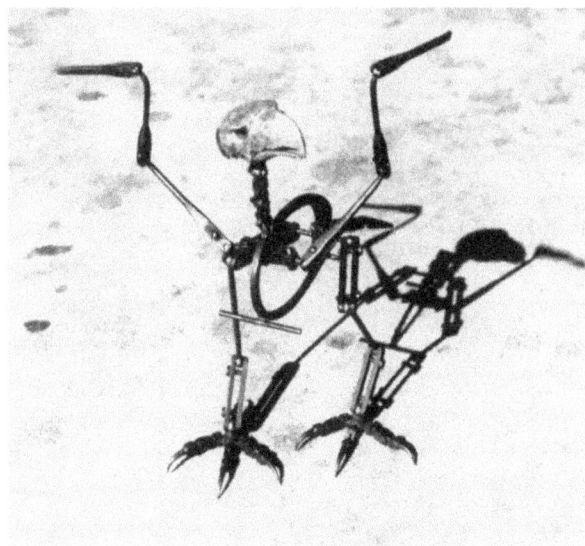

And there is one final still image. Long-circulated among collectors, it had little context until much of the artwork and documents that make up this account came together. It is a partial composite shot from the last scene planned for shooting on the ill-fated second Technicolor test. In the "Allosaur Capture Sequence" it seems to corresponds to Scene 23: Set 9. Long shot, looking down into the valley below. In the right foreground a birdman is standing beside his eagle. We see the procession far below him. He mounts eagle and flies away. The scene is one of the most illustrated in the surviving *War Eagles* material, existing as a doodle on the last page of the sequence notes, a rough sketch by an unknown artist, and a finely finished drawing by Harry Stevenson. The still shows the cliff and background, but there is a only a dark matted area for the eagle and rider present.

There are vertical scratches visible, marking the image clearly as a piece of motion picture footage. The shot is unfinished, but there is an outline of the rider, sitting on the edge of the cliff, peering into the valley below. I confess an identification with the figure, since I have spent many a year now, peering at action in the far distance. In my case the distance is composed of decades. In the script, the rider mounts up and flies away to make his report, and now I have made mine.

Will War Eagles itself ever take flight? As Ray Harryhausen is often fond of saying:
"It's in the lap of the gods..."

The final frame? Only time will tell. From the author's collection

278

Presented here are screenwriter Harold Lamb's "Notes on the Great Eagles and Their People", probably delivered after conferences with Merian C. Cooper and prior to his full duties as scenarist on *War Eagles*. They bear all the marks of his experience as an author of historical fact and fiction, with references to the many cultures he regularly wrote about, and they refine the idea that the bird people are actually the descendants of a lost Viking tribe. True to

Lamb's habits as a fiction writer, they are heavily researched and a rarity in period screenwriting. With the advent of television series in the early 1950's, it became a regular practice to create a similar document known as a "Writer's Bible" to give series writers a grasp of background and history for a show and its characters, but Lamb's interesting effort occupies a unique position for fantasy films of the era.

NOTES ON THE GREAT EAGLES AND THEIR PEOPLE

CHILDREN OF THE CLAN

At birth a boy-child might be plunged in the sea (at the island) or exposed to the snow, to harden him. (Cossacks did this, to "salt down" their children for the hardships of life.)

Young boys and girls might be flocked together in the tribe. They play with the fledgling eagles ~ getting clawed, and tumbling together with the birds.

These boys learn to ride the wiser, older birds on the training ground. (As Mongol boys first learned to ride by holding themselves on sheep, clinging to the wool.)

They also have to bring water to the tethered birds, as the boys of the elephant lines tend the beasts they will master later on.

Young children are carried in the air slung beside women in woven baskets, slung across the eagles. And they are tied by cords about the waist when left to play on the cliffs of the valley.

When the boy reaches warrior age, he must be able to manage a grown eagle in the air. To dive with the eagle, and cast his winged javelin. He must have trained the eagle that is to be his companion-steed.

Perhaps he has to make a leap from the eagle. That is, to jump from the bird's back into the air. Then the bird dives after him (as a hawk goes down after a fish dropped from a gull's claws) and comes beneath him, so the young warrior can gain its back. If the boy or the bird fails in this, the boy will be killed.

If he is accepted as a man by the warriors of the clan, he is allowed to carry weapons, to go with the men on hunts, and to war. Then he is anointed with the blood of the eagle he has trained. Thereafter the two of them, the man and his steed, will be free in the air; they will be masters of the heights.

Then ~ when he can protect her ~ the young warrior is allowed to take a bride.

The marriage, like tribal mating, would be simple and barbaric ~ a betrothal rather than a ceremony. The warrior would come to the girl's dwelling where other women wait as if to protect her.

Breaking free, he mounts his own eagle, flying after the girl, and snatching her from her eagle, flying with her up to the eyrie he has made for her apart from the tribal swellings. In this love-chase the girl may still escape, if she can. If she submits, she joins the warrior in his eyrie, which is roofed with woven feathers and floored with down (Like the wedding "bower" of the Vikings)

THE WOMEN

Are apart from men at feast and council.

They are as daring as the men, because they have equal share in great trek. Like the Spartans they take part in the games when young, to fit themselves for the air riding.

When married, with children, they have the care of the household, and its defense when the men are off hunting or at war.

They prepare the honey-mead, or wine of this Viking folk. And they pour the wine, at a feast from jars into the drinking cups of the warriors. These are made from eagle beaks ornamented with gold or turquoise and mica. (Like the drinking vessels of the Norsemen, made from curved horns.)

The older women have the care of young eagles ~ fledglings. They nurse injured birds, putting oil on gashes, or splints on broken wings. The men sharpen the eagles' talons with rubbing stones.

On the trek, the women have the children slung by them, and their few utensils. They also have the care of the tribal fire, carried in a large metal vase, shaped like a censer. They feed it with charcoal and dried wood during the flight.

The young girls are daring, and will not submit as brides to the young warriors unless the men have greater courage.

These women weave fibres from the inner bark of trees.

They make the garments of down. And the thatch of great feathers, or woven grass that roofs their small dwellings.

THE SKY

The eagle people know the sky as sailors know the sea.

They can tell approaching weather by a glance at cloud formations at vast distances.

In their trek, they guide themselves by the Southern constellations, at night. Perhaps Orion's square is visible. The Milky Way, to them, would be the Path of the Wild Geese. A falling star is a sign, a good omen.

So, to them, light is a blessing. And darkness a curse. (The eagles are reluctant to fly at night, but do so when driven.)

The sun and warmth, and the coming of spring, are to the eagle people what green grass, water and shade are to the animal-nomads. Security, and life. Their arrival in the sunlight on the heights of the Valley is their festival, their spring.

To them, white is a royal color. Naru wears a white tunic or kaftan of down. (The soft down feathering of such garments and robes gives protection against cold and wet, as with birds.) So White Eagle is distinguished from the other eagles by his color.

Blue, the color of the clear sunlit sky, is also linked by the eagle folk. (White is the imperial color of the nomad Mongol tribes. Their Kha Khan was seated on a white horseskin. They also favored blue as the color of clear beneficent skies.)

Black, to the eagle people, would be repulsive. Black is the color of the depths, and of night. And red the color of volcanic fire, the servant of their enemies in the hell below the Valley.

THE WINDS

The wind means more to the eagle people than to sailors in the time of sail on the sea.

They ride the winds. The eagles themselves have the trick of taking advantage of air currents. Eagles can not rest in still air. They glide with the wind, and across air currents, resting their wings.

It is a gigantic task to ride the cyclonic winds of the Antarctic. The struggle with the forces of the air has given the eagles great power of wing, and developed the men physically. These men have become hardened to cold. They can breathe in the thin air of vast heights. They are free of disease. Like the birds they can exist for days without food. (The ordeal of the long trek has accustomed them to this.)

When they ride, they watch the cloud signs for approaching wind, to take advantage of it.

The coming of the Great Wind (the eighty to a hundred mile Polar hurricane) might be the time of their migration from the island to the warmth of the Valley, and security. This wind might make the island uninhabitable by the eagles, or the men.

In their prayers or salutation to the dead, the eagle folk might cast the petals of flowers or small feathers out over the cliff into the air currents - watching to see if the offering is carried up or down. (As the Kirghiz burn paper prayers, and watch to see if the burnt wisps are carried up by the heat of the flames toward the sky. That is a good omen.)

THE CHIEFTAIN

The Chieftain of the tribe has the power of a king.

Upon the great trek, or in a tribal hunt, or war, this chieftain has authority of life or death. When the eagles are in the air, his command may not be disobeyed.

He has power to judge a man, to direct the flight of the tribe, to signal for the gathering of the warriors.

In the summer island, or in the heights of Valhalla, when the tribe is at rest, the Chieftain must call the Council of the Warriors, to ask their decision. Any man of the warrior caste has a right to speak in this gathering.

It is the duty of the leader to protect every living member of the tribe, to guide the tribe to the best places in their isolated world for gathering food or fish. And, above all, to lead the tribe in battle against its enemies.

Probably the Chieftain wears head-gear in the air that distinguishes him from the others. This might be a feather crest, or a headband with an emblem of wings. He might wear white ~ possibly wearing a reflector shield on his arm. And his eagle, the fiercest of the war birds, would be marked by a crest, or gleaming metal like thin gold plates in its harness trappings

The laws of the tribe are simple and few.

To harm an eagle, even by accident, is a crime.

To fail to give aid to a member of the tribe injured on the trek, or in battle, is the greatest of crimes. That is, to leave someone behind, when there is danger.

To bring anyone from the outer world into the tribe might be an offense against their law.

To fail in a test of daring is a disgrace.

Every warrior must protect his mate, on the trek or in conflict. (As the eagle will fight for its mate.)

The worst punishment is exile from the tribe. In such a case the guilty man would usually prefer death, by leaping from a cliff, or from his eagle.

Among the eagle folk, who know nothing of writing, or the laws of civilization, a man's word is held binding. They take no oaths, and care nothing for the contracts of civilized folk. Lying, or stealing, or subterfuge is unknown among them.

They have neither soothsayers, nor witch doctors, nor physicians. Their life of endurance keeps them free of disease. And they enjoy life. As with birds, the freedom of the air is their element. Like aviators afoot on earth they are reckless of hazards on the ground.

Like the horse-nomads, they are uneasy when afoot. They can fight on the ground with bows and swords, but they are more accustomed to fighting from the air.

SIGNALS

In the air, the eagle people follow the signals of their chieftain. During the migration, he controls the movement .

of the flight. The others watch the flight of his eagle, as pilots in a plane formation watch their squadron leader. When his eagle ascends or descends, or swerves, they follow.

Commands are passed by voice from rider to rider during a quiet flightPerhaps the wind-instrument, the Aeolian harp, is used at times to attract attention.

At night, or in the Antarctic gloom, the rider of the leading eagle might carry a horn lantern -- the others following the gleam of it through the sky. (As the early seamen carried a mast light on the leading ship, so the others would not lose company during the darkness.)

In rapid action, the chieftain of the eagle folk directs the others with arm signals.

In the heights of the Valley of the Eagles, the long horns are blown that echo between the cliffs.

The signal for the gathering of the warriors of the tribe might be: a single eagle rider takes off from the Meeting place at great speed with a basket of fire on a long lance, or swinging behind him at a rope's end -- if it is dark at the time. So the sky rider and the flame appear almost like a rocket. As the eagle people along the cliffs see the flame rising into the sky, they answer by lighting torches. So that the vast circle of the heights of the Valley is illumined by moving flames, gleaming against the snow and ice above. Possibly the women have a way of signalling the warrior-flight, if the riders are in the air, distant from the encampment. These women have mirrors of polished metal or fragments of mica. By flashing the mirror surfaces toward the eagles, many miles away, they can attract the attention of the riders -- call them back. (This primitive sun-telegraph was used by several peoples. Especially the Byzantines, who had a chain of posts in the heights, fifteen or twenty miles apart. The furthest post was at the edge of the frontier in Asia, overlooking the Tigris. The last post of the sun telegraph was in Constantinople. In this way news was flashed hundreds of miles in an hour or so.

THE GREAT TREK

Geographically.

From the unknown island in the Pacific, below the equator. Here the vegetation is drying up. The rushes and grass are dying, and water pools failing, with the change in season. The eagle tribe is camped on the high plateau of the island (resembling the bare slopes of Baluchistan.) On the crest of a volcanic mountain, around which clouds are beginning to gather, or heat lightning to play -- as the season changes.

On this island (where they boy and his companion are picked up by the eagle folk, when they are near death) may be a stopping point in the trek over the sea. In this case we do not see the starting point of the trek. But our men from civilization would find signs of the previous passage of the eagle people -- claw marks on the hard earth, or strange remnants of an encampment where no human being exists.

From the island, the trek would lead into the gloom of the end of the Antarctic night. The great birds would be flying low over the sea, and would head into the near darkness. At this point they would meet the first wind of the Antarctic. And they would follow the guiding light on the lead-eagle.

They would head toward the flaming sky lights of the aurora australis, miles overhead. As if they were winging into the sky itself. But the wind increases to a blizzard, while they search for the first glimpse of ice (on the Antarctic fringe) under the aurora. This blizzard forces the tiring birds down. They land on the great, drifting iceberg.

On the iceberg, they have to shelter themselves against the blizzard. The birds gather together for warmth. The old people and children are put into the best shelters by the warriors. And the great berg drifts before the wind. In the blast of the storm, it begins to crack.

Now perhaps the air clears and the aurora is seen again. Or the blizzard continues. But a section of the berg is cracking loose from the main mass. The breaking has the force of an explosion, and the whole mass shakes.

Some groups of the tribe are caught on the part breaking away. The eagle men have to fetch the older people and children back to safety, across the widening cracks as the berg breaks up. Some men fall to death down the chasm. Others are brought across on ropes.The broken part slides away, or overturns. Now the main mass is toppling under the wind. The eagle people have lost supplies, etc., in the catastrophe. Now they have to rush to take off on the giant eagles. The women catch up the children, and the warriors send them up on the first birds.

In flight again, the tribe is over ice that rises to the heights of the barrier range. Here, perhaps they have to force the Gate of the Winds, where the Antarctic hurricane rips between two remote ice peaks. In the flight from the iceberg, the tribe has been separated. But the birds head toward the distant Valhalla.

Beyond the barrier range, out of the wind, they come down into the valley where fruits and wild grains grow. They have almost no food left, and they must get more from this life giving plateau.

But here other life exists, the primordial life of the depths -- the prehistoric beasts and beast-men. And to get their food, the eagle folk have to fight off the monsters and the men of the depths, who swarm out to capture their women. (In this plateau, they have come into the light of the first sun of the Antarctic summer, circling low around them.)

High up, in the remote distance at the end of the food plateau -- or far beyond it -- they can now see the sun of the heights of Valhalla.

When they have destroyed their enemies, the beast-men, they rise to the heights of Valhalla. Into the sunlight, and clear air beneath the snow peaks, where they can feast at the end of the trek. The eagles have come home, and the warriors come in from their victory.

FEAST OF VALHALLA

This is the gigantic rejoicing of the Viking brook coming home. The eagle riders regaining their heights. In the sunlight of the heights, with food aplenty and the wine or honey-mead of the Valley.

(Perhaps some elder men have been left, like herders on these heights, with the old eagles. And fledglings - - if this is the breeding ground of the eagles.)

The arrival in Valhalla means release from care. It isthe mating time of the warriors and girls. The fitting up of their bridal dwelling apart from the others.

Perhaps the tribal fire that has been carried on the great trek is lighted now on the stone in the Hall of the Vikings. (This would be a space open to the sky, at the edge of the cliffs, with great stones for tables. Ancient dolmens would mark the hall - a Stonehenge effect, in which the natural stone columns would be the pillars of the roofless hall.)

The warriors sit with their wine, while the elder men chant the story of the trek, and the battles. An athlete might dance the eagle-dance of the tribe, from stone to stone and along the cliff. (The eagle dance of the Hopi Indians is a striking example of a tribal-religious dance.)

Young girls would go up on their eagles, in the love-chase, trying to escape - - or not to escape - - the younger warriors who pursue them, to snatch them off their eagles, and carry them off to the mating bowers. Such would be the wedding of the boy from outside and the girl of the eagle folk.

It would be the spring in this remote Valhalla, the blooming of flowers through the snow. Freedom in the warmth of the new sun. And delight in the falling cascades of water, from the snow. The younger spirits let themselves go, down the falling water.

Under this, the chanting of the Viking saga.

SPORTS OF THE EAGLE PEOPLE

These are not arranged games, but spontaneous.

Two warriors cast the long winged javelin-spears at each other. When the spear is thrown, full at the second man, he bends his body, and catches it as it flies by, hurling it back at the first thrower. They are close together, and it would be fatal to be struck. It is a disgrace to miss the catch.

They might shoot arrows from a height at a gossamer veil floating down. And fly down to recover the target on the eagle.

They leap from the war eagles, and save themselves when the eagles swoop down after them.

They would be free with their wagers. (With an instinct for laughter in all their doings). They might have the world-old knowledge of dice. Their dice would be flattened pebbles or agate bits, and a man would cast the dice standing up, upon a board or stone marked off into squares. He would win or lose by the squares on which the rolling dice settled.

A man might bet another that he could not throw his lance down from a cliff, to strike the earth some hundred feet below. The unsuspecting warrior would throw his lance. As he did so, the eagle of the wagerer - - which had been trained to do this - - would take off from the cliff beside them and dive after the lance, catching it before it struck the ground, and bringing it up again to the men.

If a giant among them, a massive bear of a man, had a chum who was a shrimp (like a small Cockney, quick with his wit and tongue where the other is slow) the big warrior would manhandle the little one, throwing him into water, to drop over a fall. The little one would be expert at a kind of shell and pea game. And he would get his revenge bywinning the garments and gear of the big fellow, who couldn't puzzle out the trick.

And then, when they were both in danger, the big chap would go through everything to pull the little one out by the scruff of the neck.

They are men who laugh when they pull out of danger. (Nomads, unlike most civilized people, are good-humored as soon as hunger or long privation is over. They are gay when they eat or drink.) An eagle rider who had to scramble to get himself and his gear up on his eagle, to take off from the iceberg before it crashed over, would be hugely amused at himself.

They joust in the air. This would be a test of the war eagles. (As elephants, matched in a fight, try to knock the mahout of the other's back to earth). The great birds in this mock fight, would try to outmaneuver the other - - circling away and dropping on the other's back - - to make the other rider fall. In such a case, the riders might wear safety belts attached to their waists, and the necks of the eagles.

The men might race each other through cloud formations,

The girls might be skilled archers. Perhaps the warriors rather look down on the bow as a woman's weapon - -or an arm for a man on the ground. They'd call the arrows "flying thorns" or "needles."

Like tree-dwelling animals, the eagle men would be skilled in falling without harm. They would be able to drop through the branches of a tree, or go over a waterfall, keeping their wits and balance.

CUSTOMS

The eagle people would be watchful of the sky for signs of wind and weather.

In Valhalla they might have a great bird's wing, or marker mounted on a pole above the Meeting place, as a wind-vane. They could judge the wind from the smoke of the tribal fire.

The periods of their day would be those of the birds. Beginning, in the first hour, with daybreak. Mid-day would be the time of warmth and rest, of bathing. (When the men go into the water, the great birds sometimes take their baths in the spray of the largest fall.) Toward the close of the day - - after they descended to camp, in the trek - - they would eat. And at nightfall they would go to their dwellings, as the birds go to the perches, to sleep.

To the eagle-folk, a rainbow would be a good omen.

And a red sun (which would mean smoke in the air, or a coming storm) would be a harbinger of evil.

Rain would probably drive them, like the birds, to cover. Unless they were migrating.

Like the birds, they would leave the sky when lightning or thunder came around them. (In the last battle over New York, they would fly through all this.)

GIANT BIRDS

The Encyclopedia Britannica - 11th Edition - Vol XVII - pp. 630-31

The Moa of New Zealand.

". . . 'The natives added that, in times long past, they received the tradition that very large birds had existed, but the scarcity of food, as well as the easy method of entrapping them, had caused their extermination' (Polack - "New Zealand" London, 1838. . . In the South Island they seem to have lingered much longer, possibly, according to H.O.Forbes (Nat. Sci.11. 1893, pp 374-380) 'down even to the time that Captain Cook visited New Zealand.' But these are only surmises, based upon the fact that in various dry caves limbs still surrounded by the mumified flesh and skin, feathers, and even eggs with the inner membrane have been found. Great quantities of bones have been found in caves and in swamps, so that now nearly every part of the skeleton, of some kind or other is known.". . . (Harpagornis, a tremendous bird of prey, died out with the pleistocene)."

". . . The most striking features of the moas, besides the truly gigantic size of some species, is the most complete absence of wings. . ."

MADAGASCAR - Palaeontology - p. 272

"Researches in various parts of the island have revealed the existence, in subfossil state, of the bones of numerous birds of the family Struthidae. These have been arranged in 12 species, belonging to two genera, *Aepyornis* and *Mulleromis*, which varied in size from that of a bustard to birds much exceeding an ostrich, and rivalling the recently extinct moa of New Zealand, the largest species being about 10 feet in height. One species of these great wingless birds laid an egg which is the largest know, being 12 ½ inches by 9 ½ inches." (Prehistoric remains)

". . .the bones of some enormous terrestrial lizards have been brought to light, belonging to Sauropodous Dinosaurs of the general *Bothridiospondylus* and *Titanosaurus*. . . AUSTRALIA - p948

". . .There is also a white eagle."

ALBATROSS P. 491 (VOL. 1)

". . .The best known is the common or wandering albatross. . .which occurs in all parts of the Southern Ocean. The length of the body is stated at four feet, and the weight at from 15 to 25 pounds. It sometimes measures as much as 17 feet between the tips of the extended wings, averaging probably from 10 to 12 feet. Its strength of wing is very great. It often accompanies a ship for days. . .without ever being observed to alight on the water, and continues its flight, apparently untired, in tempestuous as well as in moderate weather."

"TRAVELS OF MARCO POLO - Yule, Edited by Cordier - Vol 11, pp. 412-21

"'Tis said that in those other islands to the south, which the ships are unable to visit because this strong current prevents their return, is found the bird Gryphon, which appears there at certain seasons. . .persons who had been there told Messer Marco Polo that it was for all the world like an eagle, but one indeed of enormous size; so big in fact that its wings covered an extent of thirty paces, and its quills were twelve paces long, and thick in proportion. And it is so strong that it will seize an elephant in its talons and carry him high into the air, and drop him so that he is smashed to pieces, having so killed him the bird gryphon swoops down on him and eats him at leisure. The people of those isles call the bird Ruc, and it has no other name . . .they are not half lion and half bird as our stories do relate, but enormous as they be they are fashioned just like an eagle.

The Great Kaan sent men to those parts to enquire about these curious matters. . .both envoys had many wonderful things to tell. . .about those strange islands, and about the birds I have mentioned. They brought (as I heard) to the Great Kaan feathers of the said Ruc, which was stated to measure 90 spans, whilst the quill part was two palms in circumference, a marvelous object! . .

"Note 5. - The fable of the RUKH was old and widely spread. . .The *Garuda* of the Hindus, the *Simurgh* of the old Persians, the *Angka* of the Arabs, the *Bar Yuchre* of the Rabbinical legends, the *Crype* of the Greeks, were probably all versions of the original fable. . .

"The circumstance which for the time localized the *Rukh* in the direction of Madagascar was perhaps some rumour of the great fossil *Aepyornis* and its colossal eggs, found in that island. According to Geoffrey St. Hilaire, the Malagashes assert that the bird which laid those great eggs still exists, that it has an immense power of flight, and preys upon the greater quadrupeds. Indeed the continued existence of the bird has been alleged as late as 1861 and 1863!

"On the great map of Fra Mauro (1459) near the extreme point of Africa which he calls *Cavo de Diab*, which is suggestive of the Cape of Good Hope, but was really perhaps Cape Corientes, there is a fabric inscribed with the following remarkable story: "About the year of Our Lord 1420 a ship or junk of India in crossing the Indian Sea was driven by way of the Islands of Men and Women beyond the Cape of Diab, and carried between the Green Islands and the Darkness in a westerly and south-westerly direction for 40 days, without seeing anything but sky and sea, curing which time they made to the best of their judgement 2000 miles. The gale then ceasing they turned back, and were 70 days in getting to the aforesaid Cape Diab. The ship having touched on the coast to supply its wants, the mariners beheld there the egg of a certain bird called *Chrocho*, which egg was as big as a butt - (*De la grandeza de una bota d' anfora'* - - The lowest estimate that I find of the Venetian anfora makes it equal to about 108 imperial gallons, a little less than the English butt. This seems intended. The ancient amphora would be more reasonable, being only 566 gallons.) And the bigness of the bird is such that between the extremities of the wings is said to be 60 paces. They say too that it carries away an elephant or any other great animal with the greatest ease, and does great injury to the inhabitants of the country, and is most rapid in its flight."

". . .Hilaire considered the *Aepyornis* to be of the ostrich family; Prince C. Buonaparte classed it with the *Inepti* or Dodos; Duvernay. . .with aquatic birds! . . . . . Professor

Bianconi. . . concludes that it was most probably a bird of the vulture family. This would go far, he urges, to justify Polo's account of the Ruc as a bird of prey, though the story of its lifting any large animal could have had no foundation as the feet of the vulture kind are unfit for such effort. Humboldt describes the habit of the condor of the Andes as that of worrying, wearying, and frightening its four-footed prey until it drops; sometimes the condor drives its victim over a precipice.

"Bianconi concludes that on the same scale of proportion as the condor's, the great *quills of the Aepyornis would be about ten feet long and the spread of the wings about 32 feet, whilst the height of the bird would be at least four times that of the condor.*

"We give, in the first edition of this work, a drawing of the great *Aepyornis* egg in the British Museum of its true size, as the nearest approach we could make to an illustration- of the Rukh from nature. The actual contents of this egg will be about 3.25 gallons, which may be compared with Fra Mauro's *anfora*! Except in this matter of size, his story of the ship and the egg may be true."

Recently fossil bones have been found in New Zealand, which seem to bring us a step nearer to the realization of the Rukh. Dr. Haast discovered in a swamp at Glenmark in the province of Otago, along with remains of the *Dinornis* or Moa, some bones. . .of a gigantic bird which he pronounces to be a bird of prey, apparently allied to the Harriers, and calls *Harpagornis*. He supposes it to have preyed upon the Moa, and as that fowl is calculated to have been 10 ft. and upwards in height, we are not so very far from the elephant devouring Rukh. . . This discovery may possibly throw a new light on the tradition of the New Zealanders. For Professor Owen, in first describing the *Dinornis* in 1839, mentioned that the natives had a *tradition that the bones belonged to a bird of the eagle kind.* . . And Sir George Grey appears to have read a paper, Oct. 23rd 1872, which was the description by a Maori of the *Hokiol*, an extinct gigantic bird of prey of which that people have traditions come down from their ancestors, said to have been a black hawk of great size, as large as the Moa.

"I have to thank Mr. Arthur Grote for a few words more on that most interesting subject, the discovery of a real fossil Ruc in New Zealand. He informs me. . . that Professor Owen is now working on the huge bones sent home by Dr. Haast, "and is convinced that they belong to a bird of prey. . .probably a Harrier, double the weight of the Moa. . .

"Sinbad's adventures with the Rukh are too well-known for quotation. . .The story takes a peculiar form in the Travels of Rabbi Benjamin of Tudela. He heard that when ships were in danger of being lost in the stormy sea that led to China the sailors were wont to sew themselves up in hides, and so when cast upon the surface they were snatched up by great eagles, called Gryphons, which carried their supposed prey ashore, etc. It is curious that this very story occurs in a Latin poem stated to be a least as old as the beginning of the 13th century, which relates the romantic adventures of a certain Duke Ernest of Bavaria.

"It is the China Sea that Ibn Batuta beheld the Rukh, first like a mountain in the sea where no mountain should be, and then, "when the run arose," says he, "we saw the mountain aloft in the air, and the clear sky between it and the sea." Kazwini also says that the 'Angka carries off an elephant as a hawks flies off with a mouse, his flight is like the loud thunder. While he dwelt near the haunts of men and dealt them great mischief. But once on a time it had carried off a bride in her bridal array, and Hamd Allah, the Prophet of those days, invoked a curse upon the bird. *Wherefore the Lord banished it to an inaccessible island in the Encircling Ocean.*

"The *Simurgh* or 'Angka, dwelling behind veils of Light and Darkness on the inaccessible summits of Caucasus, is in the Persian mysticism an emblem of the Almighty."

According to the Research department there is a record of a Golden Plover who flew 2500 miles across the sea. This was a sustained flight as they do not alight on water.

save New York

REVERSE ANGLE   LONG SHOT

The whole sky over Jersey full of American
pursuit ships rushing to ▓▓▓▓▓▓

in full retreat,

LONG SHOT   STATUE OF LIBERTY

In the f.g. the bombers bank, and sweep o.s.
out to sea ▓▓▓▓▓ FULL SHOT   STATUE OF
LIBERTY. Perched on its shoulder is White
Eagle. Slim and Naru stand together beside
him. O. S. a huge roar of motors, above the
circling, screaming eagles, and behind a
magnificent sky of broken clouds. As the
American pursuit ships flash through, squadron after squadron headed out to sea,
INTERCUT WITH FLASHES of SLIM'S previous army
flying mates, recognizing him, saluting him.
▓▓▓▓▓ Suddenly the last flight
has swept ▓▓▓▓▓. As the ▓▓▓ of motors

past.

thunder

diminishes, and the steady victory roar of
New York City, punctuated by steamer sirens,
becomes audible below, BOOM INTO A CLOSER
SHOT   STATUE OF LIBERTY, SHOWING only head
and shoulders. ▓▓▓▓▓▓▓▓

Slim stands beside White Eagle, one arm
around Naru, the other raised after the
departing planes. BOOM SUDDENLY into a
big magnificent CLOSEUP   WHITE EAGLE, as he
screams in triumph, and wildly beats his
great shining wings.

FADE OUT.

the

▓ end

The actual last page of *War Eagles* that Cyril Hume turned in on October 10, 1939, with his hand notations. Courtesy of the Estates of Cyril Hume and Richard Maibaum.

Bibliography
Books

Ackerman, Forrest J. *Mr. Monster's Movie Gold.* Norfolk, VA: The Donning Company, 1981.

Apostal, Jane. *Duncan Gleason: Artist, Athlete and Author.* Los Angeles: Historical Society of Southern California, 2003.

Archer, Steve. *Willis O'Brien: Special Effects Genius.* Jefferson, NC: McFarland & Co., Inc., 1993.

Behlmer, Rudy, ed. *Memo From David O. Selznick.* New York: Viking Press, 1972.

Berry, Mark F. *The Dinosaur Filmography.* Jefferson, NC: McFarland & Co., Inc., 2002.

Birdwell, Michael E. *Celluloid Soldiers: Warner Bro.'s Campaign against Nazism.* New York: NYU Press, 1999.

Cooper, Merian C. *Grass.* New York: G.P. Putnam, 1925.

D'Arc, James V., ed. *Register to the Merian C. Cooper Papers.* Provo, UT: Brigham Young University, 2000.

De Chevrieux, Marcus. *Joe Duncan Gleason: Rediscovering California's Marine Art Master.* Newport Beach, CA: Newport Harbor Nautical Museum, 2003.

Goldner, Orville, and George E, Turner. *The Making of King Kong.* Cranberry, NJ: A. S. Barnes and Co., Inc., 1975.

Gottesman, Ronald & Harry Geduld, eds. *The Girl in the Hairy Paw.* New York: Avon Books, 1976.

Harmetz, Aljean. *The Making of the Wizard of Oz.* New York: Alfred A. Knopf, 1981.

Harryhausen, Ray & Tony Dalton. *Ray Harryhausen: An Animated Life.* London: Aurum Press Ltd., 2003.

Harryhausen, Ray & Tony Dalton. *The Art of Ray Harryhausen.* London: Aurum Press Ltd., 2005.

Hume, Cyril. *Myself and the Young Bowman.* New York: Doubleday, Doran & Company, Inc., 1932.

Jenson, Paul M. *The Men Who Made the Monsters.* New York: Twayne Publishers, 1996.

Kaplan, Martin & Johanna Blakley. *Warner's War: Politics, Pop Culture & Propaganda in Wartime Hollywood.* Los Angeles: The Norman Lear Center Press, 2004.

Karolevitz, Robert F., and Fenn, Ross S. *Flight of Eagles: The Story of the American Kosciuszko Squadron in the Polish-Russian War 1919-1920.* Sioux Falls, S.D.: Brevet Press, 1974.

Lamb, Harold. *The March of the Barbarians.* New York: The Literary Guild of America, Inc., 1940.

Marz, Samuel. *A Gaudy Spree.* New York: Franklin Watts, 1987.

Nelson, Arthur A. *Wings of Danger.* New York: Robert M. McBride and Co., 1915.

Pettigrew, Neil. *The Stop-Motion Filmography: A Critical Guide to 297 Features Using Puppet Animation.* Jefferson, NC: McFarland & Co., Inc., 1999.

Rovin, Jeff. *From the Land Beyond Beyond.* New York: Berkley Publishing Corp., 1977.

Schatz, Thomas. *The Genius of the System: Hollywood Filmmaking in the Studio Era.* New York: Pantheon Books, 1988.

Turner, George E. *The Cinema of Adventure, Romance & Terror.* Hollywood: The ASC Press, 1989.

Van Hise, James. *Hot Blooded Dinosaur Movies.* Las Vegas, NV: Pioneer Books, Inc., 1993.
Vaz, Mark Cotta & Craig Barron. *The Invisible Art: The Legends of Movie Matte Painting.* San Francisco: Chronicle
 Books LLC, 2002.

Vaz, Mark Cotta. *Living Dangerously: The Adventures of Merian C. Cooper.* New York: Villard Books, 2005.

Weaver, Tom. *Monsters, Mutants and Heavenly Creatures: Confessions of 14 Classic Sci-Fi/Horrormeisters.*
Baltimore, MD: Midnight Marquee Press, Inc., 1996.

Wells, H. G. *The War in the Air.* Lincoln, NE: Bison Books, University of Nebraska Press, 2002.

Wray, Fay. *On the Other Hand.* New York: St. Martin's Press, 1989.

Periodicals

Ackerman, Forrest J. "Rare Treats." *Famous Monsters of Filmland* #136, August 1977.
"Admiral Byrd's Antarctic Expedition Finds 900 Miles of New Coastline." *Life* Vol. 9 No. 2, July 8, 1940.
Behlmer, Rudy. "Merian C. Cooper is the Kind of Creative Showman Today's Movies Badly Need."
Films in Review Vol. 17 No. 1, January 1966
Cappa, William. "Merian C. Cooper–Take Two." *Cult Movies* #20, 1996.
Creelman, James Ashmore. "How to Stay Out of the Movies." *The Bookman,* November 1924 & April 1926.
Dello Stritto, Frank J. "Monstrous Ambition: The Nightmares of Merian C. Cooper." *Cult Movies* #19, 1996.
Lybek, Al. "Harold Lamb and Adventure: Cossacks and Crusaders." *ERB-dom/ The Fantastic Collector* #260 & 261.
Mandell, Paul. "The Brothers Delgado: The Titans of Miniatures." *Cinemagic* #29, 198?
Murray, Doug. "The King Kong You'll Never See." *Closeup* #3, 1977.
Shay, Don. "Willis O'Brien–Creator of the Impossible." *Cinefex* #7, January 1982.
Turner, George E. "A Lost World of Dinosaurs." *Retrovision* #3, August 1998.
Turner, George E. "Marcel Delgado: Kong & Beyond." SPFX #10, 2002.
"What? Color in the Movies Again?" *Fortune* Vol. 10 No. 4, October 1934.

Other

"Motion Picture and Entertainment Memorabilia." Camden House Auctioneers, Inc. Catalog,
 November 4 & 5, 1989.
"Profiles in History Presents: The Ultimate Sci-Fi Auction / Hollywood Memorabilia Auction 14.
"Profiles in History Auction Catalog, April 26, 2003.
An unpublished book manuscript by special effects artist A. Arnold Gillespie covering his techniques and
Oscar-winning career at MGM, courtesy of Robert Welch.